THE LAST MISSION OF THE WHAM BAM BOYS

ALSO BY GREGORY A. FREEMAN

Troubled Water: Race, Mutiny, and Bravery
on the USS Kitty Hawk

Fixing Hell: An Army Psychologist Confronts Abu Ghraib
(with Col. [Ret.] Larry C. James, PhD)

The Forgotten 500: The Untold Story of
the Men Who Risked All for the
Greatest Rescue Mission of World War II

Sailors to the End: The Deadly Fire on the
USS Forrestal *and the Heroes Who Fought It*

Lay This Body Down:
The 1921 Murders of Eleven Plantation Slaves

THE LAST MISSION

OF THE

WHAM BAM BOYS

COURAGE, TRAGEDY, AND
JUSTICE IN WORLD WAR II

GREGORY A. FREEMAN

palgrave
macmillan

First published in 2011 by PALGRAVE MACMILLAN® in the U.S.—a division of St. Martin's Press LLC, 175 Fifth Avenue, New York, NY 10010.

Where this book is distributed in the UK, Europe and the rest of the world, this is by Palgrave Macmillan, a division of Macmillan Publishers Limited, registered in England, company number 785998, of Houndmills, Basingstoke, Hampshire RG21 6XS.

Palgrave Macmillan is the global academic imprint of the above companies and has companies and representatives throughout the world.

Palgrave® and Macmillan® are registered trademarks in the United States, the United Kingdom, Europe and other countries.

ISBN: 978-0-230-10854-7

Library of Congress Cataloging-in-Publication Data
Freeman, Gregory A.
    The last mission of the Wham Bam boys : courage, tragedy, and justice in World War II / Gregory A. Freeman.
        p.   cm.
    Includes bibliographical references.
    ISBN 978-0-230-10854-7
    1. World War, 1939–1945—Atrocities—Germany—Rüsselsheim.
2. Lynching—Germany—Rüsselsheim.   3. Rüsselsheim (Germany)—History—20th century.   4. United States. Army Air Forces—Airmen.   5. World War, 1939–1945—Aerial operations, American.   6. World War, 1939–1945—Campaigns—Germany.   7. Bombing, Aerial—Moral and ethical aspects.
8. Civilians in war—Germany—Rüsselsheim.   I. Title.
D757.9.R87F74   2011
940.54'05—dc22

                                                                              2010044091

A catalogue record of the book is available from the British Library.

Design by Letra Libre

First edition: June 2011

10   9   8   7   6   5   4   3   2   1

Printed in the United States of America.

For my father, Jerry Freeman

A man is truly dead only
when we stop speaking his name.

CONTENTS

Eight pages of photographs appear between pages 96 and 97.

PRINCIPAL CHARACTERS

Note: Ages listed are ages at the time of the incident in 1944.

CREW OF THE *WHAM! BAM! THANK YOU MA'AM*

Second Lieutenant Norman J. Rogers Jr.: Pilot, from Rochester, New York, twenty-four years old

Second Lieutenant John N. Sekul: Copilot, from the Bronx, New York, twenty-two years old

Flight Officer Haigus Tufenkjian: Navigator and bombardier from Detroit, Michigan, twenty-three years old

Staff Sergeant Forrest W. Brininstool: Engineer from Munith, Michigan, twenty-eight years old

Staff Sergeant Thomas D. Williams Jr.: Radio operator from Hazleton, Pennsylvania, nineteen years old

Sergeant William A. Adams: Nose gunner from Klingerstown, Pennsylvania, nineteen years old

Sergeant Elmore L. Austin: Left waist gunner from Edinburg Falls, Vermont, nineteen years old

Sergeant Sidney Eugene Brown: Tail gunner from Gainesville, Florida, nineteen years old

Sergeant William A. Dumont: Belly gunner from Berlin, New Hampshire, twenty years old

RESIDENTS OF RÜSSELSHEIM, GERMANY

Josef Hartgen: Foreman at the Opel plant, Nazi Party member, air raid warden, forty-one years old

Kathe Reinhardt: Sister of Margarete Witzler, thirty-eight years old; husband is in the German army, serving on the Russian front; runs a tobacco shop in Rüsselsheim with her sister Margarete Witzler.

Margarete Witzler: Sister of Kathe Reinhardt, fifty years old

Johannes Seipel: Farmer, sixty-five years old

Otto Hermann Stolz: Nazi SA member, or "brown shirt," thirty-one years old

George Daum: Machinist at the Opel plant, forty-five years old

Lonie Daum: George Daum's wife, mother of three, age unknown

Heinrich Barthel: Instructor at the Opel plant, forty-three years old

Johann Opper: Railway switchman, Nazi Party member, sixty years old

August Wolf: Machinist at the Opel plant, forty-three years old

Friedrich Wüst: Blacksmith, Nazi Party member, forty years old

Karl Fugmann: Efficiency manager at the Opel plant, forty-two years old

Phillip Gütlich: Farmer and tavernkeeper

Franz Rinkes: Member of the Hitler Youth, sixteen years old

Georg Jung: District Catholic priest of Rüsselsheim

Jacob Hoffman: Evangelical minister in Rüsselsheim

WAR CRIMES GROUP

Major Luke P. Rogers: American war crimes investigator

Lieutenant Colonel Leon Jaworski: American chief of the Examination Division of the War Crimes Branch, Chief of the Investigation Division, prosecutor in the Rüsselsheim case

Germany

DENMARK
SWEDEN

Stralsund

Hamburg
Hamburg

Mecklenburg-Vorpommern

Oldenburg

Niedersachsen

Brandenburg

POLAND

Osnabruck
Minden
Langenhagen

Berlin

Potsdam
Frankfurt

NETHERLANDS

Greven

Sachsen-Anhalt

Nordrhein-Westfalen

Sachsen

BELGIUM

Hessen

Thuringen

Frankfurt
Hof
CZECH
REPUBLIC

Rüsselsheim

LUX
Darmstadt

Rhineland-Platz

Nurnberg

Saarland

Bayern

Stuttgart

FRANCE

Baden-Wurttemberg

AUSTRIA

SWITZERLAND

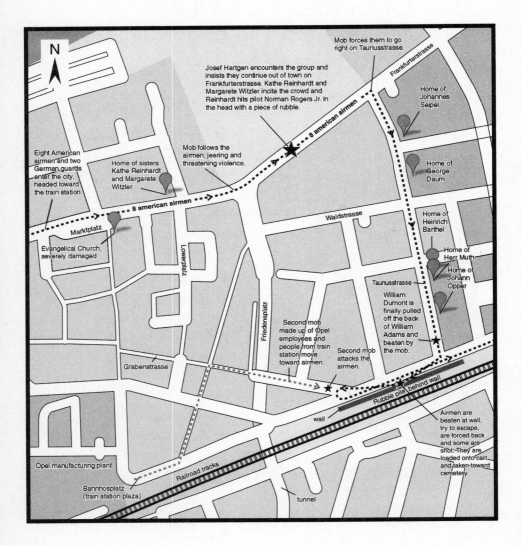

N

Josef Hartgen encounters the group and
insists they continue out of town on
Frankfurterstrasse. Kathe Reinhardt and
Margarete Witzler incite the crowd and
Reinhardt hits pilot Norman Rogers Jr. in
the head with a piece of rubble.

Mob forces them to go
right on Taunusstrasse.

Frankfurterstrasse

Home of
Johannes
Seipel

8 american airmen

Home of
George
Daum

Mob follows the
airmen, jeering and
threatening violence.

Eight American
airmen and two
German guards
enter the city,
headed toward
the train station.

Home of sisters
Kathe Reinhardt
and Margarete
Witzler

8 american airmen

Waldstrasse

Home of
Heinrich
Barthel

Marktplatz

Home of
Herr Muth

Home of
Johann
Opper

Evangelical Church,
severely damaged

Lowerplatz

Taunusstrasse

William
Dumont is
finally pulled
off the back
of William
Adams and
beaten by
the mob.

Friedensplatz

Second mob
made up of Opel
employees and
people from train
station move
toward airmen.

Second mob
attacks the
airmen.

Grabenstrasse

Rubble pile behind wall

Airmen are
beaten at wall,
try to escape,
are forced back
and some are
shot. They are
loaded onto cart
and taken toward
cemetery.

wall

Opel manufacturing plant

Bahnhosplatz
(train station plaza)

Railroad tracks

tunnel

INTRODUCTION

THE FIRST WAR CRIMES TRIAL AFTER World War II did not involve concentration camps or Nazi policy making, and the defendants were not high-ranking German military officers and political leaders. They were ordinary men and women, some elderly, all residents of a small city in Germany that had no prison camps or SS facilities. There was no obvious reason for them to be the first target of the Allies' attempt to restore justice after a terrible war.

They were on trial for what they did to eight young American men, good men who found themselves the focal point of a city's rage against the horrors of modern warfare. These young Americans and these otherwise unremarkable German civilians came together in what would become a historic test of morality, personal strength, and respect for the law under the most horrendous conditions.

The crew of the *Wham! Bam! Thank You Ma'am,* a B-24J bomber based in England, clashed with the residents of Rüsselsheim toward the end of a conflict that brought a type of warfare and a level of destruction almost unimaginable only a few years earlier. When the war in Europe ended in 1945, sixty German cities had been destroyed and 593,000 people had died—most of them civilians—from Allied bombs. Ninety-one thousand Allied airmen died in the European bombing campaign—55,000 British and 36,000 Americans. Most of the German deaths came in 1944 and 1945, during the last year of the war, a result of the Allies becoming increasingly proficient with their bombing campaign, which showed little mercy when it came to inflicting damage on civilian targets as a means to hasten the end of the war. The airmen who flew the bombers were mostly young men who wanted to help end the Nazis' takeover of Europe, and the Allied bombardment was successful in that respect. But destroying Hitler's war machine came at a steep price, both for the Germans on the ground and the Americans in the air.

The *Wham! Bam!* story reminds us that behind every statistic about the airmen, soldiers, and sailors killed in war is a man with a family, a man whose absence leaves questions and heartache that linger for generations. And for some families, the nature of the men's deaths is an added burden, as their loved ones died not quickly or easily but in terror and agony.

THE DEATH OF EACH MAN LOST in World War II left a trail of sorrow that his family would trudge through for decades, but the way in which the crew of the *Wham! Bam! Thank You Ma'am* died also opened a new chapter in the debate over the rules of war and what can reasonably be expected of a civilian populace battered by incessant attacks from their enemy. The questions raised by this debate still resonate today; only the locales and the technology of war have changed. In 1944, the debate was about bombers dropping hundreds of tons of high explosives and incendiaries on civilian targets—both Allied and Axis—and whether those in the right were going too far in adopting the methods of those clearly in the wrong to win the conflict. The same debate lives on in the Middle East, with ordinary citizens under siege, victims of a larger conflict. It continues with the controversy over alleged torture by American forces during the wars in Iraq and Afghanistan, with parallel concerns that American servicemen and women are now overly constrained by strict rules of engagement, designed to keep civilian casualties to an absolute minimum and spare culturally important structures, such as mosques.

The same rage that fueled the violence in Rüsselsheim lives on today in streets all over the world. In 1944, the streets of Rüsselsheim were filled with hundreds of average citizens venting their fury on the young men from America who had the bad fortune to walk through their town. In 1992, the same rage reared its head in the Rodney King riots in Los Angeles and other cities, with mobs attacking innocent men and women because of their race or ethnicity. In 1993, a mob in Mogadishu, Somalia, dragged the bodies of two servicemen through the streets in a joyous celebration of the deaths of young Americans who had come as part of a humanitarian mission for the starving country. In 2004, it was American contractors working for the Blackwater security firm who were killed by locals while delivering food in Fallujah, Iraq, their mutilated bodies hung from a bridge crossing the Euphrates. Countless other examples can be found all over the world, involving not just the United States but many nations and cultures. In so many of the cases, a close study of the circumstances and the motivation behind the mob violence reveals a deep sense of injustice, a rage fueled by indisputable suffering and loss, a rage that generates some sympathy for its origins but not for its results.

The murders in Rüsselsheim are testimony to the wrath a justly outraged man or woman can inflict on an innocent, and the trials that followed were a test of whether justice can prevail over man's basest instincts.

CHAPTER 1

BLACK SORROW

RÜSSELSHEIM, GERMANY

August 26, 1944

THE WOODEN WHEELS OF THE HAY WAGON kept a slow but steady rhythm as it was pulled down the rough stone street of Rüsselsheim, Germany, the small bed loaded heavily with the bodies of eight American airmen whose blood ran off the back edge of the cart, leaving a long, thick trail of black sorrow on the road. Sergeant Sidney Eugene Brown, the tail gunner of the American bomber that had gone down near this German city two days earlier, could hear nothing but the rumble of the wheels, the low monotonous grumble a contrast to the previous two hours of screaming and cacophonous noise.

Brown wondered where they were going, but he dared not raise his head to look around. Most of the crowd was gone, it seemed, and that was the most important thing. It was quiet except for the wagon's drone, and Brown supposed that meant he and his companions were being taken out of the city. He didn't know what was going to happen, but it couldn't be worse than what they had been through already.

A long way from his home in Gainesville, Florida, the nineteen-year-old country boy now lay piled in a heap with seven of his crew-mates, some of them his best friends. Brown had been lucid enough at the end to see several young Germans pull the hay cart to where the crew members lay on the street. He could do no more than lie there and wait. First they picked up William Dumont, the belly gunner from Berlin, New Hampshire, and tossed him into the cart with no regard, and then Brown's good friend William Adams, the nose gunner from Klingerstown, Pennsylvania. As they moved down the street, Brown was the next one to be tossed in. The loading continued until all eight Americans had been heaped in a jumble, bleeding profusely, limbs broken. The heat was excruciating, especially for Brown, who still wore the heated flying suit that had kept him warm at freezing altitudes when their B-24J bomber, the *Wham! Bam! Thank You Ma'am,* made its run near Hannover, a German city about 173 miles away. In the August heat, with men piled on top of him and his throat aching with thirst from dehydration and blood loss, the flying suit was torturous. But Brown could not risk moving to ease his discomfort. He could not see who was pulling the cart, but he suspected it was more than just one man. And even if there were just one, Brown was in no shape to outrun him or fight him. The more he listened, the more he thought it sounded like a small group of people pushing and pulling the cart. And the voices sounded impossibly young.

Brown could hardly breathe. Under the men, he struggled for each breath of the hot air thick with the smell of blood, sweat, urine, and feces. His head throbbed with pain from the blows he had suffered, and he couldn't even tell where else on his body he was hurt. The pain was everywhere. The metallic taste of blood filling his mouth made him want to retch. Brown couldn't tell who was still alive. He knew for sure that some of his friends were gone already. After they had been grinding along for about ten minutes, Brown heard one of the men next to him let out a small groan when the wagon bumped hard over the road. He realized then that it was Second Lieutenant John Sekul, the copilot, jammed in next to him, his head close but turned away. Beaten severely and shot in the head, Sekul was still hanging on. Glad to know someone else was alive, Brown whispered to him. "John, hey, John . . . move over a little. I can't breathe."

Sekul edged his body slightly away, giving Brown a tiny bit more room to suck in the fetid air that was keeping him alive.

Then he heard Sekul say something to him softly, through cut lips and broken teeth.

"Brownie . . ." he whispered. "Pray."

Brown didn't say anything in return, fearful of attracting the Germans' attention. But he was thinking *John, this little old Baptist boy's been praying all day.*

As the wagon rolled on, Brown could hear Sekul saying the rosary, quietly, in a voice muddled with blood.

"Our Father, who art in heaven, hallowed be Thy name; Thy kingdom come; Thy will be done on earth as it is in heaven," Sekul whispered. "Give us this day our daily bread; and forgive us our trespasses as we forgive those who trespass against us. . . ."

The tumbrel continued and Brown made out the sound of two or three voices speaking German as they pulled the wagon along. Brown wondered what the men were going to do with the Americans.

After another fifteen minutes or so, the wagon stopped, and Brown could hear voices again. This time there seemed to be a new voice in the mix, at least one. Brown decided to risk a look. As gingerly as he could, he raised himself just slightly so he could peer over the side of the cart.

As he looked around, trying to make out the scene through the maddening pain coursing through his head, Brown's eyes fell on a man walking toward the cart carrying a two-by-four piece of lumber in his hand and looking as if he were about to get to work.

Oh my God, he's coming to finish us off, Brown thought.

Brown slumped back down and closed his eyes, knowing his only chance for survival was to continue playing dead. He did not have the strength to fight anyone. He felt the cart shake as the man pounded on the side, looking for any response from the men he thought should be dead. Then Brown could hear the man grabbing the airmen one by one and looking for signs of life, striking them hard in the head with the club if there was any doubt. Brown heard Staff Sergeant Thomas Williams, an only child from Hazleton, Pennsylvania, make a small sound as the German pulled him up, followed by a crushing blow to the skull and one last whimper.

Sekul also heard the men being finished off. He began quietly whispering again. "Hail Mary, full of grace, the Lord is with thee; blessed art thou among women, and blessed is the fruit of thy womb, Jesus. . . ."

Brown, hearing the whispered Hail Mary, was glad that Sekul was still alive but wished he would be quiet. Brown felt Sekul's hand, resting on his shoulder, and felt him wince, feebly clenching his fist, as the German clubbed him in the head. The whispering of the rosary stopped. Brown lay as still as he could, hoping the executioner would pass him by. He could do nothing as Sekul's life slipped away and his hand fell from his shoulder.

Brown was certain he would be next, and he was. The man swung the club hard, but because of the way Brown was laying on the bottom, the sideboards of the wagon prevented the German from getting a good angle. The blow hit Brown in the head but glanced off. The German climbed up on the cart to get a better angle on the fliers and continued beating some, but then air raid sirens filled the air, signaling yet another Allied bombardment like the one this crew had taken part in just days earlier. The man with the club and the two other Germans ran for the safety of a slit trench nearby, leaving the airmen alone.

The cart was silent now; there was no more struggling, no groans or moaning. The only sound was the sirens screaming through the air, and those stopped after a few minutes. Brown wondered if he was the only one alive in the cart but then the terrible moans and groans came again. When he opened his eyes and looked around, he saw a terrible, gory scene. His friends were beaten horrifically, their heads smashed in, with blood, brains, and skull scattered. He was certain they were all dead or dying. Brown felt like he was dying too, the pain overwhelming him at times and the situation forcing him into a deep despair.

Dear God, help me out of this, he thought.

Bombs never fell on the cemetery, but Brown was too deep in his own pain and fear to notice whether they were landing somewhere nearby. After a while, he did realize that the Germans were not returning to the cart.

The day was completely silent as Brown lay in the cart, wondering if he would be the only survivor of the *Wham! Bam!* or merely the last to die.

In Gainesville, Florida, Brown's parents were thinking of their boy with the wavy, dirty blond hair and hoping, praying that the war would be over soon and Gene could return home safely. In Rochester, New York, a young wife was seeking comfort with her new in-laws, reading and rereading the last letters from her pilot husband and looking forward to the next. Loved ones were doing the same in the Bronx, Pennsylvania, Vermont, New Hampshire, and Michigan.

They were worried. They were hopeful. They had no idea.

CHAPTER 2

DREAMS AND NIGHTMARES

BEFORE THE LAST MISSION

BY ANY MEASURE, THE ENTIRE CREW of the *Wham! Bam!* didn't get the lucky hand. The men were led by Norman Rogers Jr., their twenty-four-year-old pilot, the second lieutenant from Rochester, New York. Rogers, the leader in every way of his ten-man crew, was the quintessential serviceman in World War II. Young and energetic, with a long life ahead of him and family eagerly awaiting his return, he was a good man who did not resent being called to duty and was eager to serve his country however it needed him. Rogers longed to be with his family and to resume his life in Rochester, but he also knew that he was doing something important, and he had been raised to value character and a sense of pride. The other airmen serving with Rogers all had their versions of the same story: All missed their loved ones but were focused on doing their part to defeat Germany.

The rest of the crew respected Rogers as a pilot and admired him as a friend. They knew that he had the skills to be a fighter pilot, a far more glamorous position, but he had requested command of a bomber partly because he so enjoyed the camaraderie of a large crew. Six feet tall, slim and handsome, Rogers was the second oldest of six children. The son of a captain in the Rochester Fire Department, Rogers grew up in the 19th

Ward, which was like its own little village where everyone knew each other. With a sense of duty instilled in him early on, Rogers joined the Marine Corps Reserve while still at Aquinas High School, and after graduating in 1937 he intended to join the Marines. His family sent him off to New York City to join the Corps, proud to see Rogers take on such responsibility. But Rogers soon came home dejected. He had been turned down twice because of his overbite, a restriction held over from the Civil War, when soldiers had to bite off the end of gunpowder packets to load their rifles, and because he had fractured his arm as a young boy. Eleven-year-old Norm had been hitching a ride to school one morning on the ice wagon that traveled through his neighborhood, letting it pull him along as he slid down the icy winter road, when he fell and fractured his left arm badly. His parents had forbidden him from playing on the ice wagon, so Norm went on to school without telling anyone and sat through classes unable to write because he was left handed. Then he went home with his arm throbbing in pain and tried to eat dinner without letting anyone know. He never complained, sitting stoically and quietly despite the agony. The injury was discovered only when his mother noticed that he was eating with his right hand. Rogers appealed the Marine Corps' rejection but, when that failed, he entered the Army Air Corps in 1939. (In 1944, the Army Air Corps would become the Army Air Force.)

Rogers's friends and family knew him to have a tough core even though he was quiet and rather shy. He could be serious and expected his crew to do things right the first time, but they also knew him to be fair and not overly beholden to military formality. The Rogers crew avoided using military titles when they were working together, calling each other by their last names instead. The crew members and Rogers's family back in Rochester knew that he wasn't shy about jumping into a fight if he thought someone was being mistreated. In addition to defending other kids from playground bullies, young Rogers had made a name for himself by standing up to the local theater manager who ordered all the kids to leave without a refund when the projector broke before the start of Saturday morning cartoons. Ten-year-old Norman marched to the box office and informed the manager that nobody was leaving his theater until they got their money back. Soon the kids were lining up to get their nickels.

His younger brother Art was in the Marines fighting on Guadal-
canal, so the Rogers family had a wealth of worries. His older brother
Jack was in the Army Air Force like Norm, having entered the war late
because his job as a fireman had earned him a deferment from the draft.
He was training to be a bombardier. Initially Norm was assigned to the
Ninth Reconnaissance Wing of the Fifth Army, but not as a pilot. For
three years, he worked as an armorer on the bombers, loading and maintaining the big guns that helped them fend off enemy fighters. While
serving on tropical bases—the Panama Canal Zone, Trinidad, St. Lucia,
and others—Rogers tried to keep his dear mother, Jennie, abreast of his
activities and assure her that he was okay. Forty-seven years old in 1940
but looking much older, Jennie was a prolific writer of letters to the editor of the Rochester newspaper and eagerly awaited letters from Norm
and her other boys, because each one meant they were safe—at least recently. Trying to overcome the military censors who would remove from
his letters any mention of where he was stationed, Rogers once wrote to
his mother: "Now I can honestly say I've been everywhere Art has been."
He knew she would piece together his previous deployments and realize
he was in Iceland. Norm's letters home, however, also showed a slow dis-
illusionment with Army life, and he told his family he was looking forward to coming home to Rochester after his enlistment was finished in
October 1943.

But then the Japanese bombed Pearl Harbor. Rogers was not discharged, after all, and at that point he didn't want to be. His disillusion-
ment with Army life turned into a frustration with not being in combat,
and not being able to make a real contribution to the war effort.

When he returned home to Rochester on his second leave in 1943,
Staff Sergeant Rogers reunited with his family and asked his sweetheart,
twenty-four-year-old Helen Monna, to marry him. A pretty strawberry
blonde with a big laugh and a warm smile, Monna proudly showed off
the ring that Rogers bought her, knowing all the while that her fiancée
would be gone again in just days.

When the opportunity arose to become a pilot, Rogers was ready to
make the move. It was his nature to be a leader, to rally men and show the
way. After preflight training in Nashville, Tennessee, and Maxwell Field

in Alabama, Rogers went on to flight training at Chatham Field in Savannah, Georgia, now the Savannah/Hilton Head International Airport. He became an Army Air Corps pilot with the rank of second lieutenant in January 1944. He was given the option of staying stateside as an instructor, but he turned that down. He was offered training as a fighter pilot, but he turned that down too. He chose to become the pilot of a B-24 bomber and work with a crew of men rather than fly solo. When he told his mother he would be piloting a bomber, she worried about him right away. "Fly slow and go low, Norm," she told him. He laughed and told her, "That's the surest way of getting hit!"

While in bomber pilot training in Savannah, Rogers wrote to Helen and suggested that she come there to marry him right away. They both realized this was their opportunity to get married because he was shipping out soon and had no idea when they would be together again. Helen wrote back right away saying she was coming and jumped on a train from Rochester to Savannah to meet her man. When she arrived in Georgia, she found that Rogers had never received her letter, didn't know if she had accepted his proposal, and had no idea she was showing up that day. Ever calm and cool, Rogers set about making the arrangements, and he and Helen were married in the Cathedral of St. John the Baptist on April 17, 1944. They dreamed of returning to Rochester as soon as the war was over and raising a family.

The next day, the new wife wrote to her in-laws, using some of Norm's stationery and proudly handwriting "MRS" in front of "Lieut. Norman J. Rogers" at the top. After explaining that Norm probably wouldn't be able to write that day because he was so busy with work, she told Jennie and Norman Rogers Sr. that Norm had gotten in from work in time to go to an 8 A.M. mass in the cathedral, then went to obtain the marriage license and a wedding ring and met two of Norm's friends who would serve as best man and altar boy. "We were married right on the altar at the chapel," she wrote. Then she went on to fill in her in-laws about her adventure in marriage.

Savannah is pretty much like Albany. Only I think there are about a thousand more soldiers here. It is very hard to find a decent place to live. I am still at the hotel.

I missed your company on the way down. Darn it, I had to do all my own worrying.

Did you write and tell Norma and Jack? I don't think Norm has. In fact, everything happened so fast I don't think he realizes yet that he is a married man. He never got any of my mail, even my telegram, until Thursday. I guess I took him by storm or something.

What do you hear from Art? Does he know any more about coming down? I know Norm would like to see him.

I am an Indian-giver. I gave this paper to Norm and now I am using it all up.

How is everybody? Are you still breaking bottles, Mr. Rogers?

I guess I will break this up. I just wanted you to know that everything worked out and that we are very happy.

Just one more thing. I want to thank you for having such a nice son. I will try and take as good care of him as you did.

Love, Mrs. N. J. Rogers (Helen)

On April 20, Rogers wrote his own letter to his parents, starting with an apology for being so busy that he couldn't write sooner. He recapped the wedding day and added that he had scammed some time off after the wedding by having a buddy answer for him at roll call the afternoon after he was married, when he was supposed to be in ground school. The next morning he was supposed to be in physical training, but his buddy fixed it up for him again so he could be off from Monday morning to Tuesday at noon, a real treat for lovers who had spent so little time with each other recently.

We think we did the right thing and I'm only sorry that we didn't do it while I was home. We got your telegram and we also got one from Mr. & Mrs. Monna. I haven't written to Jack or Norma yet but I suppose by now you have already told them. I imagine they were sort of surprised. What did uncle Frank and the rest of them say when they heard about it?

Everything around here is going fine so far. I got checked out yesterday so I'll be starting to fly with my new crew before long. We haven't been doing much flying lately because the weather has been pretty bad. I'm anxious to get working with my crew to find out just what kind of a bunch I've got. . . .

So Long, Norm

Helen and Norm were together until July 6, 1944, stationed at Langley Field in Virginia, while Rogers and his crew waited for their orders to deploy overseas. With the rest of the country, they had eagerly followed the news of D-Day and the invasion of France, alternately elated at the success of the troops engaged in the epic event and distraught over the idea of so many young men, just like Rogers and his crew, being mowed down on the beaches of Normandy. Rogers and his wife knew that he would be sent to England at some point, and they both worried about the dangers of flying missions into Germany and other bombing sites in Europe. They knew the death rate for bomber crews was high. Rogers never expressed hesitation or fear to any of his crew or his family, but his wife knew there was a deep worry that he kept hidden. One night in July, Rogers awoke from a nightmare, flustered and worried. Helen asked him what was wrong, what the nightmare was about.

"I don't think I'm coming back," he told her. It was the last time he said anything about his worries, and she never mentioned the nightmare to anyone.

When the orders came, Rogers learned that he and his crew were to fly to England and join the 491st Bombardment Group H, 854th Squadron of the Eighth Air Force. Sworn to secrecy about the details of their deployment, Rogers couldn't even tell his wife he was leaving. The couple had agreed earlier that whenever Rogers was shipped out, he would break formation and dip his wings over their apartment as a last good-bye. For weeks, every day that Norm went to work on the base, Helen would sit on the porch of their apartment listening for bomber formations. As each formation passed overhead, she would look to the sky and wait, hoping none of the planes broke formation. But on July 6, one plane did. Helen knew what it meant: Norm was on his way to England, and she should go back home to Rochester.

They didn't know how long it would be before they could see each other again. They also didn't know that Helen was two months pregnant.

THE TEN CREW MEMBERS were new to the scene in England but they were typical of the air crews flying missions over Europe throughout the war. They were young men who went to war when called, reluctant to leave their wives, girlfriends, sons, and daughters behind but determined to do their duty, all hoping to make it through the war without getting killed in midair by a fighter attack or antiaircraft fire, going down with the plane, or being captured by the Nazis after bailing out of their plane.

Two members of the crew—Lieutenant Bernard Cassidy, the navigator, and Lieutenant Yancey Robinson, the bombardier—did not make the ill-fated mission. With just two exceptions, the crew that would fly the *Wham! Bam!'s* last mission on August 24, 1944, had never flown in combat before. Rogers had flown a few missions with other crews, and one man that day would be a substitute who had more experience. Rogers's copilot, Second Lieutenant John N. Sekul, was respected as the second officer on the plane, but he still lamented not making the cut for an assignment to a fighter plane. The native of the Bronx, New York, was otherwise a lighthearted, agreeable sort who went with the flow, but he chafed every time he saw the fighters flying alongside his bomber.

Staff Sergeant Thomas D. Williams Jr., an only child from Hazleton, Pennsylvania, was drafted while attending college and ended up as the radio operator on the Rogers crew. He had a girlfriend waiting for him back home.

Most of the other crewmen were in their teens and had been drafted right out of high school. Sergeant Elmore L. Austin of Edinburg Falls, Vermont, was on the left waist gun, and Sergeant William A. Dumont, from Berlin, New Hampshire, manned the belly gun. Austin and his girlfriend had been eager to marry, but he convinced her that it was best to wait and make sure that he returned from the war. He didn't want her waiting for a husband who would never return. Sergeant William A. Adams also left his girl behind in Klingerstown, Pennsylvania; now he was on the nose gun. Tail gunner Sergeant Sidney Eugene Brown was from Gainesville, Florida, and liked to refer to himself as "a little bit country." Everyone at home called him Gene, but his crewmates knew him as Brownie.

At twenty-eight years old, Staff Sergeant Forrest W. Brininstool, serving as the engineer, was the old man of the crew. With a wife back home on their farm outside Jackson, Michigan, Brininstool wanted to get home safely just as much as everyone else, but he also felt a responsibility to look after "the boys," as he called the rest of the crew. In a bomber, just a few more years than the rest of the team brings an obligation.

Brown and Adams struck up a close friendship as soon as the crew was formed, bonding over their common country background; one was from way down South and one was from up north in Pennsylvania, but they both knew the country life. Adams wasn't one of those know-it-all Yankees, Brown once told him. He was a good old country boy like himself. Adams knew to take it as a compliment, and he agreed it was true.

The Rogers crew was tight, as most groups of young men become when they train, work, and live together almost all the time. Military decorum still applied, however, so the enlisted men still showed respect to Rogers, Sekul, and Brininstool as officers, but once on their plane, everyone knew that Rogers ran a laid-back ship.

ROGERS'S CORRESPONDENCE with his wife and his parents continued after he arrived in England, first at Metfield, a tiny village in Suffolk, located near the border with Norfolk, about five miles southeast of Harleston and seven miles northwest of Halesworth. He wrote to his father on July 8, 1944.

> It makes me very happy to know that both you and Mom approve of Helen. However, I am awfully sorry that I didn't get married at home. There is no doubt in my mind, though, that Helen and I did the right thing in getting married now. At first I wondered about it and thought perhaps we should wait until after the war, but now I know differently and am sorry that we didn't get married even sooner than we did. She really is the nicest girl in the world as far as I'm concerned. . . .
>
> I don't know what is going to happen to me from now on but whatever my fate may be, I am sure that I have made the most of my life and lived the best I was able. That probably doesn't make sense but I am sure you know what I mean. And I appreciate all that you and Mom have done for me and I hope that some day I will be able to repay you in part. I know that I can never fully repay you and I know that I have appeared awfully ungrateful in the past.
>
> I'll leave you now for a while but I will write again soon and let you know how things are. Right now, me, my crew, and my ship, we are in fine shape.
>
> Take care of yourself,
> So Long, Norm

THE METFIELD BASE where Rogers and his crew were stationed was a simple airfield built near the village for use by the U.S. Air Force's

491st Bomb Group and the 353rd Fighter Group. From there they expected to fly bombing runs deep into enemy territory and then try to fly, or limp, back home to the safety of the base nestled in the beautiful, quiet countryside of England. Until the crew was assigned to a mission, they spent the days training, often flying simulated bomb runs on English towns, and studying flight plans and maps. While the men were still settling in and wondering about their first assignments, the peacefulness of the base was rocked by an enormous boom on the sunny afternoon of July 15. As Rogers, Brown, Dumont, and the others raced outside to see what was happening, they saw a dark cloud billowing up from less than a mile away. Were they under attack? Could a German bomber possibly have made it there in broad daylight without anyone even hearing it?

Then came a series of explosions, each one sending more black smoke and pyrotechnic sprays high into the air. Pretty soon Rogers and his crew realized what had happened. Somehow, the base's ammunition dump, situated at the edge of the airfield, had caught fire. Now 1,200 pounds of bombs and other incendiaries were rocking the beautiful, quiet English countryside.

When the explosions stopped and the damage could be assessed, the airmen found that five men had been killed in the blasts, although none were from the 491st. Five B-24s were lost and six others were badly damaged. The military investigation followed promptly, with the already legendary Lieutenant General James Harold "Jimmy" Doolittle leading an inspection committee that arrived two days later. Most of the men at the base had already pinpointed the cause of the explosion as what was supposedly the munition crew's standard way of unloading bombs from a truck: drive it in reverse at high speed, then slam on the brakes and let the bombs slide off. The 491st took three days off to help clean up the mess at the base.

On July 23, 1944, Rogers wrote to his mother, first apologizing for having to use V-mail—a tiny photograph of his actual letter, sometimes required during the war to reduce the volume of mail—and then telling her that he hadn't flown any missions yet but that he expected to soon. "I am sort of anxious to get started because I'm afraid that the war might end before I get a crack at them," he wrote. He couldn't tell her about the excitement and the tragedy of the ammunition dump explosion, but he probably wouldn't have wanted to worry her with that sort of news anyway.

AS JULY WORE ON, the Eighth Air Force was worrying about the performance of its B-24s and the changing tactics of war. In the last week of July 1944, the U.S. Air Force ordered the removal of all ball turrets from the Eighth's B-24s to reduce weight and improve maneuverability. The ball turret, mounted on the belly of the plane, was heavily armed with two 50-caliber machine guns. It was a small, cramped space, but it did give the gunner a good view of attacking fighter planes. Each turret rotated horizontally and vertically so that the gunner could fire in any direction. Although the turrets had been welcomed as an ingenious defense against fighter planes, the Eighth Air Force was now deciding that the enemy's changing strategies made them less valuable. The bigger risk these days came from the exploding shells of ground-based artillery rather than the Luftwaffe. The 88-mm antiaircraft gun shells fired from the ground were one of the Germans' strong points in the war, creating the "flak" that air crews feared so much. The term "flak" was a German contraction of Flugzeugabwehr-Kanone or Flugabwehr-Kanone, meaning antiaircraft gun. Even if the bombers did encounter fighter planes, they would fly faster and be more nimble without the ball turrets.

The B-24 was critical to the Allies' effort to bomb the Germans into submission. It had been developed in response to the U.S. Army Air Corps' request in 1938 for more bombers. Most of the first-production B-24 heavy bombers, named Liberators, went to the Royal Air Force, including those that had been ordered by France before the German occupation. American Liberators first saw action in June 1942, some time after B-24s flown by the British had already been in use. The big airplane, powered by four Pratt & Whitney R-1830–43 14-cylinder turbocharged radial engines rated at 1,200 horsepower each, was not a hit at first with either the public or air crews. The B-17 had already established itself as the "Flying Fortress" and earned a reputation among crews as a solid plane. No weak sister itself, the B-24 was armed with eleven Browning machine guns—two each in the dorsal, tail, and ball turrets; one in each waist window; and three in the nose. The plane was built with the specific purpose of delivering bombs weighing 500 and 1,000 pounds to enemy targets. On a typical combat mission, the B-24 would carry about 5,000 to 6,000 pounds of bombs, though on short missions it might carry much more.

After the B-24 proved its mettle in bombing runs against the German fuel supply in Europe, B-24 production jumped dramatically at the Willow Run, Michigan, facility, located between Ypsilanti and Belleville. Planes were rolling off the assembly lines so quickly that crews were sent to sleep outside the Willow Run facility on cots, ready to fly the planes away immediately after production was complete. By the end of the war, five production plants would produce an impressive 18,482 aircraft, meaning that more B-24 airplanes would be built than any other aircraft in American history. By 1944, when the Rogers crew was preparing to jump into the war in Europe feet first, the B-24 was already becoming known as the workhorse of the Allied bombing effort. And a workhorse it was. There was no glamour or comfort in this plane. This machine was bare boned, with the minimum machinery and metal required to take bombs where they needed to go. There was no heat onboard, even though the high altitude temperatures could reach fifty degrees below zero, so the crew usually wore bulky, electrically heated flight suits. Flying the B-24 was no easy matter either. The pilots had to maneuver the plane using brute strength to wrestle the controls; if it was raining, they might have to stick their heads out the window to see where they were going, because the B-24 had no windshield wipers.

IN THE FIRST TWO WEEKS of August 1944, the 491st flew thirteen missions in fourteen days, though Rogers and his crew were not sent out. Losses were relatively low, but on August 3, Second Lieutenant Marshall W. Field and his crew—July replacements like Rogers and his crew—were shot down by flak over France. On August 11, First Lieutenant Charles H. Christian's B-24 took a direct hit between the number 3 and 4 engines just as it began dropping bombs over Saarbrucken, Germany. Another pilot who witnessed the plane going down reported that "nine objects were seen to drop out of Lt. Christian's aircraft but we did not actually see any open chutes." Surprisingly, the crew had in fact stayed with the plane, and Christian managed to land near Nantua, France, with no significant injuries. The items seen dropping from the plane may have been gear that the crew was tossing overboard to lighten the load.

On August 13, a crew bailed out of their B-24 with two engines aflame over Le Havre, France, on their thirtieth mission. No one knew for a long time what happened to them, but as always when the crew was seen bailing out, their buddies back at the base held out hope that the men had survived and been taken prisoner, which in fact they had. Spending the rest of the war as a POW was no one's first choice, but it was the optimistic outcome you hoped for when the plane didn't come back to the base.

On August 15, Rogers and his crew, along with the rest of the 491st, were informed that they were moving to a nearby base in North Pickenham, in Norfolk. The 492nd had been flying from that base, but German fighter pilots latched on to the planes' distinctive tail markings—bare metal and silver fabric fins with black stripes, vertical for the 44th and horizontal for the 392nd group—and made sport of knocking them out of the sky. Eight B-24s from the 492nd had gone down on May 19, fourteen on June 20, and twelve on July 7. Almost sixty bombers had been lost in less than three months, effectively wiping out the 492nd Bomb Group. The 491st was sent to North Pickenham to replace the beleaguered group, and by nightfall on August 15 the 491st was at the base known as "North Pick."

Initially it was assumed that the 491st would adopt the same tail insignia that had been used by the doomed 492nd, a typical move when one group takes over operations for another. But the men of the 491st were well aware of why they were at North Pick and why the remnants of the 492nd were leaving. They quietly decided not to paint the striped insignia on the green tails of their B-24s.

Two days of housekeeping followed the move, and then on August 18, the 491st flew its first mission from North Pickenham. Again Rogers and his crew were not included. They were getting antsy to be on their first mission, partly because they were eager to serve, wanting to do more than sit around the base, and partly because they wanted to get it over with, to get that first mission out of the way so they could stop worrying about it.

SOON AFTER HE ARRIVED at North Pick, Rogers received a letter from Helen. Thrilled as always to get mail from his wife, he found a quiet spot to read it and soon realized this was no ordinary letter from home. His dear Helen was pregnant.

Rogers couldn't wait to tell his buddies, and he beamed with pride whenever one of his friends congratulated him. "I want my bouncing baby girl," Rogers often said, even before learning of Helen's pregnancy.

On August 20, 1944, Rogers sat down and wrote his bride a ten-page letter telling her how overjoyed he was with the news, how much he loved her, and how he hoped to finish his business in England soon and come home to be a father. Sadly, his wife never received the letter. A young boy in her neighborhood had a habit of taking mail from people's mailboxes, and eventually Helen found shredded parts of Norm's last letter to her moldering in a ditch. She couldn't read any of it and wondered if Norm even knew she was going to have his baby. Helen had been robbed of her husband's passionate correspondence at a uniquely joyous time in their lives, a loss that would be compounded when she realized it had been the last letter he ever sent her.

On the same afternoon, Rogers wrote a six-page letter to his father. Because of wartime delays in mail delivery, it arrived some time after the letter to Helen had been destroyed.

> It seems sort of strange to me that I'll have kids of my own. I knew, of course, that it would happen eventually, but now that the time has come I can't picture myself as a father.
>
> All I can say is that I'm sure lucky that I had the father I had. At least I have a perfect example to follow.
>
> Things have been pretty dreary over here for the past few days and we've just been sitting on the ground doing nothing. Just like a big pack of vultures walking around on the ground after somebody clipped all their

wings. This war isn't going to last much longer and we'll be in the air again soon doing our best to get it over with in a hurry. We've got to finish it up now so that I can get home by February.

The baby was due in February.

THE MEN WHO WOULD soon join the thousands of American fliers in the skies over Europe all dealt with their own worries in their own ways, rarely voicing them even to each other. If anyone knew what fears were hidden in their hearts, it probably was the girlfriends, wives, and mothers back home, the women in whom men could confide their deepest worries. Helen Rogers knew that her husband had been fearful of his assignment to England, having dreams that he would never return. But he went on without complaint, like so many other men during the war.

And so did radio operator Thomas Williams, who never told his crewmates about the dream that still haunted him, the images that came back to him at night as he lay down to sleep in Pickenham, awaiting their first mission. His girlfriend back in Hazleton knew, but she couldn't comfort Williams as he struggled to make the nightmare go away, to convince himself that it was nothing more than that. Before coming to England, even before training for the bomber crew, Williams had spent a night at his girlfriend's home and woke up the whole house with screaming from a nightmare. Not of his plane flying through clouds of flak, hot shrapnel ripping through the fuselage. Not of his bomber on fire and spiraling down to a terrible end. Not the usual ways a bomber crewman would expect to meet his end. Something worse.

His girlfriend had assured him it meant nothing, that it was just a bad dream. She held him and promised him that he would be okay, that the dream didn't mean anything at all. Williams wasn't certain she believed what she said any more than he did.

As the months passed, Williams tried to put the nightmare out of his mind, but as the date for his first mission grew closer, the images and the sounds came back to him regularly. When he closed his eyes at night, the sights of a rubble-strewn street in Germany appeared to him and he was gripped by the chest-tightening fear again. He could see his friends and crewmates around him, all of them running, trying to escape a mob of angry townspeople. The dream had no ending, just an endless loop of running, panic on the faces of the crew, and brutal, horrific beatings.

Williams knew what the dream meant. He was going to be beaten to death in Germany.

CHAPTER 3
WINDING DOWN

THE AMERICANS WHO ARRIVED IN ENGLAND in July 1944 knew they were coming late to the show. No one knew exactly when the war would end, but everyone knew that it couldn't go on much longer.

D-Day had changed the tide of the war, just as the Allies had hoped. They invaded northern France and, after reassigning several of their divisions from Italy and southern France, they defeated the German army units in France. A Soviet offensive on June 22 in Belarus resulted in the near destruction of the German Army Group Centre (two strategic army groups that fought on the Eastern front) and then another Soviet offensive forced German troops from western Ukraine and eastern Poland. Resistance forces in Poland, emboldened by the Soviet push, initiated several uprisings against the German occupiers, but German troops crushed the largest one, in Warsaw. Another Soviet offensive in eastern Romania isolated the German troops in that country and prompted revolts there and in Bulgaria, after which both countries shifted their allegiance to the Allies.

The war in the Pacific raged on, but there were encouraging developments on that front as well. Forces in Southeast Asia had repelled the Japanese sieges in Assam, pushing the Japanese back to the Chindwin

River. The Japanese were still strong in China, capturing the cities of Changsha in June and Hengyang in August. American forces were driving the Japanese back in the Pacific, most notably in June with an offensive against the Mariana and Palau islands. That successful drive, which was such a crushing loss to the Japanese that it led to the resignation of Prime Minister Hideki Tojo, made air bases available to the Army Air Force that could be used to launch bomber attacks on Japan itself.

Everything was changing in the war. The 491st started its combat tour just as the European Strategic Air Offensive against the German aircraft industry—previously of top priority—was being replaced by tactical support of the invasion and then by campaigns against such targets as oil, nitrogen, and transportation. The Luftwaffe had lost air superiority over the continent, and since June 1944 antiaircraft flak was killing more Allied serviceman than fighter planes were. Although Rogers and his crew were coming in late, there was still plenty to do. When they arrived in England, less than 25 percent of the bomb tonnage that eventually would be dropped on Europe by the Eighth Air Force had been delivered.

Concentrating its attacks on strategic objectives in Germany, the 491st dropped thousands of bombs on communications centers, oil refineries, storage depots, industrial areas, shipyards, and other targets that provided material support to the war. Its planes struck Berlin, Hamburg, Kassel, Cologne, Gelsenkirchen, Bielefeld, Hanover, Magdeburgon, and even the headquarters of the German General Staff at Zossen, Germany.

The 491st also supported ground forces at Saint-Lô in July 1944 and assaulted V-weapon sites and communications lines elsewhere in France during the summer. The group would go on to drop supplies to paratroops during the airborne attack in Holland, and it would bomb German supply lines and fortifications during the Battle of the Bulge from December 1944 to January 1945. Rogers and his crew participated in none of these missions, either arriving too late or not being assigned that day.

ROGERS'S CREW AND THE REST of the 491st were the fresh fish in the 14th Bomb Wing, which was commanded by Brigadier General Leon

W. Johnson, famous among crews for his flying in Operation Tidal Wave on August 1, 1943. An audacious and incredibly dangerous effort to destroy nine Romanian oil refineries in Ploesti, Tidal Wave was one of the costliest air operations of the war. Fifty-three aircraft were lost and 660 crew members were killed on what the 14th Bomb Wing would come to call Black Sunday. Johnson and four others were awarded the Medal of Honor for their heroics that day. Flying alongside the crews of the 44th, which had participated in the operation, and the 392nd, which had far more experience than the new guys in town, Rogers and the other men of the 491st felt they were finally in the big leagues.

Rogers and his crew settled into the routine at North Pickenham, sometimes shunned by the more experienced crew members who did not want to get too friendly with guys who might not be coming back. Better to wait and see who has luck on their side before making a new buddy. The realities of flying into enemy territory were hitting Rogers and his crew in the face every day now, from the smart-ass heckling from the "old guys" who had survived a few runs to the practical aspects of preparing for a trip in which you might end up in enemy hands. Each man had to pose for photos wearing a haircut and civilian clothes of a fashion that could pass in Europe, the images carefully posed and lighted to look like identification photos from any number of government bureaucracies—Germany, France, Italy, Romania. Fliers carried the small photos in their "escape and evasion kits" so that they could be used on forged documents if the men found themselves bailing out and on the run, with help from local resistance fighters. The crew members did their best to pose with a blank expression and the stern demeanor you would expect of someone having the all-important identification papers processed in a government office in Berlin. Sekul's photo was especially effective, looking every bit the serious Aryan dedicated to the Führer, and Brininstool could have passed easily as a railroad clerk in Bucharest. Rogers looked like he was suppressing a grin at the thought of such charades, and Williams looked like he was ready to pick up his glove and get back to his baseball game in Pennsylvania.

The crew also gathered helpful information along the way. More than one experienced bomber crewman told them to leave their sidearms behind. "That thing won't help you and will just end up getting you in more trouble," they said. "If you're on the ground and being chased, one little pistol's only going to make 'em mad. Better off without that heavy thing."

As the Allies continued marching onward after D-Day—nearly to Paris by mid-August—Rogers and his crew worried that they would still be sitting on the ground when the war ended. How crazy would that be, to go home and say you never even flew a mission?

And then on August 20, the teletype at the base clicked out the order that would change so many lives. Attacks planned for the next day would require a great deal of the Eighth Air Force's resources and pretty much every plane at North Pick. In Mission 568, the Eighth was sending a total of 1,319 bombers and 739 fighters deep into Germany to hit sixteen targets. This would be the largest formation of aircraft to leave England so far in the war. Rogers was notified that his plane would be the backup lead in their formation, the one that would take over guiding the formation to its target if the lead aircraft were hit. That meant Rogers and Sekul would have to attend extra briefings the next morning.

Unfortunately, two of the regular crewmen—Lieutenant Bernard Cassidy, the navigator, and Lieutenant Yancey Robinson, the bombardier—were away, undergoing training in advanced radar systems. They would miss the crew's first mission and, as it turned out, the last flight of the *Wham! Bam!* In their stead, Flight Officer Haigus Tufenkjian would serve as both navigator and bombardier. The Detroit, Michigan, native had volunteered to go to war in 1942, and his training in electrical engineering at the Ford Motor Company had made him a good candidate for the more technical positions on a bomber crew. Tufenkjian, a round-faced, jovial Armenian American, was at the Pickenham base recovering from wounds he suffered on a bombing run with his own crew when the call came for a volunteer to fill the empty slots in Rogers's crew. Tufenkjian stepped forward. The men in the Rogers crew had never met him.

Rogers and the rest of his crew were not happy to be setting out on their first mission without Cassidy and Robinson, and to make matters worse, their regular B-24—the one in which they had trained and with which they had become intimately familiar—was down for removal of the ball turret gun. They had planned to come up with a nickname and logo for their plane after earning the rights by flying it on a mission, but now they had to settle for a spare B-24J—a variant of the original B-24 that differed slightly in terms of armor and had a few mechanical improvements. The plane already had a flashy name, the *Wham! Bam! Thank You Ma'am,* and a cartoon logo of a reclining rabbit. As they prepared for the mission, both apprehensive and excited about finally being able to make use of their training, they realized that the *Wham! Bam!* had more experience than they did.

Their lack of experience, however, would play no role in the fate of the *Wham! Bam!* For many bomber crews, the likelihood of returning safely to the base depended more on chance, sheer dumb luck, whether a piece of flak zipped this way or that way, than on anything else.

The mission was scrubbed two days in a row because of bad weather over Germany or somewhere along the flight path, so the Rogers crew had to wait along with the rest of the more than 12,000 men on this mission, wondering if the next morning would finally be the day for them to fly.

On Wednesday, August 23, Rogers and Sekul flew practice runs over Germany in a different plane, then they and the rest of the crew whiled away the evening playing poker in the barracks. Brininstool was the big winner, which was no surprise. A few months earlier, Brown had been playing craps with the boys while they waited to fly a training mission, and Brininstool was taking everything he had. In the middle of the game on that day, while Brininstool was winning, Sekul walked up and ordered everyone on to the plane.

After they were in the air for a while and everything was quiet, Brown called to Sekul on the intercom.

"Brown to Sekul," he said, knowing that Brininstool would hear too.

"Go ahead, Brown," Sekul replied.

"That's the last time this little old Southern boy gets in a craps game with a bunch of Yankees."

On this night before their first mission, they got to bed soon after the sun set, anxious about the next day's mission and knowing they would have to wake long before sunrise. Rogers and Sekul, along with the volunteer bomber and navigator Tufenkjian, awoke at 1:30 A.M. to attend briefings on the bombing strategy, flight plans, and many details about coordinating their flight with the huge number of other planes in the air for this assault. Everyone else woke up at 2:30 A.M. and was ready for breakfast by 3, each man taking the time to shave so that the oxygen mask needed at high altitudes would make a good, tight fit. As the men trudged along in the rain on their way to the chow hall for an early morning breakfast, they wondered if the mission might be canceled again because of the weather. Brown was counting on it, because he had an excruciating toothache that he knew would make him miserable during the flight. He had considered going on sick call but didn't want to be scrubbed from the mission. If the rest of the boys were going, so was he. He wasn't going to let his buddies risk their lives while he lay around with a toothache. In fact, he was so sure they would not be flying that day that when he realized he had left his dog tags in the shower stall, he did not go back for them.

The crew found a treat awaiting them for breakfast: real eggs instead of the powdered eggs they usually found on their trays. The men enjoyed the scrambled eggs with toast, oatmeal, grapefruit juice, and coffee, talking all the while about the mission and what they could expect.

After breakfast they boarded two half-ton trucks for the rainy ride to a briefing session. Brininstool, the engineer, and the gunners went to one session, while Williams joined Rogers, Sekul, and Tufenkjian in the last of their series of meetings.

In their session, Rogers, Sekul, and the other officers learned the details of their mission. After the door to the meeting room was closed, the flight commander began by pulling down a map to reveal the secrets of the day. When Rogers and Sekul saw the red ribbon pinned to the map, delineating their flight path, they realized they would be taking their crew deep into dangerous territory.

The commander explained that this was a big operation and then broke it down for the men. The crew would be part of the first of four groups the Eighth was organizing for that day's assault. This group would consist of 433 B-24s, including the Rogers crew, escorted by 248

P-38, P-47, and P-51 fighters. Once near their targets, the group would separate, and 125 bombers would attack Brunswick/Waggum, 99 would go after Brunswick/Querum, 88 would hit the oil refinery at Misburg, and the Rogers crew would be among 72 bombers targeting the Langenhagen airfield near Hannover.

So it was Langenhagen. This would be their first mission as a bomber crew. This target was well into the heart of Germany, and the two pilots knew the mission would be extremely dangerous.

After the commander's briefing on the elaborate route the planes would take, breaking off into their smaller groups at certain waypoints, the meteorologist took over to explain the weather conditions for the day in England, over the Channel, and at their target sites. He was followed by the armament officer, who discussed their bomb loads, and a signalman, who went over details of radar use for the mission. The last person to speak was the intelligence officer, who described the targets and their significance, along with what was known about antiaircraft batteries and Luftwaffe defenses in the area. Rogers and Sekul, like all the other officers in the room, were paying close attention and making notes they would need during the mission. When the intelligence officer was finished, the commanding officer stepped forward again and asked if there were any questions. When there were none, he told the men to synchronize their watches and then they were dismissed.

Rogers and Sekul picked up their crew's escape and evasion kits on the way out of their meeting, each one a bag measuring about four inches by five inches and containing currency from several countries, maps, a compass, and the faux civilian photo that each crew member had made. Williams stayed behind as the rest of the crew left their session to get geared up. As radio operator, he needed to be briefed on call signs, radio frequencies, and codes, which were new for each mission. The information was crucial to the plane's mission and safe return, so it was sandwiched between two heavy pieces of clear celluloid to give it weight and make it less likely to fly away in the ferocious gusts that could blow through a bomber during a mission. When Williams joined the rest of the crew in the trucks waiting outside, he found the gunners all suited up in their electrically heated flight suits, harnesses, oxygen masks, and Mae West life vests, carrying their rations for the day.

Brown was realizing that the mission wouldn't be called off and regretted not having his dog tags. Before the truck pulled away, the officers handed each man his escape and evasion kit.

As they rode out to the plane they would borrow that day, the crew members had plenty on their minds. They went through all the technical details on which they had just been briefed; the officers and radioman had plenty to remember, but the gunners had been given the good news that they probably wouldn't run into much resistance from Luftwaffe fighters. All of the men, however, were occupied with the same thoughts of their loved ones back home. One thing they tried not to think too much about was the effects of the 2,893 tons of explosives they and the rest of the Eighth Air Force were about to drop on Germany. For bomber crews, it was important to focus on your mission, doing your job, and the moral certainty that you were on the right side and doing your best to end the war.

Thinking too much about what was happening on the ground could drive a man crazy.

THE ROGERS CREW HAD NOT yet seen the destructive power of a bombing raid on a European city, but they still knew what they were doing. They knew they were going to drop 500- and 1,000-pound bombs that could devastate a wide area within minutes, setting off uncontrollable fires. The bombing campaign had been effective in these later years of the war, and the crew members knew that this success came, in part, through the destruction of civilian areas as well as military targets. They probably had no way of knowing what it was like to be on the ground as a B-24 like theirs passed overhead with the bomb bay doors open, probably couldn't even imagine the horror they wreaked on the ground with the simple push of a bombardier's toggle switch, but they couldn't deny the nature of their job. On every mission, bomber crews were in life-and-death struggles to survive long enough to drop bombs that would kill hundreds, perhaps thousands. Regrettably, many of them would be civilian men, women, and children. It was a burden, if the men let themselves dwell on it. Most bomber crews sought solace in the knowledge that they were aiming for legitimate military targets, and any civilian deaths were unfortunate but unavoidable facts of war.

That was easier for American crews to believe than it was for British bomber crews. As the war raged on into 1944, the two allies took different tacks with their bombing campaigns, to the extent they could separate their strategic decisions. Both parties agreed early on about the war-winning potential of bombing, but the U.S. Army Air Force, led by Lieutenant General Henry H. "Hap" Arnold, contended that the way to win the war was by knocking out the enemy's key industrial sites. For the British, who were far more war-weary and ready to go for the jugular against this enemy, the right strategy was to bomb civilian targets and destroy the German morale. The British relied on "area bombing" to wipe out entire cities at a time, through the years developing sophisticated bombing techniques that assured near-total destruction rather than just extensive damage. During the war in Europe, the Royal Air Force (RAF) was largely responsible for the bombing of Germany while the U.S. Eighth Army was tasked with defeating the Luftwaffe—both by shooting the planes out of the air and by bombing airfields, production plants, fuel refineries, and any other industrial target that supported the German air force. The Eighth Army's success with this effort was why, at this point in 1944, the ball turrets on the B-24 were seen as unnecessary and why antiaircraft fire from the ground was considered the bigger threat to bombers over Germany.

Even with their focus on military targets, however, American bombs still killed great numbers of civilians. The reason was partly because dropping bombs from thousands of feet while being buffeted by flak and fighting off enemy planes can take a real toll on a crew's accuracy. And it was partly because the American dedication to bombing only military targets was sometimes just a semantic cover for what actually happened in battle. The architects of the bombing missions, as well as the pilots and bombardiers, knew that only military targets were acceptable, but they also knew that Air Force policy was that any city with a population of more than 50,000 was automatically considered a military target because it was assumed to have military or industrial assets. When it was impossible to conduct precision bombing because of weather or other restraints, bomber crews could legitimately target such a city. In this situation, the pilots and bombardier were empowered to make that call if they arrived at their military target and found it unavailable.

The RAF Bomber Command tried to use the same semantic cover even though it was acknowledged openly that the goal was to bomb German civilians until the country lost the will to fight. Publicly, the RAF stated that it was not indiscriminately bombing civilians and was focusing on German industrial targets. What it did not say was that it was bombing industrial workers—and all other civilians in the area—not only to undermine the military supply line but to demoralize the entire populace, specifically with the goal of "dehousing" the citizens and making them refugees and causing other privations. In the latter part of the war, especially when Rogers's crew was about to make its first mission, the Eighth Air Force often was able to conduct more precise bombing raids on strictly industrial targets because the Luftwaffe threat had been greatly diminished and weather conditions over the targets trended favorably. Under the same conditions, the RAF Bomber Command continued bombing and even stepped up efforts to attack cities previously untouched, such as Würzburg and Hildesheim, both known for their historical significance and beauty rather than military assets.

The American adherence to precision bombing, at least when conditions allowed, did not carry over to the Pacific theater. In Japan, General Curtis LeMay, heading the U.S. XXI Bomber Command, practiced area bombing for the same reasons espoused by the British. And like the British, and sometimes like the Americans in the European theater, LeMay found ways to rationalize the widespread killing of Japanese civilians. After the firebombing of Tokyo on March 9 and 10, 1945, LeMay said that there are no innocent civilians. "The entire population got into the act and worked to make those aeroplanes or munitions . . . men, women, and children."

Critics of area bombing in Germany were often met with the response that the Germans did it first in Britain, and the argument was not easily dismissed. The British people suffered terribly during the Blitz, the vicious German bombing campaign which began in June 1940. The first targets were industrial, in an effort to soften up Britain for a German invasion, but targeting technology was relatively primitive in 1940 (although it would advance greatly during the war), and bombs often fell on civilian neighborhoods. The civilian death toll was high: 258 killed in July 1940 and another 1,075 in August. The August figure included 136 children and 392 women. The Germans intensified their efforts, and on September 2, 1940, Hermann Göring ordered that London be destroyed. Three days later Hitler ordered the Luftwaffe to pursue a general bombing campaign against urban targets, specifically with the intent of destroying British morale.

Area bombing continued for nine months. The Luftwaffe rained hell down on the British people, dropping 350 tons of bombs on London alone by September 17. The bombing escalated at a shocking rate; by April 1941, more than 1,000 tons of bombs were dropped on London in a single night. The civilian death toll also continued to mount, with a single raid on Coventry killing 5,000 people. By the time the Blitz ended in May 1941, the Luftwaffe had killed 40,000 Britons and left 750,000 homeless. The bombs had destroyed more than a 1.25 million homes.

British prime minister Winston Churchill said in a speech at London's County Hall, on July 15, 1941, that the British people supported retaliating against German citizens. "If tonight the people of London were asked to cast their vote whether a convention should be entered into to stop the bombing of all cities, the overwhelming majority would cry, 'No, we will mete out to the Germans the measure, and more than the measure, that they have meted out to us.'" It was classic Churchill, rousing the spirit, but he may not have been accurate. Interestingly, the theory justifying the German area bombing as retaliation for the Blitz was accepted the least by the British people who had suffered the most as German bombs rained down on London and other targets. An opinion poll conducted in 1941 during the Blitz asked "Would you approve or disapprove if the RAF adopted a policy of bombing the civilian population of Germany?" In the northernmost counties of England, where there had been no bombing at all, 76 percent of the respondents approved bombing German civilians. But in the most heavily bombed areas of London, the people were split 45 percent for the reprisal bombing and 47 percent against. The people who had seen the horrors of what area bombing can do were the least likely to inflict it even on their worst enemy.

There was, to be sure, considerable debate and conflict in the British government over the targeting of civilians. After the bombing of Hamburg and Berlin, House of Lords member George Bell spoke to the House on February 9, 1944, condemning the wholesale destruction of civilian areas, in response to others who had spoken in support.

"It had been said that area bombing was definitely designed to diminish the sacrifice of British lives and to shorten the war," Bell said. "Everybody wishes with all his heart that these two objects could be achieved, but to justify methods inhumane in this way smacked of the Nazi philosophy of 'might is right.'"

The government spokesman replied succinctly: "These great war industries can only be paralyzed by bringing the whole life of the cities in which they are situated to a standstill."

Proponents of area bombing argued strongly that the British public should be told that the RAF was intentionally targeting civilians, that it was a legitimate and productive strategy of war, rather than pretending it was an unfortunate result of trying to hit military targets. The strongest and most influential proponent was Sir Arthur "Bomber" Harris, the head of the RAF Bomber Command. He argued incessantly with government leaders, including Churchill himself, that the facade of military targeting with accidental civilian deaths made the RAF look unskilled and weak to the enemy, especially in comparison to the American Eighth Air Force, which could claim more accuracy in hitting military targets. As the war was winding down and the Soviets became a growing threat, Harris argued that the inaccurate perception of the RAF bombing campaigns must be corrected.

"That aim is the destruction of German cities; the killing of German workers; and the disruption of civilized life throughout Germany," he said. "It should be emphasized that the destruction of houses, public utilities, transport, and lives; the creation of a refugee problem on an unprecedented scale; and the breakdown of morale both at home and at the battle fronts by fear of extended and intensified bombing, are accepted and intended aims of our bombing policy. They are not by-products of attempts to hit factories."

The debate, of course, has to consider how the enemy would have responded in the same situation. The British knew firsthand that the Germans had no compunction about killing civilians, especially as the V–1 and V–2 rockets continued to terrorize London late in the war, and one has to wonder how the Nazis would have bombed American targets, if it had been possible for them to do so. Historians believe it is unlikely that the Nazis would have restricted themselves to purely military and industrial targets and instead would have opted for the every-city-is-full-of-war-industry-workers theory and carpet bombed civilians en masse. In reality, the Germans likely would have killed American men, women, and children indiscriminately and tolerated no debate about the propriety. Killing Rosie the Riveter while firebombing Pittsburgh and Atlanta would only have been a bonus for the German war effort, rather than having to use the death of war workers as a ruse for the real goal of decimating the population.

Proponents of area bombing could be coldly rational. British author George Orwell defended area bombing, saying that the effect on women and children was overstated and that killing civilians was not necessarily any worse than killing men in uniform. On May 19, 1944, he wrote in the *London Tribune:*

> I can't feel that war is "humanised" by being confined to the slaughter of the young and becomes "barbarous" when the old get killed as well.
>
> Obviously one must not kill children if it is in any way avoidable, but it is only in propaganda pamphlets that every bomb drops on a school or an orphanage. A bomb kills a cross-section of the population; but not quite a representative selection, because the children and expectant mothers are usually the first to be evacuated, and some of the young men will be away in the army. Probably a disproportionately large number of bomb victims will be middle-aged.

Orwell was arguing not only for the bombing of German civilians; he was justifying the German attacks on English cities also. He went on to say that German bombs had killed between 6,000 and 7,000 children in England during the Blitz but that that was fewer than the number killed in road accidents over the same period.

The debate over the bombing strategies would continue past the end of the war, even as the numbers of the dead were still being tallied. The numbers revealed that the bombing of civilian targets changed the nature of war: Between 1939 and 1945, an estimated 15 million soldiers, sailors, and airmen from both sides were killed in World War II. Three times as many civilians were killed: 45 million. Historians generally agree that the Allied bombing campaigns were decisive in the victory over Germany and Japan.

The crews flying those missions, most of them young men straight out of high school, were not responsible for debating the merits of their orders, and they rarely questioned them. They flew where they were told to fly and dropped their bombs on the targets they were assigned, trusting that their work was part of the larger effort to shorten the war and defeat an unquestionably evil enemy. Seldom low enough to see the carnage created by their bombs, nevertheless they knew, as they flew away and hoped to make it back safely to their bases, that they were leaving behind a new kind of horror on the ground.

Some of the British RAF crews had seen the devastation firsthand in London, and others had heard about it. The Americans had seen the newsreels of firestorms in London, the buildings caved in, the civilians dead in the streets. And they had seen the reconnaissance pictures of German cities after Allied attacks. The crews of the Eighth Air Force were good men, and they must have thought sometimes about the stories they heard of Hamburg.

The horrors on the ground were the stuff of Dante. A year before the Rogers crew arrived in England, on July 27 and 28, 1943, Allied bombs began falling on Hamburg, Germany, at 1 A.M., the city targeted because of its ports and industrial operations. The fires were still burning from the previous evening's attack, providing easy targets for the bombers. When the air raid warning sounded late on July 27, the citizens of Hamburg began racing to their safe havens once again—either the public shelters with thick concrete walls specially built to withstand the force of explosives or shelters in the cellars of their homes. But then nothing happened for more than an hour. The bombers didn't come, the pounding of the flak guns was missing, and so people hesitated before going into the shelters, miserable, cramped spaces with unbearable heat in which strangers would be jammed together for hours at a time. Many of the residents found patches of grass near the shelters and lay down, preferring the cool evening air, resting their heads on the bundles they always carried to the shelters: their most important documents and their most precious photographs. Those trying to sleep outside the shelters had no way of knowing why there was such quiet after the air raid warnings had sounded. This was the first mission in which the Allies tried using "Window," a secret strategy calling for bomber crews to throw out chaff—shredded tinfoil dropped to overwhelm German radar—and it was working beautifully. The RAF bombers were flying to the north of the city, convincing the antiaircraft gunners that they were passing by on their way to another target. But then they swung around and attacked from the east.

Flying as part of Operation Gomorrah, 739 bombers attacked the most densely populated districts of the city. The effects on the already battered Hamburg were particularly severe on this night. The commander of a flak battery, Lieutenant Hermann Bock, had a perfect view of the city from his post. He had seen many attacks before, but what he saw this night horrified him.

> Hamburg's night sky became in minutes, even seconds, a sky so absolutely hellish that it is impossible to even try to describe it in words. There were aeroplanes held in the probing arms of the searchlights, fires breaking out, billowing smoke everywhere, loud roaring waves of explosions, all broken up by great cathedrals of light as the blast bombs exploded, cascades of marker bombs drifting down, stick incendiary bombs coming down with a rushing noise. No noise heard by humans—no outcry—could be heard. It was like the end of the world. One could think, feel, see and speak of nothing more.

On this night, the bombing was more successful than the Allies could have hoped. They benefited from unusually warm weather and good flying conditions that allowed the bombers to drop their bombs on target, concentrating them in a way that they could not on most missions. The weather conditions also created something that the Allies could never have predicted. The city of Hamburg burned, as it had many other nights, but now a vortex and whirling updraft of superheated air created a 1,000-foot-high tornado of fire.

By 1:20, an inferno was blowing through the neighborhood of Hammerbrook with hurricane speeds and temperatures of nearly 1,800 degrees Fahrenheit. The bombers were still dropping their loads and would continue doing so for another half hour. All the air in the city seemed on fire. Asphalt streets burned, flames leaping from the pavement. Fuel oil leaked from ships, barges, and storage tanks into the city's canals, setting the water ablaze.

Those caught outside ran, with nowhere to go. Those in the bomb shelters were no better off. Though protected, for the most part, from the bomb blasts, the growing fires sucked the oxygen out of the shelters, leaving many to suffocate or slowly roast as they struggled for air. The men, women, and children in the bomb shelters faced terrible choices: They could stay in the underground shelters as they became smoky ovens, or they could go out into the fires of hell. Those who ventured outside and lived to describe it told of hot, dry winds so strong that even grown men struggled to walk upright, winds so strong that they blew open doors and broke through the windows of homes and businesses. People were swept into the air like dry leaves on a fall day. The winds carried a blizzard of sparks and embers that looked like red snowflakes. Anything light was immediately whipped into the air and ignited. Roaring clouds of fire would burst out of buildings with no warning as the contents suddenly ignited all at once. Whirlwinds of fire raced up and down the streets, turning some people into human torches but sparing others only a few feet away. The survivors all spoke of the shrieking, roaring, howling storm of fire.

The firestorm continued through 3:30 A.M., at least an hour after the last bomb had dropped on the city. Four square miles had been incinerated, with virtually no trace of anything left except brick and stone facades that would not burn. Roughly 50,000 people died in the raids that night and the following days, and the city of Hamburg was all but destroyed.

After the firestorm, many of the survivors were in shock, severely traumatized by their own experience and how they had seen others die.

Police reports documented how some survivors clung to the last remnants of their families by carrying the charred bodies, or pieces of them, for days. One report quoted witnesses who had seen refugees from Hamburg trying to board a train in Bavaria and in the process dropping a suitcase that broke open and spilled its contents: toys, singed underwear, and the burned corpse of a child. Those entering the city after the firestorm were shocked at the devastation, and they saw evidence of a new way of death. Many had died not from the bombs themselves but from the horrific effects of the firestorm, which could suck the oxygen out of even the few spaces untouched by fire. Cellars and bomb shelters were opened to find families huddled together, all dead from suffocation. One man, arriving to search for his brother, found piles of bodies on the steps of a large office building, all lying facedown. Thinking at first that they had been blown out of a bomb shelter by a direct hit, he then realized that they had been smothered after leaving the shelter en masse when conditions became unbearable, only to find that there was no oxygen outside either.

The firestorm in Hamburg, like the similar horror of Dresden later in 1945, was the result of a confluence of factors, mostly weather, that the Allies could not have anticipated. That is not to say, however, that the Allies did not welcome the result and do everything to make it possible. Like the German bombing of London, the RAF bombing was designed to unleash fire in the most effective way and let it do its dirty work. The first wave of bombers dropped high explosives that smashed open buildings, sending flammable material flying in every direction. Then other bombers dropped incendiaries. More than just bombs or ignition sources, incendiaries were meant to start and fuel fires in the most effective ways. Germans who had been through the nightmare enough times could distinguish the different types of incendiaries being dropped on them by their unique sounds. A sudden crack of an explosion was a 26-pound firebomb that could shoot flames out 260 feet on impact. The sound of a splash came from the 30-pound firebomb spreading liquid rubber and benzene over an area with a 165-foot radius. If it sounded like a wet sack falling on the ground, the source was a five-gallon canister of benzol. A sharp explosion might be either a 233-pound bomb throwing rags soaked in benzene or heavy oil or a 246-pound bomb that scattered 1,000 benzol-and-rubber patties. A sound like a flock of birds taking flight came from a stick of incendiaries breaking apart near the ground and scattering fire starters in all directions.

Perhaps the worst of the lot were the bombs carrying phosphorous and magnesium, which burned at extremely high temperatures and could not be extinguished easily. People splashed with phosphorous would often leap into canals or rivers to douse the flames, only to find that the phosphorous reignited instantly when they emerged from the water.

The Americans about to fly their first mission into Germany weren't responsible for that carnage. They were on their way to a legitimate military target, an airfield with relatively few enemy combatants present and practically no civilians. To German citizens who had lived through the horrors of Allied bombing, they were still *die terrorflieger*—the terror fliers.

But to the families and loved ones back home, they were Norm, John, Forrest, Bill, Gene, Bill, Tom, Elmore, and Haigus. These were good men.

CHAPTER 4
ROOKIE RUN

ROGERS'S CREW ARRIVED AT THE LOANER B-24J about an hour before they were to take off. The rain was easing up, and the gunners went about the business of readying their .50-caliber Browning machine guns for the flight. Rather than being left in place on the planes between missions, the heavy guns were removed, cleaned, and repaired if necessary, then the gunners on each flight had to reinstall them. Rogers inspected his airplane, filled out the necessary forms with the crew chief of the *Wham! Bam!,* then checked that each crew member was prepared for the flight. He found that Brown was having trouble getting his guns installed and working properly in the tail mount, and was getting frustrated. The gunners trained relentlessly with these weapons, learning to assemble and disassemble them in the dark, but Brown still couldn't get them mounted right. No doubt, the throbbing tooth wasn't helping any.

"Don't worry, Brownie. You'll get it," Rogers told him in his typically reassuring way. "Just keep working on it."

With less than an hour to go, Tufenkjian still hadn't shown up, and the crew was starting to wonder what they would do without a navigator and bombardier. After milling around outside the plane while Brown wrestled with his guns, the two pilots, radio operator Williams, and engineer Brininstool put on their heated flying suits. Rogers gave the order for everyone to assume their positions for takeoff. The crew climbed in through the bomb bay doors and made their way down the catwalk that traversed the length of the plane. Rogers and Sekul took their positions as pilot and copilot, Brininstool on his feet behind them keeping an eye on the instrument gauges. Williams was manning the radio at his little desk in the cockpit, and the gunners were sitting in the fuselage, where they would wait until the plane was airborne before manning their gun stations. Brown still hadn't gotten his tail guns fixed, but Rogers told him he would have time to work on them during the long flight.

Just before it was time to start engines, Tufenkjian's head popped up through the bomb bay doors and he hustled down the catwalk. He continued all the way forward and to the right of the nose landing gear to his cramped station with the beautiful panoramic view in the nose of the plane. Nobody on board got a good look at him. Belly gunner Dumont and left waist gunner Austin might have glimpsed him but never really saw his face; Adams, Brown, and the other crew up in the cockpit area never saw him.

The four engines on the *Wham! Bam!* rumbled to life, and before long the plane was taxiing for takeoff. Rogers and Sekul used every inch of the runway to get the heavy plane in the air and then joined the other planes in the complicated and extremely difficult process of getting 1,319 aircraft together in formation. It would take a while, and most of the crewmen had little to do until they were closer to Germany, so the gunners rested in the fuselage and Brown tried to ignore the throbbing in his head. The pilots and Tufenkjian, meanwhile, were busy trying to get the plane on the right course to meet up with the rest of the Eighth. After the ninety minutes it took to climb to 20,000 feet, Rogers took up the backup lead's position: behind, to the right, and above the lead Liberator. Soon other B-24s were finding the formation and taking up their positions, the group slowly building until it numbered 72. That combat wing then followed the flight plan to a point on the English coast where it met up with the rest of the 1,247 aircraft that would penetrate Germany.

The formation was awe inspiring. More than 1,000 aircraft flying in formation across the English Channel, the deafening roar a precursor to the destruction that would rain down on the enemy.

Somewhere over the Channel, Rogers ordered the gunners to their positions. Adams took up his position at the nose gun, and his buddy Brown went to the back of the plane and manned his guns. He put on his heavy, electrically heated flight suit and plugged into the oxygen supply. Squeezing into the tight confines of the gunner's seat—*Dang, I can't make my butt any smaller than this,* he grumbled as he got into position—he was mesmerized by the sight of so many planes. For a country boy from rural Florida, seeing nearly the entire Eighth Air Force assembled in the air was astounding. Brown stared for a moment and then went to work on his guns again. He had to get the barrels seated just right in the threads and then screwed in just enough. The barrels needed to be tightened a certain number of revolutions, rather than just making them as tight as you could, to accommodate the expansion and contraction as the gun fired and then cooled in the freezing cold of high altitudes. Too much or too little, and the guns wouldn't fire properly and even could explode in your face. Brown had seen it happen to another gunner in training.

He couldn't see what he was doing in the tight quarters, so he had to do it all by feel. Twisting, feeling with his bare fingers, hoping he had the barrels in right, knowing they were getting closer to the target every minute. Finally he decided they were right, or rather he really hoped they were. He wouldn't know until he had to shoot at a Luftwaffe pilot; he wasn't allowed to test fire the guns yet. Earlier in the war, pilots would give gunners an order to test fire their weapons early in the flight, while they still had time to address any problems, but that practice was discontinued when too many gunners accidentally shot other planes in their formation.

After working on the guns, Brown placed an extra flak jacket under his seat—a common maneuver by young men who wanted to protect their more sensitive areas—plugged in his heated flight suit, and settled in. He looked up and out the rear of the plane, and this time he was startled to see none of the 1,000-plus planes he had marveled at just moments earlier. In the few minutes he had been busy, his formation of 72 bombers had broken off from the larger mass—the huge, intimidating group that offered protection in numbers—to go to its own targets. The massive formation was splitting up as it neared Germany.

Brown couldn't see all the planes ahead of him, and it suddenly felt very lonely up there, looking back at nothing but empty sky.

Old Gene's the last one in the bunch, he thought.

The *Wham! Bam!* flew on with the other bombers, closer to Langenhagen every minute. Soon Rogers ordered Dumont to his belly gun, which he manned only at the last minute because it was so cramped, and instructed the gunners to test their guns. Brown was relieved when his functioned perfectly.

So far there had been no enemy fighters and no flak. But the crew knew that the flak would come when they got closer to the target. Before long, they heard the bomb bay doors open. That meant that they were only about five minutes from the target. The men donned their flak suits—heavy vests that draped over the shoulders, offering some protection from the flak bursts. The gunners put on their M–3 helmets, modified versions of the standard M–1 "steel pot" helmets used by the infantry. The M–3s had ear cutaways to accommodate the bulky earphones that all the crew wore as part of the soft flying helmet, with big, hinged metal ear flaps that came down over the ear cutaways. The outside of the helmets felt like soft fur because they were sprayed with flocking to keep bare hands from freezing to them at high altitudes.

Continuing the Window experiment, Brininstool went to a side window and started throwing out chaff, the tinfoil-like strips that would fill the air with radar-reflective material and confuse enemy attempts to hone in on the bombers.

And then it began. The antiaircraft shells began bursting all around the *Wham! Bam!,* black clouds appearing in an instant as the explosives detonated at preset altitudes. With the pilots unable to divert from their course to take evasive action, the crew was at the mercy of the exploding shells and bits of metal ranging from the size of a pea to a baseball, shooting through the air in all directions, usually missing anything important, such as a fuel or hydraulic line or a crew member, but sometimes not.

The plane shook violently with every nearby burst, and when one shell exploded directly under the number-two engine, the shock wave sent the left wing rising high into the air, almost standing the plane straight up on its other wing. Rogers and Sekul couldn't do much but try to hold on as the plane went vertical, with everyone on board wondering if the plane was about to "pancake," or flip over on its back. Then the plane slowly settled back down in the right direction and continued on through the black bursts of metal and gunpowder.

The first mission of the Rogers crew was every bit as terrifying as they had feared, worse than any stories they had heard from the old hands back at the base. They saw one B-24 take a hit and drop out of the formation, but so far the *Wham! Bam!* was making it through, buffeted left and right, above and below, by the concussions of exploding shells but not taking a direct hit that did real damage. If fighters came, Adams decided he could do more good on a waist gun near the center of the plane than at his position on the nose, so he went back and manned one of the .50-caliber guns there. Still in formation with the other planes, the *Wham! Bam!* was bouncing up and down as Rogers and Sekul struggled to keep it on course and give Tufenkjian a chance to hit his target.

In the nose of the plane, Tufenkjian had flipped up the red lever protecting the bomb release toggle and was looking through his bomb sight, waiting for the right moment. It came, and he pushed the toggle to initiate the release of the entire bomb load from the *Wham! Bam!* onto the airfield at Langenhagen.

"Bombs away," Tufenkjian calmly called on the intercom.

"Roger that, bombs away," Rogers replied.

The crew felt the plane rising as its load lightened. A few of the men called out in celebration; all were relieved that they had successfully carried out their first mission and could turn for home now.

And it was then that their luck ran out. After they dropped their load on target, an antiaircraft shell exploded just under the bomb bay, its doors still wide open, taking out the hydraulic system and one engine while damaging two others. The burst shot shrapnel into Brininstool's gut as he stood near the cockpit, and Adams took some in his arms and buttocks. Brininstool had been wearing a flak jacket to protect his torso, but the shrapnel had found a weak spot in a fold of the suit and made its way in, through the thick protective material, through his Mae West life vest. Despite being knocked to the floor by the shrapnel, Brininstool hurried into the cockpit to help assess the damage. When he got there, he asked Rogers how bad it was.

"We've got one good engine," Rogers told him. "That won't be enough to get back over the Channel." Rogers immediately radioed for fighter escorts to help them as they limped back toward safe territory.

In the split second it took one shell to explode, the fate of the *Wham! Bam!* and her crew had changed. Brininstool started making his way to the rear of the plane, wanting to check on the gunners.

The bomb bay doors were stuck open, creating a bad aerodynamic drag on the already faltering plane. Normally pilots closed the doors as soon as possible after dropping their load. Fifteen miles south of Hannover, Germany, the faltering *Wham! Bam!* dropped out of formation, with one engine smoking but Rogers and Sekul keeping the plane under control. The plane was descending quickly, and the rest of the formation had no choice but to proceed without it, the lone wounded plane becoming what fliers knew as the rabbit, easy prey for an enemy fighter. Rogers knew his crew was going to have to bail out, but he wanted to keep the plane flying as long as he could. The crew marveled at how Rogers and Sekul were keeping them in the air. They hoped they could make it far enough to avoid landing right into enemy hands.

With the hydraulics out, the tail turret was useless because Brown could not move the guns to aim at enemy fighters—not that any had shown up. So Brown left his position in the tail without having fired a single shot to go forward and check on the other men. Brininstool was making his way back, stumbling and clutching his abdomen, and Brown found Adams bleeding and in pain, unable to use his right arm. Adams was pretty shook up, so Brown helped him take off his flak suit and put on his parachute, then he threw the flak suit back over Adams's shoulders, letting it rest over the parachute harness. Brown tried contacting Rogers and Sekul by intercom to ask what was going on, whether they should bail out or not.

"Rogers! Rogers!" Brown called out, screaming into the microphone over the drone of the engine noise and the rushing air. "Sekul! Can y'all hear me? What are we doing?"

There was no response. The flak burst had taken out the intercom system. Brown watched the plane descend lower every second, still impressed that Rogers and Sekul were keeping them in the air. He tried to guess how high they were, wanting to make sure that they were below the point where oxygen was needed. Brown knew that if they were still too high to breathe safely on their own, there wouldn't be any warning before they passed out. Passing out at this critical juncture could be disastrous; by the time you woke up, you'd be riding the plane down to the ground. He had unplugged from the plane's main oxygen system when he left his position at the tail gun, switching his breathing line to a small bottle of emergency oxygen that he carried in his hand.

He peered out the side of the plane and could tell that Rogers and Sekul were keeping the *Wham! Bam!* on a steady glide path down, and Brown estimated that they were low enough to forgo the oxygen supply.

That looks like something between 6,000 and 10,000 feet, Brown thought. *We can breathe, but we have to get out of this plane.*

The plane was making wide, low circles over Wentrup and Hüttrup, Germany, to the west of their target, as Rogers and Sekul tried any maneuver to keep it in the air, both looking for anywhere that might offer an opportunity for a crash landing. Unfortunately, the local "home guard" saw the plane and thought it might be attacking the canal road bridge in Ladbergen, so it opened fire with an antiaircraft battery when the *Wham! Bam!* was at about 2,600 feet, firing three ten-round volleys as the plane circled past.

Brown and the rest of the crew felt the rounds explode near the plane, rattling it hard again. They cringed and ducked, hoping the *Wham! Bam!* wouldn't take another hit, because that surely would finish them off. At this altitude, they wouldn't have time to do much of anything after a direct hit.

The rounds didn't hit the plane, but the maneuvering couldn't last. Rogers realized they were rapidly losing altitude and there was nothing he could do about it. He told Brininstool to order the men out while he and Sekul held the plane steady as long as possible. Brininstool made his way back through the fuselage, clutching his bleeding torso, and gave the order to abandon ship. The crew had never practiced a parachute jump: The Army had decided it was too risky after fliers had been injured and taken out of action during training jumps. So this would be everyone's first jump. The crew had discussed beforehand that they would rather jump out of the bomb bay doors than the Army-prescribed exit at the rear door, where they feared their chutes would become entangled in the B-24's twin tails.

Brown looked through the hatch that led to the catwalk, which had blown open from the blast, and saw a parachute spilled open, its silk folds flapping in the wind. At first he thought there might be someone attached to it, that the chute had popped open when the man was hit. But then he could see that there was no one there, so he looked out the window by the waist gun and saw chutes already drifting down. Dumont and Williams had already bailed out.

Brown went to his wounded buddy and said, "Bill, we gotta get out of here! They're jumping!"

Adams had already taken off his fur-lined flying boots and put on his regular shoes, a smart move when you might be running from Nazis in the sweltering August heat. Brown had been too preoccupied with trying to contact the cockpit to switch his footwear, so he was going to have to jump in his boots. He looked out the window and saw that the plane was still descending fast.

Brown could tell that Adams was worried about jumping out of the plane, so he thought that maybe if he went first it would encourage his buddy. Brown turned to Adams and shook his hand firmly.

"I'll see you on the ground," he told Adams.

Brown rolled over and out from a kneeling position. Adams watched his friend disappear through the bomb bay.

Brown pulled the handle to release his chute almost as soon as he left the plane, rather than waiting the ten seconds that the Army had taught the crew members. His silk parachute opened in a huge WHOMP! and jerked Brown up, then he slowly drifted down. As he hung there in the air, in the curious quiet after the noisy pandemonium on the plane, Brown watched the *Wham! Bam!* and saw another body tumble out of the bomb bay. He knew it had to be Adams.

Brown watched as the body fell, and fell, and fell, for what seemed forever without the chute opening.

Oh my lord, his chute ain't gonna open, Brown thought.

Finally the chute popped open and Brown could breathe again. He watched as Adams floated to the ground far beneath him. Adams had been following the procedure he was taught and had waited ten seconds before pulling his rip cord.

Then Brown saw Tufenkjian, Austin, and Brininstool jump out. Sekul was next, and then finally Rogers, who had stayed at his position behind the controls as long as he could, was the last to leave the *Wham! Bam!*

All of the men of the *Wham! Bam!* had made it out alive. Now, as they drifted down to earth, they were hoping to survive being captured and sent to a POW camp. They thought that would be the worst outcome.

CHAPTER 5

WELCOMING

THE *WHAM! BAM!* WOULD BE THE ONLY BOMBER not to return to Pickenham that day. Seventy-one other bombers were headed back to their base while, on their first mission, Rogers's crew was parachuting down into Germany.

The nine men drifting to the ground near Greven, Germany, knew they were in serious trouble. They hadn't even made it through their first mission, and now they were falling into Germany and an unknown fate.

Continuing to circle downward after Rogers and Sekul gave up the controls, the *Wham! Bam!* crashed beside the Bedkersjürgen farm, wreckage scattering across the field and road, the engines traveling the farthest and settling in the farmyard. The last flight of the *Wham! Bam!* was over.

The home guard that had been shooting at the plane recorded seeing the *Wham! Bam!* crash at 12:15 P.M. near Hüttrup. A lookout saw the plane go down and alerted the local fire brigade, which dispatched one fire engine from Hüttrup. The lookout also alerted the military detachment at the nearby airfield, Feld L.M. Lager 2/6, and a master sergeant, Oberfeldwebel Spintler, sent a team to cordon off the crash site until it could be searched. Once they arrived, they saw that there was no danger of fire and turned the fire truck away. A bomb disposal crew was on its way to search the wreckage for live ordnance, but the immediate concern was locating the crew. The lookout and several residents had reported seeing parachutes from the crippled plane, so Spintler dispatched several teams to start looking for the Americans.

BROWN COULDN'T QUITE SEE exactly where his friend landed, but it seemed that Adams had gone down well. It took Brown a good two or three minutes longer to drift down because Adams's ten-second free fall had given him a head start, but Brown was headed for a landing in the ideal soft spot: a freshly plowed field. He started thinking back through the Army instructions for how to land safely but, before he could gather his thoughts, he slammed into the ground and his face dug into the soft earth. It happened so fast that Brown was left thinking the bail-out instructions were not worth anything.

Thank God for this plowed field, Brown thought. *That happens so fast that it's no wonder folks break their legs.*

Before he could pick himself up, Brown heard someone shouting. He rubbed the dirt off his face and blinked hard to try to clear his eyes as he lay tangled in his parachute, raising his head enough to look around for the source of the commotion. About fifty yards away he saw a farmer running toward him with a pitchfork. Behind him was a crowd of about twenty Germans who looked ready to tear the flier apart. Brown struggled out of his parachute harness and tried to get to his feet, but the crowd was on him before he could get his balance, one man hitting him on the head with some sort of stick or pole and the crowd pushing him around, shouting in anger. Brown got the sense that he was not the first American flier these civilians had encountered.

Brown had no options, so he tried to protect himself from the blows as well as he could, becoming distracted at one point by a little boy who was standing at the edge of the crowd watching. When the boy spoke to Brown in English, saying "What is your name?" an adult shooed him away quickly. Soon some of the men began screaming at Brown to pick up his parachute, gesturing so he would understand. The twenty-four-foot parachute was difficult to gather up on his own, but Brown managed to get it all in his arms and the Germans seemed insistent that he carry it with him. Every time he dropped part of it, they yelled at him to gather it up again. Brown had no idea why they were so determined that he carry his chute. He didn't want it, and usually locals were happy to have the parachute silk. *Maybe they see it as some sort of evidence,* he thought, *and they want me to take it with me when they turn me in to the authorities.* The crowd pushed Brown along and he stumbled through the field in his flying boots, which already were unbearably hot in the August heat. Sweating furiously, he managed to rip off his flying headgear with its bulky earphones and lay it on top of the parachute. But after more marching and stumbling, the headgear fell off the slippery silk, prompting one German man to pick it up and hit Brown across the head with it several times. Then the man placed the headgear back atop the parachute silk in Brown's arms, so gently that Brown wondered why the German was treating the equipment with such care. He understood later that the locals considered it evidence and now the property of the Führer.

After they left the field, the crowd stopped while several men discussed what to do. Brown just stood there, trying not to drop the parachute or the danged headgear again. After a few minutes, the men reached some sort of decision and the crowd began to disperse, several of them giving Brown a good shove and making a few remarks to him before they left. One man gestured for Brown to follow him, and the two went to a small house, where the German got his bicycle and pointed down the road, gesturing for Brown to start walking. Brown figured he was being taken to the local police or military unit, which might be good, considering the way that crowd had been acting. So Brown started trudging along, guessing the temperature must be at least in the eighties—not so bad for a boy from Gainesville, Florida, but he didn't walk around country roads in fur-lined boots. The German was following behind him, pushing the bike alongside, apparently having brought it along for the ride back home, as he couldn't ride slowly enough to stay behind a tired American country boy with little motivation to hurry. If Brown did not move fast enough, the man would bump him in the rear with the bicycle tire. That got old really fast, so Brown made a point of walking in the sandiest paths between the hard-packed tracks in the road, which made it harder for his captor to push the bike along.

Approaching the town of Greven, a village southwest of Osnabrück, seventy-five miles west of Hannover, Brown could see that they were expected. Locals had gathered on either side of the road, waiting to see the captured American. The catcalls and angry shouts started as soon as Brown came into sight, and, once they were in the town, one man stepped out of the crowd and took position behind Brown as he continued walking. For about a block, the man kicked Brown in the rear end with every step, then he drifted back onto the curb. The crowd was shouting angrily and shaking their fists at Brown the whole way. Soon the procession reached a two-story building on the right side of the street in the middle of the village. A stone building, Brown thought it must be the town hall because it looked so much like the Gainesville County courthouse back home, even down to the same room layout on the first floor. He was led up some steps and down the hall to an office, where Brown found Austin and another man in a flight suit that he didn't recognize—Tufenkjian—already there. They looked like they'd been through hell, their faces battered and bruised, both of them bleeding and looking more than a little scared. Then Brown found out why. Right after he stepped in the door, a civilian pounced on him and began beating him furiously, Brown all the while trying to hold on to the parachute and headgear. The stocky man, about forty years old, five foot eight, and two hundred pounds, beat Brown, bloodying his face badly, until he seemed to tire and then pushed Brown over toward the other airmen. By this point Brown was half strangled by the small drogue chute that pulls the rest of the silk out of the pack, which had gotten wrapped around his neck during the assault. As he freed himself from the strangling silk, Brown looked at Austin and then at the other man, wondering if he was from a different flight crew. As they stood along the wall, waiting to see what would happen next, Brown refused to talk to Tufenkjian or even make eye contact. They had been warned that the Germans sometimes planted an agent among air crews to learn more as the Americans talked to each other.

Waiting with the others, Brown realized that he still had his escape and evasion kit in his pants pocket. In their hurry to beat him, the Germans had forgotten to search him and take all his possessions, as they had done with the other men. Knowing he still had the kit gave him hope.

Over the rest of the afternoon, Brown and the others waited as the rest of the *Wham! Bam!* crew began to show up, brought in by more Germans who were proud to turn over their captured fliers.

Brown had lost sight of Adams behind some trees so he didn't see his friend crash through a tree and then land safely in the backyard of a farmhouse, where he was met by a farmer who was about fifty years old. The farmer was wary but gentle with Adams, helping the flier disentangle himself from the parachute cords and harness and then taking him inside the house. The two gestured and smiled at each other, Adams not wanting to let on yet that he could speak and understand some German because of his Pennsylvania Dutch heritage. He followed the farmer's lead, unsure what his intentions were. Soon the farmer placed some cornbread and buttermilk in front of Adams and indicated that he should eat. Although he was too worried to be hungry, Adams ate some of the food to satisfy his host, who then set about bandaging Adams's shrapnel wound on his arm.

Before long, another man, about seventy years old, walked into the house. Adams suspected it was the man's father, and the elder man apparently did not respond well to finding an American bomber crewman sitting at his kitchen table. The man argued with the other in German, gesturing toward the door and seeming to give orders to his son. Adams got the idea that the father wanted the American out of his house and turned over to the authorities. The younger farmer did not seem happy with the decision, but he complied and gestured for Adams to get up and go outside. The farmer took his bicycle and the two set off, leaving the farm by the little country road that would lead to Greven. For the mile walk to the village, Adams walked alongside the farmer on his bike, neither of them speaking and the German making no effort to restrain him. It was as if the two were out for a casual trip to the village, or as if the farmer simply had to make a delivery.

As they approached the village, the farmer stopped and spoke to Adams, gesticulating in a way that told Adams he should now walk in front of the bicycle. The farmer also pulled a pistol from his belt and pointed it at Adams. In this manner, the farmer victoriously entered the village with his captured airman. Residents stopped on the street and peered out of windows to see the American paraded through town by the brave farmer as Adams was nudged along to a stone building. As he entered the building and was taken to an office, Adams was relieved to see that Brown and Austin were already there and seemed to be in relatively good shape. There was another man in a flight suit but, like Brown, Adams did not know who it was because he had never laid eyes on the navigator/bombardier replacement. As he was wondering who Tufenkjian was, the one-man welcoming committee set upon Adams. Adams got the same beating that the other fliers had already received.

Soon the other men were brought in, one at a time. Williams and Sekul were in pretty good shape when they arrived, but Rogers and Dumont both had injured their ankles on landing, Dumont quite severely, and Brininstool had the serious flak injuries to his abdomen. Brininstool had been taken in by an elderly couple when he landed on their farm. They took him into the house and cleaned his flak wound with hot water, acting very kind. In return, he had tried to give them his silk parachute, a valuable item for peasants during the war. They politely declined, telling him "Nein. Es gehört zu den Reich." It belonged to the Reich.

All the enlisted men were beaten by the civilian man as they entered the holding room. The officers were spared, apparently a courtesy to their rank.

Once all nine fliers were present, the Germans began interrogating them one at a time. Each man was pulled into another office where a tall uniformed officer, about sixty years old, tried to pry information out of them. The men were not sure what branch of the military he was in, but they suspected some sort of home guard or local authority. Adams was one of the first to be taken for interrogation. The German officer could speak only a few words of English, but it did not matter much because Adams was not going to tell him anything.

"Name your unit," the German officer ordered.

"Adams, William N. Sergeant. 33833051."

The officer was angered by Adams's insistence on providing only his name, rank, and serial number. He tried again.

"Unit!" he yelled at Adams.

"Adams, William N. Sergeant. 33833051."

The stocky civilian who had beaten Adams and the other men was standing in the corner of the room, glowering. Adams was scared, but he was not going to be intimidated into giving the Germans any useful information. He had to hold fast.

"What is target?" the German asked him.

Adams looked over at the man and swallowed hard. "Adams, William N. Sergeant. 33833051."

The officer became enraged, screamed something in German, and then called the civilian man over. The man backhanded Adams with all his might, then slapped his head back in the other direction. He did this over and over again, spinning Adams's head each time. Adams could do nothing but sit there and take it. The German officer was screaming at him in German. A couple of times he used his broken English to make sure Adams knew why he was being beaten.

"This what you get for bombing our women and children!" he screamed at Adams. "This what you get for kill German people!"

With the civilian breathing heavy from exertion on the hot August day, his shirt soaked with perspiration, eventually the officer gestured for him to stop. Then the officer leaned down toward Adams, whose head was hanging limp, with blood pouring from his mouth and nose, and spoke quietly.

"Adams, William N. What is your unit?"

Adams hesitated because his mouth was swollen and filled with blood. He managed to mumble a response.

"Adams, William N.," he said softly, his voice thick and slurred. "Sergeant. 33833051."

The officer was done with Adams and had the civilian drag him out of the room and past the others, then down to a small room in the basement. The rest of the men were dismayed to see Adams's condition but not surprised, because they could hear it all happening. They also knew they would get their turn. Each man was taken into the room where Adams's blood already stained the floor and seated in the same chair. Each man was asked for information, each refused to give anything but name, rank, and serial number, and most were beaten for their insolence. As before, the officer adhered to the military courtesy of not treating the officers—Rogers, Sekul, and Brininstool—as violently as the other men. After the interrogations, all of the fliers were taken down to the basement room, which appeared to be a storage area, and was barely large enough for all nine men to sit on the floor.

Once all of the men were there, in relative privacy, they started comparing notes and checking on one another. Rogers vouched for Tufenkjian, confirming that he was the replacement that day and could be trusted. Nobody had much information to pass on, except the tale of their own capture. Adams conveyed the bits and pieces of German that he had overheard, but Rogers agreed with him that they shouldn't reveal that Adams could speak their language. Brown did bring up a problem with Rogers.

"Rogers, I ain't got my dog tags," he told his pilot. "I left them back at the base. I hope that won't mean anything to the Germans."

"Well, don't worry about it," Norm told him. "I don't have mine either, so you won't be the only one."

The German officer came down with the civilian thug and a couple more men. They opened the locked door to the room and singled out Adams and Tufenkjian, gesturing for them to come forward. The officer looked at them carefully and then asked Adams, "Sie sind Juden, nein?" Adams seemed confused at first, not understanding the question. "Juden? Ja?" the officer said again. Then Adams understood and quickly said, "No, no, I'm not Jewish. I'm not Jewish."

The officer wasn't convinced, but he turned to Tufenkjian. "Du bist ein Jude."

"No," Tufenkjian said. "I'm not a Jew."

The officer thought for a moment and then gestured for all of the Americans to take down their pants or flight suits. The men did not comply immediately, looking around at one another in surprise. But they were powerless and so they slowly began to undress. They stood there with their clothing piled around their ankles and feet, wondering what would come next. The German officer was not satisfied.

"Die Unterwäsche. Entfernen Sie es!"

Some of the men understood what was going on and did as the officer wanted, pulling their underwear down to their ankles. The others soon followed, and all nine men were standing there with no pants or underwear. The officer then moved around the small room, taking a good look at each man's genitals, trying to find a circumcision that in 1944 Europe, though not in the United States, would have been a good indicator that the man was Jewish. He looked closely at Adams and Tufenkjian and seemed not to find what he was looking for. He looked at Tufenkjian's face again and said, "Ja, ich glaube du bist ein Jude." He still thought Tufenkjian was a Jew.

After the Germans left, the men dressed and waited for a time in the locked room. Everyone was dejected, depressed, and apprehensive. As they waited, Rogers took the lead as always and told the men not to worry too much.

"We're American, and we'll be treated like POWs according to the rules of war," he told them. "Just stick with name, rank, and serial number. That's all you have to tell them, and, other than that, we'll just cooperate as best we can. We'll get out of this."

Then the Germans returned and the Americans were led outside to a waiting truck. With several local officials acting as guards, they boarded as the locals jeered at them, and then they rode for a few minutes to a train station. There they boarded a train with their guards and went to an unnamed Luftwaffe airfield, where they were handed over to air force officers. They were all interrogated again by two German officers, but this time there was no beating or other harsh treatment, possibly because the Luftwaffe officers had some respect for fellow fliers. Although the Americans were tired and roughed up, all of the men thought they were okay without a doctor's care, except for Brininstool, who obviously had a bad stomach wound. Dumont's ankle was broken, but they didn't think the Germans would do much but wrap it up and the men decided he was better off sticking with the rest of them. Rogers reported to the Germans that his engineer needed care, talking with an officer who spoke English. When the Germans replied that they had no doctor at the base so Brininstool would have to wait, Rogers informed them that they would get no cooperation from his crew until a doctor was found.

Later that evening, after the men had been taken to a single-story building on the air base where they would spend the night, guards came for Brininstool. Adams helped Brininstool get up, and the guards indicated that Adams should come along to help carry the wounded man. The two Americans were put in a truck and driven to a small field hospital near the airfield, where Adams watched as a doctor wearing swimming trunks—he must have been summoned on short notice—operated on Brininstool with no anesthesia, cutting into his belly to remove a piece of shrapnel. After the doctor closed the wound, the Germans loaded Brininstool into an ambulance and took him to a hospital in Münster, where he would undergo a second operation. Adams returned to the rest of the crew at the airfield.

The men slept at the airfield that night, all of them nursing wounds—broken or twisted ankles, swollen jaws, black eyes, bloody lips. The next morning they were given a breakfast of potatoes and soup, which they ate eagerly: It had been nearly twenty-four hours since their last meal, and their ordeal had made them ravenous. Then three Luftwaffe guards took them to a nearby railway station and the group boarded a train headed south at about noon. Brown remarked to one of the other Americans that they were riding second class.

"Hard to believe they won't spring for first-class tickets, huh?"

The Luftwaffe guards gave the men a box to carry, and when they looked inside, they saw that it was all the personal belongings that had been taken from them—watches, lighters, family photographs—along with their escape and evasion kits. The guards did not want to carry it, so the men took charge. The Germans did not tell the men where they were going, but in fact the destination was the Dulag Luft aircrew interrogation center at Oberursel, north of Frankfurt. Specialists there would try to get information out of the fliers before they were sent to a POW camp. The crew ate bread and margarine on the train, which they would ride for the rest of the day. At every stop along the way, after German civilians noticed the Americans on the train, crowds would form at the windows, shouting in anger at the "terror fliers" and shaking their fists, spitting on the windows.

THE AIRCREWS BACK AT North Pickenham didn't know what was happening with the men of the *Wham! Bam!* They only hoped the crew was alive. They thought they were probably POWs. The chances seemed good since the crews of other planes in the formation had filed reports stating that they saw the *Wham! Bam!* losing altitude with one or two engines out but generally under control.

The day after the shoot-down—on August 25, as the *Wham! Bam!* crew was traveling south by train—the 491st was picked to lead the entire Eighth Air Force into Germany again. The mission was a success, with the bombers placing their loads on target with uncommon accuracy. Also on the same day, Paris was liberated by the local resistance assisted by the Free French forces. The war in Europe was winding down fast.

THE TRAIN RIDE CONTINUED into the night of August 25, but the train had to be abandoned before midnight because the Allies were bombing the local cities. The American bomber crew had to run for the safety of a German air raid shelter, squeezing into the dark, hot confines with their guards, the rest of the train passengers, and locals, none of them happy to be sharing space with Americans who, if not for being caught one day earlier, might be the ones dropping bombs on their city right at that moment. The Americans were startled by how the whole shelter rumbled and shook as the bombs fell all around them. It was the first time they had any real sense of what it was like to be on the receiving end of all that Allied firepower.

One of the cities targeted that night, as the crew of the *Wham! Bam!* huddled in the air raid shelter, was Rüsselsheim. On the Main River, about fifteen miles southwest of Frankfurt in the state of Hesse, Rüsselsheim's primary employer was the Opel automobile plant, which had contributed to the German war effort by manufacturing military engines, torpedo detonators, and other munitions. The plant alongside the railroad tracks on the western side of the train station had been a constant target of Allied bombing, which, like all bombing of that era, often missed its mark, and the city itself also was considered a legitimate target because it supplied labor to the factory. Because of the Opel plant, which had been a primary employer for more than twenty years, the people of Rüsselsheim had suffered more than perhaps any other Germans in the immediate area.

Before the bombing, Rüsselsheim had been a quaint small town, with tile-roofed houses lining neat, well-kept streets. The steeples of Protestant and Catholic churches soared high over the red-tile roofs. By August 1945, Rüsselsheim looked nothing like that. It was a city in ruins.

In addition to about 8,000 people employed at the Opel plant, which included many workers from other countries, Rüsselsheim also had forced labor in the form of men and women captured and shipped back to Germany to keep the war machine moving. The forced laborers were guarded to some extent but had limited freedom to move about the city. They were not, however, accorded the same rights as German citizens and sometimes were excluded from shelters during air raids, left to fend for themselves as the bombs fell.

On this night, as the crew of the *Wham! Bam!* huddled in the bomb shelter with Germans who did not welcome them, the British Royal Air Force attacked Rüsselsheim with particular ferocity, sending 116 Lancaster bombers to try to destroy the Opel motor factory. The air raid sirens sounded after 11 P.M., rousing the people from their beds to begin yet another night of hurrying down to the shelters. One was a sixteenth-century fortress at the eastern end of the city that had been converted with benches, electricity, and other basic amenities for the citizens there. The Opel plant also had built two large concrete bunkers near the plant for its workers and their families by excavating down and then building three-story shelters with walls seven feet thick and roofs fourteen feet thick. Originally designed to hold about 7,000 residents in all, the bunkers often were crammed with far more. Other citizens chose to ride out the raids in their own cellars; on this night they included George and Lonie Daum with their three children, one very sick with scarlet fever.

With the first sound of the air raid sirens, thirty-eight-year-old Kathe Reinhardt and her fifty-year-old sister, Margarete Witzler, who together

ran a tobacco shop in Rüsselsheim, hurried to get their elderly and frail
mother out of bed. Working together, they lifted the crippled old woman
onto a small handcart, covered her with a blanket, and began pushing her
toward one of the bunkers near the Opel plant. It was slow going in the
dark of night, the two women pushing the cart over rubble-strewn
streets, taking twenty minutes to reach their destination. Other residents
of Rüsselsheim were converging on the shelter, each bringing their own
burdens, some families with five or six children in tow, all frightened,
many crying. Forty-year-old Josef Hartgen, an air raid warden and
deputy Nazi chief for the city, arrived with his family and helped herd
everyone into the shelter, ensuring some degree of order in the near
chaos. Then the bunker shook with the first of the bombs falling on Rüsselsheim, the ones designed to blow apart the buildings and create kin-
dling for fires. Hartgen maintained order and relayed information from
those arriving late to the shelter and messengers brave enough to venture
out for updates during the bombing.

Only ten minutes into the raid, the Daums heard someone banging
on the door to their cellar. It was the local block warden crying "Daum!
George Daum! Your house has been hit by two gas cans!" Daum jumped
to his feet and told his wife he had to go. "Gas cans"—incendiary bombs
with flammable liquids—would destroy their home. Leaving his wife and
children in the shelter, Daum raced out as bombs continued to fall. He
found his home afire, the liquid from the gas cans burning in different
spots. He set about trying to put out the flames, hoping his house would
not suffer another direct hit.

Daum's wife waited anxiously, as did so many others in their own
cellars and in the municipal shelters. As more information came in to
the big bunkers, some men left to try to save their homes or shops. For
the next hour, the people of Rüsselsheim endured the bombing, waiting in fear, the fetid air and hot summer evening make it impossible to
sleep in the bunker, even if they could ignore the rumbling of bombs
outside and the constant wonder about what was happening to their
homes and shops. They had no way of knowing until they left the
bunkers, but this attack would be the worst yet on Rüsselsheim. The
British were dropping 674 two-thousand-pound bombs and more than

400,000 incendiaries on Rüsselsheim, more by far than any previous attack. The British crews reported that Rüsselsheim could be seen burning from one hundred miles away.

Toward the end of the bombing raid, Hartgen and other city leaders mobilized the remaining men in the public shelter to begin saving what was left of their city.

"All men, out of the shelter now! We must begin putting out the fires! All men out now! Hurry!" The men left the relative safety of the bunkers to begin their dangerous work, risking their lives as the bombs continued to fall, some of them dying in the process. When the all-clear signal sounded and the women and children left the shelters about 1:30 A.M., they found their city on fire. They set to work dowsing the flames, digging their homes from the rubble, and recovering the bodies of those who had died that night. They would work all through the night and into the morning. No one in Rüsselsheim slept. Many wept as they slowly moved bricks and broken mortar, searching for the irreplaceable mementos, the family photos, anything they could salvage from their modest homes. Wives sat in shock next to the bodies of their husbands, parents cradled the bodies of their lost children.

Afterward the RAF claimed that the bombing had been highly accurate because the factory had been clearly marked first by Pathfinders, elite squadrons of fliers that swooped in before the bombers and marked targets with flares. German reports, however, indicated that while the forging and gearbox assembly areas of the Opel plant were knocked out of action, 90 percent of the rest of the factory escaped serious damage— almost certainly a positive spin on what was indeed serious damage.

The effect on the Opel plant was incomplete at best, but the effect on Rüsselsheim was extreme. The already battered city was knocked flat and still burning long after the bombers were gone. The bombing killed 198 men, women, and children, of whom 177 were forced laborers who were not allowed in the bunkers. Many of the forced laborers had children with them, and all they could do was hold them as the bombs fell and the fires raged. Some of the laborers were left holding the lifeless bodies of their children as the Germans emerged from the safe refuge of the shelters. Twenty-one Germans had died during the raid, a major toll for one night's bombing, twenty-one added to the many before.

AT THE SHELTER WHERE THE *Wham! Bam!* crew was waiting out that night's raids, the all-clear signal sounded at 3 A.M. on August 26. They emerged with their guards, stumbling back out into the utterly dark, rubble-covered streets. Brown was taken by how black the night was, with no moon, no electric lights. He knew he could run off and the guards would never be able to stop him, but he had no idea where he would go. Running blindly from the guards and finding himself in a crowd of Germans, looking obviously like an American flier holding an evasion kit, would only get him killed or captured again. He stayed with the rest of his crew as they shuffled along, holding on to one another so they wouldn't get lost in the dark, prodded along by the guards.

The Americans boarded the train again and soon were headed south. They didn't know it, but they still had a long way to go before reaching the interrogation center. Only three hours later, however, the train pulled to a halt outside of a city that was about fifteen miles southwest of Frankfurt. Soon a railway worker walked down the aisle and announced something in German, which prompted everyone on the train to get up and start reaching for their bags. The German guards stood and ordered the Americans to get up too. As they moved off the train with everyone else, Adams quietly told the other men that he thought the Germans were talking about the railroad tracks being bombed out so they couldn't pass through the city ahead. They would have to walk around the damage to catch a different train on the other side of the damaged track, inside the city.

As their German guards were talking and looking at a railway map, the Americans heard the name of the city: Rüsselsheim.

CHAPTER 6

STATIONS OF
THE CROSS

THE TRAIN HAD STOPPED JUST SHORT of Rüsselsheim, so the passengers began trudging into town to find the station. When they stepped out of the train, the airmen could smell the fires that smoldered throughout the city and the salty, chalky smell of crushed stone, mortar, and concrete. There also was the distinct, stomach-churning smell of burned flesh. Even in the early hours of the morning, just as dawn was breaking over the rubble and burned-out buildings of the town, the heat was beginning to build. The Americans could tell this was going to be another very hot day in Germany. The men moved along at the guards' direction, jeered and ridiculed every step of the way by people shaking their fists in anger and spitting on them.

The crew had no idea what awaited them, and they could not begin to understand the local townspeople's hatred of Allied bombers—not just of the Allies in general, but specifically of the men who flew planes high over their communities and rained hell down on their homes, shops, and farms. The Allies had bombed this region day and night for several months now, and nearly everyone had a relative who had been killed in the attacks.

Soon after dawn, the eight Americans and the three Luftwaffe guards walked into a city that had been bombed flat. Brown looked around and was amazed by the devastation. There was hardly a building left standing more than one story high. Rubble was piled everywhere. The people were bedraggled, dirty from the smoke and dust in the air. Civilians were still trying to put out the fires and removing the dead from the demolished buildings. The crew stood there for a moment, waiting for instructions from their guards, who themselves did not seem to know what to do, talking among themselves and looking off in different directions. One of the guards, a fat man about forty years old with one stripe on his arm, seemed to be the senior of the three. He and another of the other guards, a slightly younger man with no rank on his uniform, walked away from the group, presumably to get directions around the break in the railroad. The group would never see the senior guard again.

The third guard waited with the Americans by the tracks, making no effort to dissuade the Germans who shouted at their prisoners. Almost two hours later, only the junior guard had returned. The two guards decided to march the Americans to their destination without the other man, following the train passengers who were walking the half mile into the center of Rüsselsheim. They prodded the Americans in the right direction, shouting orders the prisoners did not understand. The men formed a column to file through the ruins of Rüsselsheim, with the younger Luftwaffe guard at the front of the line, followed by Rogers, who had to be assisted by Sekul and Tufenkjian because of his ankle sprain. The rest came along after, with Brown carrying the injured Dumont piggyback, since his ankle injury had worsened. The second Luftwaffe guard brought up the rear. The Americans joined the throngs of people trudging along, some evacuating that part of the city, others passing through the city in the other direction. Adams thought there must be four or five thousand people moving. As the men were marched through the bombed-out city, they passed by Marktstrasse, the street that would have taken them directly to the train station. Instead of turning right at the Evangelical Church with its roof caved in, they continued along Frankfurterstrasse because their German guards didn't know the city any better than the Americans did.

As they continued their slow march, the men hobbled by injuries, heat, and fatigue, they picked up followers who walked venting their anger at the bombers. Unable to understand the Germans, the men did not realize that the townspeople were angry at them not just for being the enemy, not just for being a bomber crew, but because they thought this crew was from one of the bombers that had brought such horror to the city hours earlier. Word spread among the local people that the crew was from a Canadian bomber that had been shot down the night before. Soon the crowd walking along with the crew had grown to nearly three hundred.

The Americans kept looking at the Luftwaffe guards for help, hoping they would intervene and calm the crowd down, at least keep them from getting violent. But the guards showed no interest in interfering, and the men were growing concerned that the guards didn't know where they were going.

Making their way up Frankfurterstrasse toward the city center, where the bomb damage was somewhat less and many buildings still stood, the Luftwaffe guard in the front of the line was approached by forty-year-old Josef Hartgen, deputy Nazi chief for the city, propaganda chief, and air raid warden. A few inches over five feet tall, lean and with a strong jaw line, Hartgen was a man dedicated to the party and serious about his role on the home front. Handsome and cocky, he thought of himself as a senior authority figure in the war-stricken city. Everyone in Rüsselsheim knew him well, the little big man who always seemed to march rather than walk, who never spoke normally but always snapped out his words as if he were delivering a speech in front of Hitler himself. He was wearing a gray-green pair of pants and a silver shirt with a light summer hat, along with a green band on his left arm that said "NSDAP AIR RAID" in German, the party insignia for rescue workers. He also carried a 6.35-mm pistol.

On his way to the damage control center at the police station, Hartgen was pushing his bike when he stopped to inquire about the disturbance caused by the Americans. He spoke with the lead Luftwaffe guard and instructed him to take the prisoners eastward on Frankfurterstrasse and out of the city. The Americans watched as the two men argued, the Luftwaffe guard seemingly refusing Hartgen's instructions and insisting that the group proceed to Taunusstrasse, where they could board another train to their destination.

Just then the airmen heard more shouting from behind them. Although they could not understand the words, they understood the anger. If they had understood the language, they might have started running sooner.

"Beat them! There are the terror fliers!" shouted Kathe Reinhardt in German, using the term "terrorflieger" for the most reviled of all enemies: bomber crews. Still holding a fresh loaf of bread from the Bopps Bakery down the street, she could have passed for an American housewife in her attractive skirt, blouse, and heels. "Beat them! Tear them to pieces! Beat them to death! They have destroyed our houses!"

Williams could not understand the shouted threats any more than the other men, but he knew what was going on. He had dreamed of a scene exactly like this. The street in a German city edged in rubble, the angry townspeople. He knew that they were about to be attacked.

The tension overtook Williams and he began to sob, looking around to see who would attack first, frantically looking for any way to escape. Brown noticed Williams's breakdown and was disgusted by the apparent cowardice. They were all in this together, damn it, and they didn't need one of their own falling apart now.

"You're a soldier in the army! You act like a soldier and stop crying!" Brown shouted at his friend. "Just stay with us and take it like a man!" Williams did his best to straighten up, but he was distraught at the prospect of dying in this place, in this way.

The men waited anxiously as their guards continued talking with Hartgen. Reinhardt continued shouting, and then she bent down and picked up a brick from the plentiful rubble in the streets and hurled it toward the airmen. The petite woman's aim was true; the brick hit Rogers directly on the left side of the head, cracking his skull and causing him to bleed from the nose and mouth. Hartgen, startled by the attack and furious that the Luftwaffe guards were disrespecting his authority, pulled his pistol and fired a shot in the air in an attempt get everyone's attention. Reinhardt ignored the gun shot and continued shouting at the Americans, whose eyes darted around nervously, watching for the next brick.

"These are the gangsters! These are the criminals! These are the ones who have killed our husbands!" she screamed.

The tension on the street remained, no one knowing what to do next or what would happen. Reinhardt's older sister, fifty-year-old Margarete Witzler, was nearby, looking matronly and old-world European in her long black dress and shawl. Responding to her sister's screams, she bent down and picked up a brick. When she hurled it toward the Americans, a flood of fury erupted.

"Amerikanische!"

"Piloten!"

A mob of at least fifty townspeople descended on the airmen, throwing more bricks, stones, pieces of slate from shattered roofs, pipes. As the attack began in earnest, Williams realized that this was his nightmare. It was just as he had dreamed and he knew what was coming. He panicked, looking for somewhere to run, but there was nowhere to go.

A farmer and tavernkeeper named Phillip Gütlich began beating the airmen with a large stick. Another man, Lorenz Wendel, tried to tell the crowd to stop but made a hasty retreat when the angry Germans threatened to turn on him. The two guards pushed the airmen around the corner of Taunus and Frankfurter Strassen, where they momentarily escaped, but as the group passed by a mound of stones collected from the bombing rubble, the mob rearmed and began throwing the stones after the fleeing men. The airmen did their best to ward off the blows, protecting each other as best they could, stopping to help when one of them fell down, but they were so outnumbered that they could do nothing. Adams was now carrying Dumont piggyback, having relieved an exhausted Brown earlier. With Dumont's ankle severely injured, he would have no chance to run on his own, but Adams was slowed by the weight.

Gütlich continued chasing the men and beating them with his stick, shouting "Tear them to pieces!" Several in the crowd started pointing to Adams and screaming "Juden! Juden!" targeting him with their stones and sticks. Trying to fend off the blows, Adams screamed back in German.

"I am not a Jew! I am German!" Then, trying to think of anything that might bring mercy from the crowd, he yelled, "Don't kill me! I have a wife and two children! We did not bomb Rüsselsheim! We bombed Osnabrück!" (In fact, the fliers did not bomb Osnabrück; Adams may have been confused and named this town because he had landed near it and may have seen the name on a road sign while walking with the farmer. Or perhaps he was intentionally lying so as not to reveal actual mission information. He also did not have a wife or children.)

Adams's plea yielded no mercy. The crowd did not let up and the airmen fled down the street, pursued by the mob. Hartgen now was leading the crowd, calling for them to follow, rallying them to more violence. People came out of their homes and businesses to join the attack. George Daum, the father who had left his sick child in the family's shelter to go out and fight fires while the bombs fell, came out of 12 Taunusstrasse with a shovel raised high, ready to strike, followed by Herr Muth, Heinrich Barthel, and Johann Opper, a railroad worker, coming out of their homes. Opper had heard rumors that the mob was an uprising of forced laborers, who were angry that they had been shut out of the air raid shelters that night. Opper had run to the homes of Barthel and Muth, imploring them to help beat back the revolt by the younger and stronger forced laborers, a revolt many Rüsselsheimers had long feared. Muth brought along his Italian rifle. All four men were surprised when they got to the scene of the action and found not slaves in revolt but "terror fliers" marching through the rubble they had created. The men's fear turned to anger.

"You must beat them!" Opper screamed to the crowd as he pummeled the Americans. By this point all the Americans were bloodied.

Muth fired his rifle in the air, possibly in an effort to get the mob's attention and calm them down, but it had no effect. Gütlich and others continued to beat the men as they approached the corner of Taunus and Grabens Strassen, landing many blows on Dumont, who was an easy target because he and Adams had fallen behind the group and Dumont could do little to ward off the blows as he tried to hang on to his buddy's back. The Germans were trying furiously to wrench Dumont off Adams's back, knowing he would be easy prey on his own. In the process, someone managed to yank off Dumont's fur-lined flying boots, leaving him barefoot. With blows landing unabated, Dumont soon fell off Adams's back and, once down, had no chance to run because of his ankle. Unable to help his friend, Adams rushed forward to the rest of the group, which was seeking safety against a brick wall alongside the railroad tracks. When Adams looked back for Dumont, he saw the flier crumpled on the sidewalk, being savagely beaten by the mob, a large piece of slate embedded in his skull. A German named Johannes Seipel, bleeding from the head because he had been struck by the flying debris, was kicking Dumont over and over.

The attack had been going on for more than an hour.

One of the Luftwaffe guards removed his pistol from its holster and began shouting for the crowd to move back, but instead the Germans turned on him. He promptly holstered his weapon and moved away, leaving the mob to do as they pleased. Fearing that the mob would make them the next victims, the lightly armed and ineffectual Luftwaffe guards did little else to resist and soon drifted away from the mob. The airmen huddled against the brick wall, doing their best to protect themselves and each other, but the attack only grew worse as railroad workers and people getting off the trains rushed over. Word was spreading, and soon another hundred people stormed down from the station to seek vengeance on the bomber crew. Women threw milk cans when they ran out of stones, and railroad workers stood on the five-foot wall above them, hitting the men with hammers and lifting a railroad tie up high to drop on them. Forty-three-year-old August Wolf was on the wall striking down at the men, as was Friedrich Wüst, who was battering Austin's head with a hammer. Soon the airmen realized that the wall offered no protection and tried to move again.

Adams fell to the sidewalk from a blow to the head. As Brown continued forward, he felt a bottle shatter over his head, spilling some sort of alcohol, which stung as it ran down over his many lacerations. Then he looked ahead, the alcohol stinging his eyes, and saw a man reaching into his pocket for something.

A knife. Lord, if he stabs me here I'm a goner.

As Brown lunged to one side to avoid being pushed into the man with the knife, he felt a sharp blow from a two-by-four above his left ear. He went down hard, his head hitting the curb. Though he never lost consciousness, Brown was smart enough to play possum, pretending to be dead so the mob would not continue attacking him.

Austin and Tufenkjian fell quickly thereafter, and Wüst knelt down to slam Austin repeatedly in the head with a hammer. The crowd set upon Tufenkjian with passion, shouting that the Jew terror flier must die.

Rogers, Sekul, and Williams were the only ones left standing. They staggered, hunched over and trying to ward off the blows and projectiles, one of them cradling the box of their personal belongings. Trying to escape from the wall, they moved west on Grabenstrasse, with the crowd close behind. The men did not get far before they ran into a second mob, this one even bigger, coming southeast down Grabenstrasse. More than two hundred people, mostly Opel employees who were milling around the plant to see the bombing damage and people stranded at the train station, had heard that terror fliers were marching through town. When they saw the blood-soaked Americans stumbling and trying to run from their pursuers, the second mob set upon them with a fresh viciousness. At some point, hands in the crowd wrenched the box of personal belongings away from the fliers, and it disappeared.

The Americans turned to run from the larger mob, making it partway back toward the wall they had just left. Soon men dressed in Wehrmacht military uniforms joined railroad workers in beating the three fliers and throwing debris at them until they too fell. The three men tried to crawl toward each other as the mob continued its assault, but soon all three fell into heaps and ceased moving. Stones and blows continued to fall for a few moments, and then the crowd realized all the airmen were down. The crowd slowly pulled back, yelling insults at the still bodies and beginning to congratulate themselves on a job well done. Gütlich stopped to chat with a nearby resident, Wilhelmina Biendl, who had watched the beatings from her window overlooking the street. "My hands hurt so from the beating!" he told her with a smile.

The members of the mob were still under the impression that the men they had beaten were Canadian, because no one had bothered to ask in the heat of the moment and the airmen wore no readily identifiable markings on their clothing. The rumor of a Canadian air crew being captured made sense because the Germans knew they had been bombed by the British the night before, which included Canadian fliers.

Back by the wall where the men had sought refuge, Warden Hartgen felt it was his official duty to bring the episode to an orderly close. Enlisting the help of a few men nearby, Hartgen had all the bloodied and battered airmen, some of them still groaning and jerking uncontrollably, lined up neatly in fine German order, their heads on the sidewalk near the wall and their feet pointed toward the street. In his booming, authoritative voice, he announced to the remaining crowd that he was going to put the men out of their misery.

Two hours after the mob had first attacked, Hartgen pulled his pistol from its holster. He started at the western end of the row and proceeded to shoot the fliers in the head. Brown continued playing dead, hearing the shots as Hartgen moved down the line, not daring to flinch. As Hartgen was shooting, someone else was kicking the man lying next to Brown, whom he thought was Sekul. With one eye just barely open, Brown could see another German man kicking Adams in the head over and over again with all his might.

Oh, my lord. Nobody can live through that.

Brown lay quietly, expecting to be shot at any moment. But then the gunshots stopped. Hartgen had made it through four of the men before his six-shot pistol ran out of ammunition. The others appeared dead already, so Hartgen called to some Hitler Youth who had been watching and participating in the attack, ordering them to get a farmer's cart and take all the bodies to the Waldfriedhof, a cemetery in the woods a little more than a mile away.

One by one the fliers were picked up by their arms and legs and thrown in the cart. Adams was tossed in and his head jammed up under the driver's bench in the front. The men's bodies were limp. Brown tried to show no signs of life as he was roughly picked up by two men, swung a few times for momentum, and tossed into the cart. He ended up on his back, his head toward the rear of the cart. Sekul was tossed in on top of him, facedown, his legs draped over Brown.

When all the bodies were on the cart, Sekul managed to raise his bloodied head and look up. He saw a sixteen-year-old boy standing nearby. The American feebly shook his head no, as if begging not to be disposed of. Hartgen called to a man nearby, Otto Herman Stolz, a thirty-one-year-old Nazi party member, and told him to help the Hitler Youth.

Stolz and the boys pulled the cart away.

CHAPTER 7

RUNNING SOUTH

SOME IN THE CROWD WEREN'T READY to give up the party, so they accompanied the cart full of Americans—most of the mob had assumed the men were Canadians and still thought so—to the cemetery, helping pull the cart and walking alongside whooping and hollering with joy about their triumph, proud to show off their war trophies. Stolz led the way, wearing the uniform that signified he was a member of the Sturm Abteilung (Storm Section). Known by the Germans as the SA but more commonly called storm troopers or brown shirts by Westerners, the SA were considered Hitler's own private army. They were the true thugs of the Nazi Party, instructed to disrupt the meetings of political opponents and to protect Hitler's mission in any way necessary. Often they were former members of the Freikorps, right-wing private armies that flourished after World War I and had considerable experience in using violence against their rivals. SA members like Stolz were valued on the home front for enforcing the Nazi way and discouraging any dissent, which is why a relatively young, robust man like Stolz was still walking around Rüsselsheim instead of fighting on the front.

The SA wore gray jackets and brown shirts that originally were intended for soldiers in Africa but were purchased in bulk from the

German army by the Nazi Party. Sometimes they also wore swastika armbands, ski caps, knee breeches, thick woolen socks, and combat boots.

When the cart reached Königstädterstrasse, the group encountered an army truck carrying captured RAF fliers from the previous night's raid on Rüsselsheim. The mob forced the truck to stop and, excited and emboldened by its previous success, tried to take the RAF fliers from their German guards. Two guards immediately stepped off the running boards, raised their rifles, and made it clear that they would shoot if necessary. With that, the crowd backed down and the truck went on its way. Ironically, the guards had saved the lives of the fliers who actually had bombed Rüsselsheim.

Losing the confrontation with the German soldiers took some verve out of the crowd, and it began to disperse, many peeling off to go home, leaving about a dozen Hitler Youth, some as young as ten years old, to continue the macabre cortege to the cemetery, on Hasslocherstrasse outside of town. Stolz sometimes helped pull the cart while the children pushed.

As they arrived at the cemetery, sixty-eight-year-old caretaker Jakob Raab and his workers were dealing with a steady stream of cars dropping off bodies from the previous night's raid. Raab stepped over to inspect the load and asked the SA man why the heavy cart was being pushed by children.

"No one else would do it," he said.

As they stood near the cart, blood dripping steadily and forming a pool underneath, Stolz and Raab noticed moaning from some of the Americans. Stolz walked off toward a pile of lumber and came back with a club about the size of a two-by-four to finish off the dying men. He was nearly satisfied when he heard the air raid siren begin to wail, signaling another bombing raid. Raab, Stolz, and the Hitler Youth abandoned the wagon and sought refuge in a slit trench, leaving the crew of the *Wham! Bam!* alone in the cemetery.

Wedged in next to Sekul and with the other men on top of him Brown stayed quiet and still for a long time, not wanting to draw attention by moving to look around. The air raid sirens stopped after a few minutes and the cemetery was quiet. Brown listened closely for any sign that someone was still near the wagon. After hearing nothing for about fifteen minutes, he slowly raised his head to look around. He saw that he was in a graveyard surrounded by a stone wall about six feet high. There was a chapel in the middle of the cemetery. He saw that the cemetery was empty, so he began trying to extricate himself from the pile of bodies. He was sure he was the only one still alive.

But then he heard a noise. Someone was trying to move under the pile of bodies. Brown was surprised but thrilled to realize he wasn't alone.

"Who's there?" Brown called softly, still afraid of attracting attention. "Who is that?"

"It's Bill," came a muffled voice from under the driver's seat. It was Bill Adams. Apparently Stolz had failed to hit Adams because his head had been jammed under the seat. Brown was glad to hear his buddy's voice and started helping him make his way out of the pile. Once they were both free, they looked around and decided that the chapel offered the best refuge for the moment, so they jumped off the cart and rushed to the small stone building. No one was there, so the two men just huddled inside for a few minutes, trying to think of what to do next. Brown took the opportunity to remove his heavy and extremely hot flight suit, stashing it in a corner of the chapel. His clothes underneath were sopping wet with sweat and blood. Both men were exhausted from the ordeal, and they were hurting in so many places they couldn't tell exactly where their injuries were. Adams had avoided many of the blows to the head by carrying Dumont and later by shielding his head with his arms when the German was kicking at him, but his arms were severely bruised. Now his arms were turning blue green and starting to swell. They turned uglier colors and swelled up more every minute. Brown had multiple lacerations on his head and his whole body ached from the beatings.

AFTER BROWN DITCHED HIS heated flight suit in the chapel at the cemetery, he and Adams made their way outside, gingerly at first, looking around for anyone who might spot them. They saw a stone wall about six feet tall, with a stone cap on top, surrounding the cemetery and about twenty yards from where they stood in the doorway of the chapel. They considered going out through the cemetery gate, but they figured that would be the most likely way to run into someone.

"Bill, we're gonna have to climb that wall," Brown said to his buddy.

Normally that wouldn't be much of a task for two healthy young men, but they were struggling just to remain upright. Brown had lost so much blood from his head injuries that if he bent over, he nearly passed out when he stood back up again. On top of that, his tooth was still aching terribly. Brown was feeling woozy as they stood looking at the wall, and he told his friend he might not make it over.

"Don't worry, Brownie. I'll help you," Adams told him. "We have to get over."

The fliers decided to go for it and took off running—really, staggering quickly—toward the wall. When they got there, Brown didn't have the strength do much more than press his body against the stone as Adams shoved him from below, pushing him up to the top, where Brown just let his body fall over to the other side. Then Adams pulled himself up and over, and the two fliers were out of the cemetery. Hoping they were alone, they looked around and realized they weren't. Maybe fifty yards away was a German on a bicycle, looking directly at them. There was almost no underbrush to hide in, just an open field. The blood-covered fliers were conspicuous. Brown and Adams stood there for a moment, staring back at the bicyclist.

"Once they see you, it doesn't make any sense to hide," Brown said softly. "That just makes them suspicious. Let's just walk."

They started walking toward a tree line to the south, figuring the woods would give them more protection than being out in the open. The man on the bicycle pedaled down the road, looking over his shoulder at them for as long as he could. When he finally turned out of sight, the fliers figured they were safe. Even if he raised an alarm, they would be gone by the time anyone showed up. Brown and Adams decided that they would keep heading south, hoping they would make it to Switzerland, which they knew would intern them and keep them out of a Nazi POW camp.

As they made their way through the woods, 412 British Lancaster bombers hummed over Rüsselsheim and opened their bomb bay doors, dropping more than 2 million pounds of explosives.

WITHOUT KNOWING EXACTLY where they had started, Brown and Adams were at a disadvantage in trying to figure out how to find help. Having no compass or other aids, they used the sun and moon to orient themselves. They longed for their escape and evasion kits, which included compasses, maps, language guides, local currency, and other helpful items, but they had been confiscated, then lost. They trudged on through the woods, wary of encountering anyone, knowing they were in no shape to fight or run. They were so nervous that when they accidentally came upon a doe and her fawn and the animals sprang up all of a sudden, it nearly scared both men to death.

The men's objective was to get as far away from Rüsselsheim as they could but also to find a good place to hide. They kept walking all afternoon, the heat wearing them down even further, and they soon became obsessed with finding water. Brown's severe blood loss was causing his throat to ache for water. The men were stumbling along through the trees when they suddenly heard noise and saw a group of people approaching on a nearby road. Brown and Adams realized that the German forest's complete lack of underbrush was both beneficial and harmful. It allowed them to see far into the distance, but it provided little cover. The airmen got as low to the ground as they could, but they were stricken with fear when they saw the group approaching. It was about two hundred Hitler Youth in brown shirts and swastika armbands, marching down the road. Brainwashed more effectively than many German adults and with the reckless abandon of youth, the teens and preteens in the group most likely would finish off the job started in Rüsselsheim, or at least would capture the airmen and turn them in. The men lay quietly, watching the group come closer, wondering if they should just jump up and run for their lives. Their hearts were pumping madly when the group made a right turn and marched away.

The men continued walking after the Hitler Youth left. After a long while, Brown and Adams came upon a marshy area with plenty of dark, murky water but it looked too bad even for desperately thirsty men to drink more than a few small gulps. Brown considered using the water to wash off some of the blood and other filth from his head, but he feared infecting the wounds, so the men just continued walking.

They had no idea where they were or how far they had traveled from Rüsselsheim, but as night began to fall, they decided to rest. There was nothing to provide shelter, so the airmen just huddled in the woods, doing their best to stay warm. Brown was wearing only socks, green Army fatigue pants, and a long-sleeved undershirt. Adams wore khaki pants, a short-sleeve shirt, and the shoes he had put on before jumping out of the plane. Brown was kicking himself for not taking the time to change into regular shoes before abandoning ship, and he wished he had merely taken the heating element liner out of the flight suit and kept the outer shell. When the heat of the day gave way to the cool night air, with no shoes, hardly any clothes, and his body still suffering from the loss of blood, Brown thought he was going to freeze to death that first night.

Recalling their training in escape and evasion, Brown and Adams decided it would be best to travel by night and hide during the day. Beginning the next morning, that is what they did. Throughout the day, they hid in the woods, camouflaging themselves as best they could with brush and leaves, hoping no hunters or farmers would happen by. Then as night fell they would go on the move, using only the light of the moon to see and to navigate southward. Finding very little water along the way, the men were constantly thirsty, and their hunger was growing. After traveling through a second night, Brown and Adams found that as dawn was breaking, they were not in a good place to hide for the day. There was not much groundcover or thick woods. But as they were wondering what to do, they realized that they were standing on an old home site. The buildings were gone, but they could see the outlines of where they had been and some belongings discarded by the former residents. And then as the sun grew brighter, they saw an old pump-handle well head. Hopeful that it still worked, they raced over to it and began pumping the handle. Water gushed out of the pump, and the two fliers drank all they could, stopping only when their bellies felt like they would burst.

Their thirst quenched, the men looked around the homestead and found Japanese plum trees with ripe fruit. They eagerly snatched the yellow plums off the overgrown trees and ate their fill, savoring the flavors of peach and apricot in the exotic fruit. Brown went to check out some apple trees nearby but found that the fruit was not yet ripe. He took some of the apples anyway, along with as many plums as he could carry, stuffing them in his pockets. After they had eaten their fill of plums and topped the meal off with a bit more water, Brown and Adams were about to look for a hiding place when they saw a man in the distance. He appeared to be working in his garden and hadn't spotted them. So they snuck away, crossing over a cabbage patch and heading toward some thicker woods. Once they reached the trees, they saw that a skinny dirt road cut through the forest and, thinking the road looked seldom used, decided to walk down it instead of taking the more difficult path through the trees and brush. Feeling confident that they were well hidden, and energized from the water and fruit, the fliers decided to keep walking for a while after dawn. It wasn't long, however, before they rounded a curve in the little road and ran right into a German coming from the other direction. They startled each other, and the Americans just stopped. Then the German said something to the men that Brown couldn't understand, but both calmly nodded their heads, saying "Ja, ja. . . ." *Yes, yes.* As they did so, both men turned and suddenly made a run for it. Both made a wild dash, fueled by a burst of adrenaline, back in the direction of the cabbage patch, Brown making a world-record broad jump across a set of railroad tracks, never touching the gravel with his bare feet. With no need to discuss plans, Adams and Brown ran into the cabbage patch and fell down between the rows, where the large, mature cabbage leaves effectively hid them. They lay still for a while as the man they encountered, along with several others, searched the area, focusing their attention on the old homestead. They beat the bushes looking for where the men might be hiding, but they never came into the cabbage patch.

Adams and Brown stayed in the cabbage patch until dark, then headed back into the woods to continue on south—after stuffing some cabbage leaves into their clothes for later. Though their spirits were generally good, the physical effects of their beating were unrelenting.

Brown's head pounded, and the rest of his body ached miserably. Adams's black-and-blue forearms were swollen terribly. As they walked they came to a river, which they later learned was the Rhine, and realized that if they were to continue to the south, they would have to find a place to cross. It was much too deep and fast to try crossing on foot or swimming. After a few hours of walking, they suddenly realized they were within direct sight of a village and had to change direction abruptly to skirt around its edges. As they did so, it seemed that every dog in town knew they were there.

Still working their way south near the river, they saw a railroad bridge and just beyond it another small village. But there was a guard house on each end of the bridge. The fliers couldn't tell if the houses were occupied, so they decided to hide out nearby until they could tell if it was safe to traverse the bridge. There were dozens of haystacks in a field about three hundred yards away from where the airmen were crouched trying to get a good look at the bridge. Adams and Brown remembered that they had been taught never to hide in haystacks. They're about the worst place you can choose to hide, their escape and evasion instructors had told them. They're obvious hiding places, and Germans really love shoving a pitchfork in to see if you squeal.

Brown and Adams thought it over and decided it was worth the risk. They were far enough away from Rüsselsheim that no one would be looking for them there, they thought. So they headed to the haystacks and tunneled their way into one before the sun rose, ready to wait out the daylight and watch the bridge all day long. Brown lay there in the haystack with his chin resting on his folded arms, just barely able to see out toward the bridge, eating unripe apples and cabbage as a light rain began to fall. They were happy to find that the middle of a haystack is dry and warm, as the hay naturally generated heat. The men were unbelievably content and fell asleep right away. When they woke up, the day was bright and no one was around. As they lay there in the hay, they whispered to each other to pass the time.

"Hey, Brownie, what do you think's gonna happen to us when we get to Switzerland?" Adams said.

"Oh, I suspect they'll lock us up a while before sending us home."

"That's fine with me," Adams replied. "Think we'll go on a bond tour?"

Brown laughed at the thought of him and Adams traveling around the country promoting war bonds, but he knew the Army liked to do that with airmen who had survived enough flights to be sent home in one piece, so he figured it would probably do the same with them. "Yeah, I bet we will. But I get first dibs on the pretty ladies."

"You know, those girls back home really like those war bond heroes," Adams said. "Heck, we'll be heroes when we get out of this mess here. We'll get back, tell our story, and we'll have those pretty girls falling all over us."

"You better believe it, Bill. Two American heroes right here in this haystack."

They both laughed quietly. Neither would let on while they were hiding and trying to reach Switzerland, but years later they admitted to each other that they were both thinking the same thing: *We're not going to be heroes. We're not going to make it home and go on a bond tour. We're going to be killed before we get to Switzerland.*

THE MEN LAY IN THE haystack for hours without seeing anything. A man on a tractor passed by at one point without stopping, then later in the day a teenage girl and boy came up toward the haystacks on bicycles with pitchforks. Brown watched as they worked, raking up loose hay around a stack and using the pitchforks to toss it back up on the top. The Florida country boy thought it was odd that they were working the hay in the rain, and he suspected the boy had brought the girl up the hill for something else. He probably knew how warm it was in a haystack. But the teens continued with their work, and Brown began to worry as they finished with one stack and then started walking toward the one with he and Adams hidden inside. The fliers remained absolutely still and quiet as the boy and girl began raking the hay around their stack. They were hidden well enough, they thought, that maybe the German teens would just do their work—or whatever else they were up to—and move on.

But then one of the Germans raked up a patch of hay right in front of Brown and the bunch of hay he had pulled down in front of his face after wiggling into the stack fell onto the ground. The first thing the boy and girl noticed was the pile of three green apples that Brown had placed near his head so he could munch all day without having to move much. Adams and Brown heard the Germans say something, which Brown assumed was "Hey, where'd those apples come from?" Right after that the girl peered into the haystack and saw Brown's face a little farther back. She screamed and jumped back as if she had seen a snake. The two Germans began talking quickly and excitedly, while the fliers stayed still, not knowing what else to do. After a minute, Brown asked Adams what they were saying.

"They're talking about whether to jab us with those pitchforks," Adams said.

But they didn't. After more conversation, the German boy and girl left the men alone and went back to raking near another haystack. The men were relieved but puzzled. Apparently the youths were not going to turn them in. Even when the tractor came back by, driven by an adult, the boy and girl didn't appear to give them away. Adams and Brown talked about what to do and decided they didn't want to get caught in the haystack so, even though they weren't sure where the boy and girl were, they crawled out of the haystack, shaking like wet dogs to shed themselves of the hay.

They walked away, never seeing the boy and girl again.

They made their way away from the haystacks and the village perimeter, still intent on crossing the river to head south. They climbed up over a dike with a roadway on top and went down to the riverside, hoping they might find a spot safe enough to swim or wade. Seeing no likely area to cross, they sat down by the Rhine for a moment to contemplate their next move, confident that they could see anyone coming from a distance. This was the second time they ignored the lessons from their escape and evasion training. They had escaped being poked with pitchforks in the haystack, and now they were sitting out in the open, where they could be seen by the enemy just as quickly as they could see the enemy approaching. They were supposed to always choose a spot that allowed them to see the enemy coming before they were spotted themselves. Tired, hungry, and still hurting from their injuries, Adams and Brown just weren't thinking clearly.

After a short while sitting at the riverbank, they saw a figure approaching from downriver. He wore the green uniform of some civil authority and had a pistol at his side.

"Dang, he sees us," Brown said. "Ain't no use in running now."

Out in the open, unable to cross the river, they had little chance of escaping. So they waited for the German—an elderly man, as most left in the villages were at this point in the war—to approach. They noticed that another man had stopped his bicycle on top of the dike and was watching to see what would happen. The official approached and said something to the fliers. Seeing Adams move as if to produce his papers from his front pocket, Brown did the same thing, both of them digging for a moment to stall. Neither flier said anything to the other, but just as in their last encounter on the road through the forest, they didn't need to speak. At the same instant, both men turned and ran as fast as they could upstream. They heard a couple of gunshots ring out as they left the German behind. Brown looked back and saw the old man furiously waving his pistol around, trying to run and catch up.

The man on top of the dike was pointing and directing another German after the fliers. Brown and Adams climbed over the dike and tried to hide in a farmer's field, tucking themselves between the rows of plants as they had in the cabbage field earlier, but they could see that the man on the bicycle was pointing right at them, so they got up and ran again. But the delay while they hid had given the old man with the pistol time to close the distance, and they heard him shouting from close by. Thinking the man might actually be able to hit them with the pistol, Brown and Adams considered overpowering him, but they figured that even if they got away, they would have made themselves known. Then it would only be a matter of time before they were captured or maybe killed. Without even having to discuss it, they stopped and raised their arms.

The old German man couldn't have been more excited and proud if he had captured Eisenhower himself.

Adams and Brown were quite a sight: still covered in dried black blood, clothing torn, Brown with no shoes, Adams's forearms black and swollen to frightful proportions, Brown's jaw huge from the bad tooth. The German yelled and gestured for them to walk back toward the village, his accomplishment giving him a newfound confidence and authority. He followed along behind, herding his prisoners to town. When the trio arrived, other old men came to help and took the two fliers to a small building that appeared to be the town's entire municipal operation. They led Brown to a small jail cell that looked like it hadn't been used in years. In fact, he had to wait while the men cleared out boxes—it was being used as a storage closet. Adams was kept in another part of the building, where village officials talked to him, trying to do their own small-town interrogation of the captured enemy flier. There was a lot of commotion outside Brown's cell; it seemed that everyone in town was excited about the prize catch. It wasn't long before villagers started coming to gawk at Brown, who had the distinct feeling of being an animal in a zoo. He just lay there and let them look, although he was tempted to leap up and growl at them, just to see them jump.

The fliers had been on the run for five days—long enough, they hoped, that nobody would associate them with the two who had escaped from Rüsselsheim. They certainly didn't want to be sent back there. What they didn't realize was that nobody was missing them from Rüsselsheim. Because the cemetery workers had left the cart with the bodies to be buried later, and they had no reason to count the bodies, no one realized anything was amiss when six bodies were buried instead of eight. Adams and Brown had made a clean escape. As far as any of the Germans knew, they were just another two downed fliers.

Brown and Adams were taken to a local clinic, where a doctor cleaned their wounds and gave Brown a tetanus shot. The doctor could not speak English, but he found a young boy who could. The doctor put a piece of paper in his hands and the boy translated for the doctor.

"It says the doctor gave you a tetanus shot. The doctor says you must keep this and tell another doctor if you see one," the boy said.

Brown left the clinic with a huge bandage on his head for his many lacerations. The town officials contacted the closest Luftwaffe base, and before long the German air force arrived to take custody of the Americans. The two men were taken to a base and locked in separate jail cells there, then guards brought them their first real meal in days: black bread and strawberry jam. The hungry Americans thought the jam was delicious, but the heel pieces of bread must have been cut weeks earlier. As hungry as they were, they couldn't choke it down. It was hard as a rock and Brown, with his aching tooth, couldn't bear even to try gnawing at it. When the guard came by his cell again, Brown got his attention.

"Hey, I sure would like some more of this here strawberry jam," Brown said, pointing to the empty cup and gesturing for more. He tried his best to put on a friendly face and smile.

The guard said something and pointed to the bread, making it clear to Brown that he wasn't getting any more jam until he ate his bread. The guard left and Brown tried the bread again. It was like trying to eat a brick. There didn't seem to be anywhere he could hide it, but then Brown looked at the skimpy mattress on his bed. It was nothing more than a cloth sack stuffed with hay. There was a slit in the side where the hay had been shoved in. Brown shoved the bread deep in the hay, but before he pulled his hand out he felt something else in there. He withdrew it and saw that it was somebody else's bread.

Somebody else had the same idea, he thought, and smiled. *I wasn't the first.*

The next morning the guard came by and, after checking to see that the bread was gone, gave Brown more bread and strawberry jam.

After a night at the base, Adams and Brown were loaded onto a truck and driven to the Dulag Luft aircrew interrogation center at Oberursel, north of Frankfurt, their original destination before the attack in Rüsselsheim. They were separated at that point, and the interrogations began. Brown's interrogation began with the German officer offering him an American cigarette, which Brown eagerly accepted, having been without a smoke for a week.

"You know, we could shoot you for a spy," the German said. "You have no uniform. You do not wear dog tags. You have no kind of identification showing you are an American airman. We could just take you outside and shoot you."

"I'm just a gunner on a bomber, that's all," Brown said.

"Well, perhaps. But maybe you are lying. We need to be sure you were not parachuted into Germany for espionage," he replied. "Maybe we should just shoot you."

After the ordeal in Rüsselsheim and five days on the run, Brown was too tired and angry to be intimidated. Instead he was just weary of dealing with the Germans. And annoyed.

"I just can't believe you would shoot a little old innocent fellow like me," he said. "I just can't believe folks like you. I can't believe you're that inhuman."

"We can. We can shoot you," the German replied.

The interrogator let the subject drop and went on to asking questions about Brown's training, his base, and his missions. Brown refused to answer each question, telling the German that he could only give his name, rank, and serial number. Trying to appear friendly, the interrogator said he understood and that, as a fellow serviceman, he respected Brown's loyalty to his country. But then he started asking questions again, almost casually, as if he thought Brown might forget he was being interrogated.

"Did you do any training at Langley Field? That was where you got your radar training, yes?"

That question startled Brown a bit, because the German was right. The Rogers crew had trained in the new radar technology at Langley.

"Man, what are you talking about?" Brown replied. "I ain't never been near Langley Field."

The questions continued, and Brown continued refusing to answer most of them, occasionally responding with a lie when it seemed that the German actually knew what he was talking about. After more questions that Brown couldn't have answered even if he wanted to—mission strategy, targets for coming raids—the American got tired of it all.

"What do you expect a little old buck sergeant on his first mission to know, anyhow?" he asked.

The German smiled and shook his head.

"You know, Brown," the German said slowly, fingering his American cigarette, "it's a strange thing to me that all you Americans who come through here are on your first mission. Isn't that odd?"

"Well, I don't know what those other boys are telling you," Brown said. "You can believe me or not, I don't care, but I was on my first one."

During the interrogation, the officer handed a postcard to Brown and told him he could fill it out if he wanted. It was a notification that he had been taken prisoner. One side was to be addressed to his family, and on the other side were several options to check: "I am not wounded. I am in good shape and everything is fine," "I am slightly wounded and receiving treatment," and so on. Brown filled out the card with his parents' address and checked the box indicating he was not wounded, choosing not to worry his parents. The card would be sent to the Red Cross, which would forward it on to the Brown family. When Brown handed it back to the German officer, the man looked at it and said, "Oh, you're from Gainesville, Florida?"

"Yes, that's right."

"I've been to Florida."

"What part?"

"Oh, some time on the east coast, and some time on the west coast."

"Anywhere around Gainesville?" Brown asked. He was trying to pin the German down to specifics.

"No, I don't think so. Just all around Florida."

Brown knew what the man was trying to do. The German was trying to get chummy with Brown by claiming to be familiar with his home area, hoping to break the ice and get a rapport going. Brown wasn't falling for it. The game continued like that for hours, the German never getting violent like the first people the crew encountered, instead trying to wheedle Brown into letting his guard down and having a real conversation. After Brown enjoyed the last of the cigarette, he pointed at the pack on the table and asked for another.

"Hold on now," the German said. "Let's talk a while before you smoke all my fine American cigarettes."

The interrogator always knew more about the flier than he let on, playing ignorant in an attempt draw out more information. At one point, the German asked him, "So, how's the weather at Metfield? Getting much rain?" Brown tried not react. He realized that the officer knew they had been stationed at Metfield in England but didn't know that his group had moved to North Pickenham.

"Yeah, it's been pretty rainy at Metfield," Brown said, laughing to himself inside.

Brown kept parrying while also trying to convince his interrogator that he truly was just a peon gunner on his first mission who didn't know anything that would be useful. The officer kept asking Brown to name his superiors, but Brown said he didn't even know their names. The only names he knew were those of his own crewmates. He couldn't have named his commanding officer if the Germans had put a gun to his head. Finally the German named the whole list of officers in Brown's bomb group, and Brown just shrugged and said he'd have to take his word for it. Eventually the officer came to accept that Brown didn't really know much, and he was sent back to his cell. Adams got pretty much the same treatment and also did not give up any useful information. Neither man mentioned that they had been assaulted in Rüsselsheim.

Both Americans stayed in their cells for almost two weeks, eating nothing but brown bread with margarine and jam and a cup of weak tea each day. The solitary confinement was particularly hard on Adams, who couldn't stand the loneliness.

The Crew of the Wham! Bam! Thank You Ma'am. *Back row, left to right: Rogers, Sekul, Cassidy, Robinson (Cassidy and Robinson didn't make the ill-fated flight).*

Front Row: Adams, Austin, Williams, Dumont, Brown, Brininstool. (Credit: U.S. Army Signal Corps / National Archives)

Second Lieutenant Norman J. Rogers, Jr., pilot of the Wham! Bam! Thank You Ma'am *(Credit: U.S. Army Signal Corps / National Archives)*

Second Lieutenant John. N. Sekul, the co-pilot from the Bronx, New York. The images of the crew members in civilian clothes are their "escape and evasion" photos intended for use if they were behind enemy lines. (Credit: U.S. Army Signal Corps / National Archives)

Staff Sergeant Forrest W. Brininstool, the engineer from Munith, Michigan (Credit: U.S. Army Signal Corps / National Archives)

Flight Officer Haigus Tufenkjian, the navigator and bombardier from Detroit, Michigan (Credit: U.S. Army Signal Corps / National Archives)

Sergeant William A. Adams, the nose gunner from Klingerstown, Pennsylvania (Credit: U.S. Army Signal Corps / National Archives)

Sergeant Elmore L. Austin, the left waist gunner from Edinburg Falls, Vermont (Credit: U.S. Army Signal Corps / National Archives)

Sergeant William A. Dumont, the belly gunner from Berlin, New Hampshire (Credit: U.S. Army Signal Corps / National Archives)

Staff Sergeant Thomas D. Williams, Jr., the radio operator from Hazelton, Pennsylvania (Credit: U.S. Army Signal Corps / National Archives)

Sergeant Sidney Eugene Brown, the tail gunner from Gainesville, Florida (Credit: U.S. Army Signal Corps / National Archives)

Wham! Bam! *pilot Norman Rogers Jr. and his new bride, Helen, at the time of their wedding in April 1944. Courtesy of Madeline Rogers Ruf Teremy*

Members of the military commission trying the residents of Russelsheim visit the wall where some of the worst beatings occurred. The rubble and railroad ties used to attack the airmen can be seen behind the wall. Brigadier General Garrison Davison, acting as judge for the commission, is at the center holding a map. (Credit: U.S. Army Signal Corps / National Archives)

The defendants during their trial.

Back Row, left to right: Barthel, Daum, Opper, Gütlich, Wolf, Wust.

Front Row: Fugmann, Seipel, Reinhardt, Witzler, Hartgen (Credit: U.S. Army Signal Corps / National Archives)

A witness, right, identifies defendant Josef Hartgen, in the lighter jacket with his arms folded. Col. Leon Jaworski, the prosecutor, is at the center. Source: U.S. Army Signal Corps/National Archives

Witzler is sentenced. She holds her head and shouts, "Nein! Nein!" (Credit: U.S. Army Signal Corps / National Archives)

Gutlich on the gallows (Credit: U.S. Army Signal Corps / National Archives)

Wust is hanged. Source: U.S. Army Signal Corps/National Archives

Hartgen is hanged. Source: U.S. Army Signal Corps/National Archives

CHAPTER 8

DEEP REGRET

ON SEPTEMBER 5, 1944, ANOOSH TUFENKJIAN answered the door and found a boy of about twelve waiting there, looking down at his feet, his bicycle lying on the grass nearby. When she saw his dark tie and the peaked hat with the Western Union badge on the front, her heart fell.

It hadn't been long since the families of the *Wham! Bam!* crew had last heard from their sons, brothers, and husbands, so they did not yet have reason to worry, at least no more than the constant worry over a loved one at war. But seeing the Western Union boy at her door that Tuesday afternoon, and the awkward way he avoided eye contact, she knew her Haigus was in trouble. She took the envelope and let the boy leave.

Tears were welling in her eyes as she opened the telegram and began to read.

THE SECRETARY OF WAR DESIRES ME TO EXPRESS HIS DEEP REGRET THAT YOUR SON FLIGHT OFFICER HAIGUS TUFENKJIAN HAS BEEN REPORTED MISSING IN ACTION SINCE TWENTY FOUR AUGUST OVER GERMANY IF FURTHER DETAILS OR OTHER INFORMATION ARE RECEIVED YOU WILL BE PROMPTLY NOTIFIED

Eight other families were receiving a similar telegram. Across America, families wept with the thought of their loved ones declared missing, knowing that a second telegram often followed with even worse news. But until that telegram came, they could still hope. And pray.

The war pressed on as the families worried and waited. The Allies continued pushing through western Europe during the latter part of 1944, trying to break into northern Germany with an airborne assault in the Netherlands, but that effort was unsuccessful.

Soviet Red Army troops advanced into Yugoslavia in September 1944, which prompted the German troops in Greece and Albania to shift closer to prevent them from being cut off.

On September 12, 1944, Adams and Brown were transferred to a POW camp, Stalag Luft IV, in Tychowo, Poland. The camp housed about 10,000 American airmen, all noncommissioned officers, along with some British fliers. Brown and Adams were able to stay together in the camp, where the Germans did not know they were part of what would become known as the Rüsselsheim Death March, and they were treated like any other prisoners: not well. The two men remained close buddies in the camp, looking out for each other. The prisoners were constantly under threat of being beaten or shot for breaking a camp rule, or stepping over a boundary line, or for no reason at all. The guards had German shepherds that barked and lunged at the prisoners relentlessly, snarling and gnashing their teeth. Brown and Adams saw the dogs set loose, mauling the weak and sick prisoners as the Germans took their time pulling them off. There was always a risk of the Germans singling you out for punishment, and Brown was distressed when Adams ran afoul of some camp rule and was taken away for several days of isolation in a hole in the ground. He knew his buddy couldn't take that kind of treatment; nobody could, really, but Brown knew it would be especially hard on Adams. He was right. The experience was nightmarish for Adams, and Brown was shocked by his friend's state when he was let out of solitary. For a long time after that, he never left Adams's side.

At one point, they heard through the grapevine that Brininstool was housed in another of the four compounds at the camp, separated from Adams and Brown only by a barbed wire fence. The prisoners weren't allowed to go to the fence, though, and guards were ready to shoot any-one who tried. They weren't even supposed to shout at the POWs on the other side and could be shot just for that. But the prisoners knew that if they stood in the recessed doorways of their barracks, the guards in the towers couldn't see who was shouting and wouldn't have a line of fire at them, so Brown stood there one day calling for Brininstool. Someone on the other side went looking for him and came back with a message.

"He was here, but he left last week!" the other POW shouted. "They shipped him to another camp!"

THE WAR CONTINUED MOVING toward the end. Partisans under commu-nist marshal Josip Broz Tito controlled much of Yugoslavia and by late 1944 were focused on delaying German troops until the Red Army could arrive. Belgrade was liberated on October 20, 1944.

In the Pacific theater, American troops invaded the Filipino island of Leyte in late October, followed quickly by an Allied naval victory during the Battle of Leyte Gulf, one of the largest naval battles in history.

Germany's last grasp at victory on the western front came on De-cember 16, 1944, when the Nazis marshaled German reserves for a mas-sive counteroffensive in the Ardennes, the hilly, forested region in Belgium, Luxembourg, and France. The goal was to divide the western Allies, encircling large portions of troops and capturing their primary supply port at Antwerp, Belgium. If successful, Hitler expected the Al-lies would be willing to end the war with a political settlement.

Confident that the end of the war was near, in December 1944, the United States War Department ordered that the Office of the Judge Ad-vocate for the European Theater establish a branch that would have as its primary function "the investigation of alleged war crimes, and the col-lection of evidence relating thereto." The branch was established soon after in Paris, and investigators began collecting evidence of war crimes from repatriates, underground sources, captured documents, and es-caped prisoners of war.

The German counteroffensive in the Ardennes had failed by Janu-ary 1945. Both sides held ground in Italy but struggled to gain domi-nance, and in January the Soviets launched an offensive in Poland, pushing from the Vistula to the Oder River in Germany, and overran East Prussia.

AFTER BEING TAKEN AWAY for medical care, Brininstool never saw his crewmates again. He was soon transferred to a POW camp, where he was allowed to write a letter home to his family, which arrived in late January 1945. He reported what he knew of the other men on the *Wham! Bam!*, telling his family that everyone got out of the plane relatively unscathed and that he was the only one seriously wounded. When he last saw the other men, they were being held by the Luftwaffe at the airfield near Greven and were being treated well; he assumed that they also had been taken to a POW camp.

The Brininstools were relieved to hear that their son was well, and they knew that the other families would be eager to hear the news, so Brininstool's mother wrote to Anoosh Tufenkjian and then Tufenkjian wrote to the other families she could contact to spread the word that the boys might be okay. Five months after their loved ones were reported missing, the letters arrived like a gift from heaven. Sam Sekul wrote back to Mrs. Tufenkjian: "Your letter certainly contained wonderful news. It has renewed our faith and hope for John's, as well as the other boys' safety. Naturally, we have been praying right along for this and knowing the boys have been seen and were not injured inspires more so."

Hildrid Austin wrote to Tufenkjian that she also had heard from Brininstool's mother, noting that it was the first news she had heard of her son, Elmore.

> *I only hope I hear from him soon. Have you heard directly from yours? We have imagined all sorts of things. When you don't hear a word for so long it is easy to imagine things. Have always felt as though he was alive but I don't think it is too pleasant being a prisoner. I know he has written if they let him but lots of things happen to the mail.*
>
> *We have two other sons in the service and another that is eighteen next month. . . . We must hope and pray this will soon be over and they can come home again.*
>
> *Sincerely yours,*
> *Hildrid Austin*

Anoosh Tufenkjian also received a grateful letter from Helen Rogers. On February 4, 1945, the day U.S., British, and Soviet leaders met in Yalta to determine how they would occupy postwar Germany and when the Soviet Union would enter the Pacific war against Japan, Helen Rogers sat down in Rochester, New York, and wrote in her beautiful, deliberate script:

> *Your letter is the first I have received in all these trying months that has given me such hope.*
>
> *It makes me feel so good to know that they all got down safe.*
>
> *I hope we won't have to wait too long before it is confirmed. As you say, with all of us praying, how can we doubt that they are safe.*
>
> *Thank you so much Mrs. Tufenkjian for your letter. You can be sure I will write to you again as soon as I get some good news.*
>
> *Sincerely,*
Helen Rogers

As she wrote the letter, Helen was only twenty days from giving birth to her daughter Madeline. When the baby was born, Helen was still hoping and praying her new daughter would someday see her father.

IN FEBRUARY 1945, the Germans marched the prisoners from Stalag Luft IV back toward the Elbe River to avoid capture by the Soviets, who were advancing quickly then. In what would become known as the Black March, the prisoners left the POW camp on February 6. About 8,000 were given the remaining Red Cross parcels and set out on a march that would last eighty-six days, taking the occasional leg on a crowded train boxcar, which was nearly unbearable because most of the men, including Brown, had uncontrollable diarrhea from dysentery. Brown became separated from Adams during the march. The conditions on the trains and on the march were deplorable, the POWs and their guards taking shelter wherever they could, scrounging for food and water. At one point, Brown found himself trying to sleep in a sheep barn, desperately sick. He prayed to God—not for relief but for endurance.

Please, God, I've been through so much, Brown prayed. *After all that, I don't want to die here in this sheep barn.*

That same night, Brown dreamed that he was talking to his father back home in Gainesville. They spoke just as clearly as if Brown were sitting at the kitchen table with his daddy. Brown woke the next morning and knew that he would survive to see home again.

The families waited, more hopeful now and clinging to the news from Mrs. Brininstool. They imagined their young men in a POW camp and worried about the treatment they were receiving there but were buoyed by the idea that the war was in its last stages and the POWs would return home.

In March 1945, Allied troops crossed the Rhine north and south of the Ruhr, encircling a large number of German troops, and the Soviets advanced to Vienna. Also in March, the U.S. Third Army, led by General George S. Patton, captured Rüsselsheim. Once free of their German captors, some of the French and Polish interred workers started talking about a disturbing incident the previous August with an Allied aircrew. Few details were available, but the Army officials in Rüsselsheim documented the story. Nothing was done to investigate, as winning the war was still the first priority. Patton was still pressing on.

The brutal war in the Pacific also wore on, but the Allies were gaining momentum. American forces advanced, clearing Leyte by the end of April and seizing Manila in March. Fighting continued on Luzon, Mindanao, and other islands of the Philippines.

Moving steadily toward Japan and what was sure to be a costly invasion of the home island, American forces took Iwo Jima in March 1945. American crews used area bombing on Japanese cities, trying to soften the island for an invasion and to break the will of the people.

April 1945 proved to be a tumultuous time. President Roosevelt died on April 12 and was succeeded by Harry Truman. Allied troops pushed forward in Italy and across western Germany. Soviet forces hit Berlin in late April, joining up with the other Allied troops on the Elbe River on April 25. Benito Mussolini was killed by Italian partisans on April 28. The Reichstag was captured on April 30, and German forces surrendered in Italy on April 29. Adolf Hitler committed suicide the next day.

German troops surrendered in western Europe on May 7, and those on the eastern front surrendered to the Soviets on May 8. The Third Reich was defeated.

THE POWS WHO SURVIVED the Black March reached Stalag 357—a new camp formed when several camps threatened by the Allies were consolidated—near Fallingbostel, Germany, around April 3, 1945. After a week, as the POWs listened to Allied artillery coming closer and closer, the Germans abandoned that camp and set out on another march. Brown was sitting next to a road near the river Elbe outside Lauenburg, Germany, on the morning of May 2 when he saw British troops arrive. The Germans quickly gave up, and the Americans were free once again.

Brown and Adams returned to the States in June, two of the three survivors of the *Wham! Bam!* crew and the only Americans who knew what happened in Rüsselsheim.

CHAPTER 9

INVESTIGATIONS

BRININSTOOL RETURNED FROM THE WAR about the same time as Brown and Adams, and all three made contact by phone. For the first time, Brininstool heard what had happened to his friends. Both Brown and Adams had reported the incident in Rüsselsheim to American authorities before being sent home, but somewhere along the way, in the often-tumultuous end of the war, their reports were lost in the Army bureaucracy and no one realized that two crewmembers had survived, that they were in the United States just waiting to be called upon.

They were more than willing to tell their story to the Army, but talking to anyone else about their experience was a different matter. They would not discuss what happened on the ground with anyone, not even the families of the men who died. Especially not them. They vowed they would never reveal to anyone what had happened to them unless the military took action against their assailants.

It wasn't just that it was painful to talk about what had happened to them and about watching their friends die. More important, they didn't want to burden the families with that knowledge. Adams and Brown didn't want the family members of their fellow fliers to know how they had died. It was too painful, too ugly.

As the war came to a close, the Allies started establishing order again, and that meant prosecuting war crimes. Some of the most notorious Nazis were either in custody or being hunted down, and throughout Europe stories were told of atrocities and inhuman treatment. There was no shortage of cases to investigate when the U.S. Army War Crimes Branch assigned Army major Luke P. Rogers as a war crimes investigator in Wiesbaden, Germany. Hundreds of incidents were reported in the file known as the Army Group records, but one caught Rogers's eye. It wasn't one of the better-documented cases, consisting only of the brief report from a Third Army officer in March and a short newspaper clipping from the *London Daily Express,* but the Rüsselsheim report intrigued Rogers. The principal function of the War Crimes Branch was to investigate crimes against prisoners of war, and this tale of a Canadian bomber crew being marched through Rüsselsheim and then beaten to death by civilians struck a chord with Rogers. He decided to flag the Rüsselsheim file for early attention, making it a contender to pursue as one of the Army's first war crimes investigations.

The task would not be easy, as the meager file contained no names or other details. Early in June 1945, Rogers set out to visit Rüsselsheim, accompanied by Lieutenant Ephraim London and his interpreter, U.S. Army Corporal Sigi Strauss. Once they reached Rüsselsheim—still in shambles from the bombing—their first stop was the local police station. The police chief, Philipp Wagner, explained that he had been appointed by the American military government after the occupation of Rüsselsheim and that he had not been living in the city when the fliers were murdered. But he had heard about the case and had already prepared a list of suspects from the town gossip, knowing that sooner or later an American investigator would come along and ask for information.

Wagner handed Rogers a list of twenty-one names and Rogers looked it over. He noticed that seven had the word "fort" in parentheses, and the interpreter explained that it meant "fled."

"So where are the others, the ones that you didn't mark as having fled?" Rogers asked through his interpreter.

"Hier. Sie sind immer noch in Rüsselsheim." Here. They are still in Rüsselsheim.

Rogers was stunned by the answer. It was almost too good to be true. Rogers had been sure that he would come to the city and find that any suspects, even if they could be identified, would have fled long ago. If some were still here and people were still talking about the murders, this case might be viable after all.

The police chief stated that the bürgermeister—the mayor—knew much more about the case than he did because he had been living in the city at the time of the killings. As Rogers and his two assistants traveled by Jeep to the bürgermeister's office, they discussed how the police chief had been surprisingly cooperative. Either he really wanted to see the murderers punished or he was just trying to ingratiate himself with the victorious Americans, they decided. When they got to the bürgermeister's office, they found he was not nearly so helpful. Ludwig Dorfler gruffly informed Rogers that he had already given the information about the murders to two other Army officers and he didn't have any time to talk anyway. He was due at a bürgermeister's meeting in another town, so he pointed the Americans toward the door.

Rogers let the mayor know that he would miss his meeting.

"You're not going anywhere," Rogers said to the German, calm and cool but with a look in his eye that said he didn't appreciate being brushed off. "It's going to be like this. We're going to take several hours of your time, and I don't give a damn how many people you've given the information to. You're going to give it to me, and you're going to give it to me right now."

With that, the bürgermeister submitted and sat down. Rogers began questioning him, with London taking notes and Strauss translating as necessary. After a few minutes, the story began to unfold in a shocking narrative. Dorfler told the story as if he had seen it all himself, but he stressed that he had not been there and was only relating what he had heard from others on the day it happened.

Probably just trying to save his own butt by saying he wasn't there, Rogers thought. *Well, whatever gets the story out of him.*

The story was a terrible one for the Americans to hear: the Canadian bomber crew marched through the city; the people in an uncontrollable rage at seeing these men on their streets so soon after bombing them; the debris thrown; the men beaten with boards, shovels, brooms, kicked and punched; and finally their bodies loaded in a wagon and sent to the cemetery.

As Dorfler told the story, Rogers used the list from the police chief to ask what each person had done in the attack. The list jogged the bürgermeister's memory, and he was able to give details about which suspects were most directly involved, which ones would be the most deserving of prosecution.

After several hours of questioning, Rogers was satisfied with the information he had gotten from Dorfler. It was too late in the day to start finding the suspects, so Rogers made it clear to the bürgermeister that he was to keep quiet about this visit.

"Do not tell anyone why we were here or what we were talking about," Rogers told him. "If you do anything to warn these people or inform them that we are investigating, you will be prosecuted. Do you understand?"

Dorfler acknowledged the warning, and Rogers felt that he had put the fear of the War Crimes Branch in him. Rogers and his men traveled back to Weisbaden, pleased that they had been so successful in what they expected to be just a preliminary fishing expedition. They were coming away with a list of prime suspects and a narrative about the murders that would form the basis of a criminal prosecution. The information from the police chief and the bürgermeister would not be admissible in court because neither was an eyewitness—although Rogers still wondered if Dorfler was lying about not being present during the attack—but nevertheless it was invaluable as a springboard for the investigation.

After the visit to Rüsselsheim, Rogers was certain that this case was worthy of prosecution. Not only was the crime heinous and a violation of every legal and moral code regarding the treatment of prisoners of war, but there was enough evidence actually to prove what had happened, and the suspects—he was still amazed by this—were still around. The next morning, Rogers made arrangements with the military government at Gross Gerau to have the suspects arrested. The Army wasted no time. Within 24 hours, fourteen suspects were taken into custody and placed in the jail at Darmstadt, a larger city a few miles south of Rüsselsheim, creating a sensation. After the fourteen were arrested, citizens informed the Army officers in town that there was another man who had attacked the fliers but who wasn't on their list. Heinrich Barthel had been seen striking the men with a club, they told the officers. He was soon found and arrested, bringing the total number of suspects to fifteen.

Rogers was not entirely satisfied, however. The two leading suspects, based on the account from Dorfler, were Josef Hartgen, the air raid warden and party official who encountered the fliers first and ended up shooting several of them in the head, and Friederich Wüst, who had been seen striking Austin in the head with a hammer. They were two of the men who had been marked as *fort* by the police chief. They had fled the city, probably realizing that the Allies eventually would come calling. Stolz, the leading SA figure in Rüsselsheim who had beaten the men with a two-by-four at the cemetery, also had fled the day before American troops arrived, but at this point Rogers did not know he was a key figure in the killings.

The next step for Rogers was to begin gathering the evidence of how the Canadian bomber crew had been killed and by whom. Rogers and London went looking for witnesses, starting with a list of names obtained from the police chief and the bürgermeister—people who had been present at the murders but not necessarily involved. Once they found some of the witnesses, those people led the Americans to others who had witnessed the attacks. Some were willing to talk, and some were not. When witnesses hesitated, Rogers explained to them firmly that they should have no fear of telling the truth but they would suffer if they lied or withheld information. All of the witnesses were interviewed, and Rogers took written statements in German.

Rogers and London were heartbroken by some of the details coming from the witnesses. When one told of how one of the fliers pleaded with the mob, screaming that they hadn't bombed Rüsselsheim, finally crying out "Don't kill me! I have a wife and two children!" Rogers and London both realized they were serving a just cause with this prosecution.

As the witness statements accumulated, it became clear to Rogers that two sisters, Kathe Reinhardt and Margarete Witzler, had been the ones to incite the crowd to violence by shouting and throwing the first objects at the prisoners. One witness told them that the sisters had been proud of their actions that day, boasting that if not for the them, the terror fliers would have proceeded through Rüsselsheim unharmed.

It also became clear to Rogers that Hartgen had taken command after he came on the scene. This was important because Hartgen, as an air raid warden and party leader, and being armed, had the capacity to drive the incident in one direction or another. Rather than calming the situation and protecting the POWs, Hartgen had inflamed the crowd and effectively became the mob leader, Rogers concluded. He was particularly disturbed by the account of one witness who described Hartgen going down the row of airmen lined up at the railroad wall and saying, "Beat this one. He's still alive."

Rogers asked every witness about the whereabouts of Hartgen and Wüst and the two Luftwaffe guards who had escorted the fliers. No one seemed to know where Hartgen and Wüst had gone, and no one even knew the names of the guards. Then Rogers checked the list of arrests made by the Army at the War Crimes headquarters and found that the Counter-Intelligence Corps had arrested Hartgen in May at Memmingen because of his position in the Nazi Party. That was good news, but Rogers still didn't know exactly where Hartgen was being held. The Counter-Intelligence Corps had arrested thousands of Nazis, and the records didn't indicate which of the retention camps they were held in. Finding one low-ranking Nazi among the thousands in custody would not be easy, but Rogers placed a special request with the Seventh Army Headquarters to locate this key suspect in the Rüsselsheim murders.

After taking statements from the witnesses, Rogers began interrogating the suspects in the Darmstadt jail. Rogers was not impressed by the men and women he faced.

What a poor collection, he thought. *All typical small-town louts.*

A few admitted playing some small role in the killings, but most claimed they hadn't done anything, although they volunteered that they saw someone else do something. They all seemed eager to implicate someone else, as if that would curry favor with the investigators and take attention away from them. After two weeks, Rogers had statements from all fifteen prisoners.

The next job was the most unpleasant for Rogers: The bodies had to be disinterred. They were evidence in the prosecution, and a forensic examination would support the allegations against the suspects. And, of course, Rogers wanted to find out the identity of the fliers and give some families peace of mind about the fate of their loved ones. Rogers made arrangements with the Army's Graves Registration Group to disinter the bodies from the cemetery where the witnesses said they were buried, but he didn't want American soldiers digging them up. He called London into his office and gave him an order.

"Go to the police chief. Have him round up six of the leading Nazis in town and bring them to the cemetery," Rogers said. "They're going to do the digging."

The Germans dug at the cemetery in the unmarked spot where the Canadians had been buried, under the supervision of Rogers and other Army officers. They found six bodies piled together, roughly thrown into a hole and covered with dirt. The Nazis kept digging, expanding from the original grave site in search of the other two bodies, but they could find no more. Rogers was not satisfied. All the witnesses had spoken of eight airmen being killed, eight airmen buried in the cemetery. Where were the other two?

"What did you do with them?" Rogers asked the Nazis as they leaned on the handles of their shovels, resting. "You take them somewhere else?"

"Nein. Hier. Wir brachten sie hier," one man replied. No. Here. We brought them here.

"Well, if you brought them here, where are they?" Rogers asked again. "I can keep you digging all day, if that's what you want."

And he did keep them digging for hours before he finally let the Germans stop. As they dug, Rogers and his men began a cursory examination of the corpses, hoping to find identifying information on each one. As they looked for the first and most obvious signs of identification, the dog tags, they were stunned by what they found. These men were not Canadian; they were American.

Four of the six bodies had dog tags on them. Rogers recorded the names and serial numbers as evidence for the trial and also to obtain additional information about the crew from Air Force headquarters.

Rogers had brought along a pathologist, Captain Max Berg, to examine the bodies as soon as they were unearthed. The bodies laid out in a row were badly decomposed, but Rogers could see that some still wore the flight overalls of a bomber crew. And one more thing was obvious, even to those untrained in forensics. Through the dirt and the decay, Rogers could see that these men had been beaten severely. Some of their skulls showed obvious fractures, and one man's skull had been broken open completely. Most of the men had been shot in the head, the bullet holes obvious in the bone. The evidence matched the stories that Rogers had been told by those he had interviewed already.

Rogers ordered the bodies transported to Bensheim, Germany, by a Graves Registration team, the unit tasked with claiming the bodies of American soldiers and identifying them. At Bensheim, which held the headquarters for Graves Registration and also an American cemetery, Berg could perform a complete forensic examination and provide Rogers with a detailed report.

The autopsy report, completed on July 9, 1945, was a treasure trove of evidence for Rogers but chilling in its flat description of the bodies and how they were found. The report identifies the bodies as Sekul, Dumont, Williams, Austin, and one tentatively identified as Rogers. He had no dog tags, but the name N. J. Rogers was imprinted over the left pocket of his flight suit. Tufenkjian's body, one of the most battered, was not identified immediately because he was not a regular crewmember with the other men and did not have his dog tags.

Berg described in his report how the bodies were unearthed in the Rüsselsheim cemetery, found about four feet down. The team found two medium pairs of sheepskin-lined boots and one extra-large pair. The bodies were clothed and there were no caskets, blankets, shrouds, or other coverings. The first body uncovered was that of Sekul, who was lying on his back with his head pointed to the west. He was identified with certainty by his dog tags, a handkerchief in his left leg pocket with his name on it, and the name and serial number printed on his Air Force–issued underwear. Berg described the body as that of a large white man, five feet ten inches tall. "In the left side of the skull was a large compound depressed fracture with irregular, jagged margins. The depressed area measured 8 by 5 centimeters. This fracture was located in the left parietal region," he wrote. Three bullet holes were seen, in the lower portion of the right parietal bone just above the junction of the suture of the temporal bone, another in almost the same spot on the left side, and a larger hole near the base of the head in the back. In addition, there was a large caved-in portion of his skull near the hairline over his left eye—almost certainly the killing blow from the man who beat the fliers in the cemetery.

Berg listed the cause of death as "(1) Compound depressed skull fracture in the left parietal region. (2) Bullet wounds in the skull." He also wrote a note explaining, "It is believed that the large depressed skull fracture in which a large section measuring 8 by 5 centimeters was depressed was probably caused by a blunt object striking with great force and probably caused the individual's death." As for the three bullet holes, Berg surmised that the larger hole in the back of the head was an exit wound for the shot to the left temple, and the shot to the right temple exited through the area that was crushed in by the blunt object. "The bullet wounds may have occurred either anti-mortem or post-mortem, from the evidence at hand this would be difficult to delineate clearly," Berg wrote. Rogers was intrigued by the evidence of two gunshots to Sekul's head, as he knew of only one from Hartgen as the men lay dying on the street. Did Hartgen shoot him twice, or did someone go to the cemetery later and make sure he was dead?

The autopsies of the other men followed in a similar fashion, with Berg documenting only the most severe injuries and those most likely to have caused death. Many injuries from the beatings would be obvious on the decayed bodies. The second body was that of Dumont, who was lying next to Sekul and slightly below on his right side, with his head toward the west. The body was clothed in an electrically heated flying jacket, with some tobacco in the left pocket. There were no boots. Berg noted a large triangular depressed fracture measuring 4 by 7.5 centimeters on the back of the head on the left side. There also was an entrance wound for a bullet at the base of the head.

The unidentified body, Tufenkjian's, was lying below Dumont. Tufenkjian's autopsy report stood out from the others because the head wounds were far more extreme, the skull broken open on the right side all the way from the top of the head through the right eye socket and even farther in the back, to the base of the head. Although the wounds to all of the men were severe, the extreme nature of Tufenkjian's head injury suggested that the crowd had targeted him.

Williams was underneath and to the side of Tufenkjian, wearing only green fatigue trousers with no shirt or undershirt. He had a handkerchief in his left pocket and carried a cotton T-shirt in the right pocket. He also had in his pocket a small piece of cloth with the number 187 on it. In the back right pocket was a comb. The only obvious sign of injury to Williams was a bullet hole in the lower portion of the back of the head and an exit wound through the nose.

Austin was lying to the side of Tufenkjian, on his right side and facing Tufenkjian. He wore the electrically heated flight jacket over a cotton shirt, undershirt, and fatigue pants. In his right back pocket he carried a handkerchief with the letter E on it. Berg described a large depressed fracture covering the area over the right eye, back to the ear, and up past the hairline, connected to a fracture that ran over the top of the head and almost down to the neckline. There also was a bullet wound entrance on the right side of the lower back of the head, with the bullet exiting through the fracture in the back of the head. The pathologist concluded that the cause of death was "a crushing injury over the right side of the skull and forehead, delivered with considerable force by a dull instrument."

The body tentatively identified as Rogers's was lying on his back below Austin. The skull had a large star-shaped depressed fracture over the left ear. There was no bullet wound.

Once Berg completed his examination of the bodies, they were interred at the temporary American cemetery in Bensheim.

ALLIED LEADERS MET IN Potsdam, Germany, on July 11, 1945, to confirm their earlier agreements about Germany and to restate their demands for the unconditional surrender of all Japanese forces. The Allies warned that "the alternative for Japan is prompt and utter destruction."

The end of the war was nearing, and when it arrived, families across America would breathe a sigh of relief as they knew their boys would be coming home. Meanwhile, families of the *Wham! Bam!* crew still waited, still hopeful.

CHAPTER 10

"I WILL REVEAL NOTHING"

THE AUTOPSY REPORTS MESHED WELL with the interviews Rogers had conducted, and he was growing more confident that justice could be done by bringing the citizens most culpable to trial. Rogers urged Lieutenant Colonel Leon Jaworski to consider prosecution. Later to become famous as the special prosecutor in the Watergate scandal, he was now becoming involved in what would become a series of high-profile prosecutions of Nazi war crimes, including those related to the Dachau concentration camp. Jaworski had strong ties to Germany because his father, a Presbyterian minister, had met his mother there after emigrating from Poland, and the couple then moved to a German community in Waco, Texas. Jaworski grew up speaking German fluently. In 1925 he became the youngest person ever admitted to the Texas bar, directing his attention first to defending bootleggers during Prohibition and then becoming known as a brash young lawyer who perhaps had more integrity than he knew what to do with. He fought hard to defend a black client accused of murdering a white couple in 1929, not a popular move with some Texans, and although he lost the case, Jaworski gained statewide fame as a lawyer willing to stand up for what was right despite risk to his career or even to his life.

Jaworski had arrived in Germany in January 1945 and realized that he was stepping into a delicate situation. With the war in its final stages and plans being made for restoring order in Europe, the judge advocate general in Washington had sent him to take charge of the prosecution of war crimes trials in the American zone, even though General Edward C. Betts, the Judge Advocate in the European Theater under President Eisenhower, didn't want him there. Betts was a West Point graduate and wanted a fellow West Pointer to prosecute the war trials.

Nevertheless, Jaworski showed up with all 132 pounds of the Pentagon's top-secret war crimes records. When he reported to Betts, he did not receive a warm welcome. Instead, the general ranted about how improper it was for Washington to put Jaworski in the prosecutor's position over his objections. Jaworski let the general rave on for a while and, doing his best not to be offended, calmly asked for any assignment, no matter how menial. Betts took him up on the offer, assigning Jaworski to an office in Paris where he would be outranked by four full colonels and where he would be serving in a lesser capacity than the prosecutor position Washington had assigned. Betts was effectively trying to put Jaworski in a corner out of the way.

Jaworski played along for a while but was quickly placed in charge of the division responsible for examining the evidence of war crimes, then a few weeks later was given charge of the division investigating the cases. Three of the other colonels moved on to other positions, and Jaworski finally found himself in the job Washington had intended from the start.

As chief of the Examination Division of the War Crimes Branch and of the Investigation Division, Jaworski became familiar with all of the investigations of alleged violations. Jaworski was made aware of the file on Rüsselsheim soon after arriving in Germany and had been following Rogers's investigation. The most frequent offense, he knew, was the mistreatment of aircrews that were taken prisoner after landing in or bailing out over Germany. The investigations had proven that, as bombing campaigns became more intense and more successful toward the latter part of the war, the mistreatment became more intense and brutal. Hitler's propaganda chief, Joseph Goebbels, had encouraged threats of violence against the airmen as a means of intimidation, and

Jaworski discovered that German police had been instructed not to interfere with civilians who attacked Allied airmen. The Rüsselsheim case, therefore, was not unique, but as Jaworski looked over the evidence, he realized this case was among the most brutal incidents of aircrew abuse he had seen.

Jaworski's review of the case files from all over Germany convinced him that the Nazis had openly violated long-recognized rules of land warfare, as agreed to by the United States and Germany in the Hague Convention of 1907 as well as in the Geneva Conventions of 1929. A true legal scholar and a man of deep faith and moral certitude, Jaworski knew that war alone was no excuse for some of the worst behavior man can exhibit. As bestial as war is, Jaworski knew, it is nonetheless governed by written and unwritten laws meant to avoid unnecessary hardships on both combatants and civilians. Special rules are intended to protect the fundamental human rights of prisoners taken by both sides. Civilized societies have long supported such laws and have prosecuted their violation, including trials held by the new American government after the Revolutionary War.

Jaworski wrote later:

> If violators went unpunished, such treaties would become meaningless. War, evil as it is, would sink to even deeper depths with no quarter given, and women and children would be slaughtered ruthlessly.
> It was evident that Nazi Germany had already reached this depth. Though German soldiers and sailors committed relatively few war crimes, many of the Nazi hierarchy and party members were responsible for some of the most shocking evils in the history of man.

But Jaworski also knew that prosecuting war crimes was no easy task, and if it was to be done at all, it must be pursued with the utmost vigor. He would not be party to a repeat of the feeble attempt to prosecute war crimes after World War I, when only twelve defendants were prosecuted out of the many thousand accused, and only nine of those even bothered to show up for court. Among those nine, charges were dismissed against three, and the remaining six received light sentences. Jaworski knew that the world would be watching the first war crimes trial pursued after the end of hostilities in Europe—with the victors trying the vanquished—watching to see how America restored justice. This first trial, whichever case Jawarski decided to pursue, would be the first conducted in the American zone of occupation, under the agreements reached by the Allies in London and Moscow, and it would be conducted under the rules of a U.S. military court martial. In contrast, the Nuremberg trials of top Nazi leaders later in 1945 would be conducted jointly by the United States, Great Britain, France, and the Soviet Union, using a combination of their legal systems.

Jaworski was deeply troubled by many of the case files he studied, unable to shake the images painted by the statements of those who had witnessed good men dying young—air crews assaulted, POWs abused, Allied sympathizers tortured and killed. His mind was still running through the many war crimes cases accumulating in his office as he and several servicemen left headquarters just before dawn on Easter Sunday and drove through the quiet streets of Paris toward the Eiffel Tower for a sunrise service organized for the troops. Parking their Jeep nearby, Jaworski and his colleagues walked through the chilly, crisp air, the morning quiet except for the sound of thousands of Army-issued boots hitting the streets. Jaworski couldn't help but contrast the sound of these boots, worn by Christian soldiers who rose early to worship their savior, with the sounds that Parisians must have heard as thousands of German troops marched into their city years earlier. On this morning, the Allied servicemen walked quietly, deep in their own thoughts, each dealing with his own troubles and his own faith in God.

Jaworski made his way up a side street and then stepped onto the esplanade around the Eiffel Tower, standing tall against a sky with just a hint of early-morning sun coming over the horizon. Coming upon the crowd of servicemen, Jaworski was amazed. He felt his heart lifting. As far as he could see in every direction, Allied servicemen and women, most of them American, stood waiting for the Easter sunrise service to begin. One of Jaworski's colleagues whispered, "We understand there are over ten thousand of us here. They came from all around Paris to be here."

Jaworski would write later:

Satisfied that the sum of the evidence was incontrovertible, Jaworski filed papers in July charging eleven German civilians, including two women, with the murder of six American airmen held as prisoners of war. Jaworski also indicated that he would seek the death penalty for all of the defendants.

Ten of the defendants were in custody—Wüst had been found as Rogers continued his investigation. Hartgen, however, was still missing. Jaworski considered him the prime defendant and did not want to go forward with the trial until he was found. Rogers still had not heard anything from Seventh Army Headquarters about Hartgen's whereabouts. He and Jaworski were frustrated knowing that their big target was in American custody somewhere and yet they could not get their hands on him. Jaworski understood that there was a tremendous amount of confusion in the arrest records of Nazi criminals, due in part to the sudden collapse of the German army, inadequate Allied resources for managing all the German prisoners, and deliberate misdirection by Germans whose true identities were not recorded. But he had to have Hartgen, so Jaworski sent a request for an immediate search of all records that included the man's name, knowing all the while that the chances of finding him soon were slim.

In only about a week, Jaworski got lucky. He received a call from the Seventh Army indicating that they had a man in custody in Bamberg by the name of Hartgen. Jaworski asked for a physical description and, once he got it, was convinced they had the right man. He ordered Hartgen put on the first available plane to Wiesbaden.

Hartgen soon arrived and was placed in the local jail, after a thorough search ordered by Jaworski. He wanted Hartgen stripped of anything that could be used to commit suicide—belts, shoelaces, anything sharp, medications. Hitler and Heinrich Himmler already had committed suicide, and he knew that a lot of dedicated Nazis were eager to imitate their heroes.

Jaworski immediately went to the jail and had Hartgen taken to an interrogation room on the first floor. He brought along an interpreter to observe the interrogation, but he intended to question Hartgen in German because he thought that would be more effective. Jaworski walked into the room before noon and sized up his foe. Sitting before Jaworski was a forty-one-year-old man of small stature, with a solid build, blond hair, and a strong jawline. He had sharp, steel-blue eyes and a face that Jaworski thought was lined with hatred and animosity. Hartgen had been a devout Nazi Party member for thirteen years, and Jaworski sensed right away that this was a hard-bitten Nazi, not just a German swept up in the events of the past years.

This is a man who abominates his fellow man, Jaworski thought, as he looked at Hartgen sitting there in front of him, his arms crossed tightly across his chest, those blue eyes staring him down. *This is a man who thrives on the hurt and oppression he can impose on others. Those eyes reflect a cruel heat, a capacity for brutality. Was he always this way? If not, what caused him to become more beast than man?*

The prosecutor would discover later that Hartgen's hard demeanor was a dramatic change from his youth, when the earnest young man, raised in a Christian home, had worshipped regularly at church. He was good to his parents and excelled in his schoolwork, coming home every afternoon to study. "He was exposed to the infectious disease of Nazism with all of its hatreds and prejudices, and from a fine and honorable young man he was transformed into a vicious beast," Jaworski would write later.

As they began to speak, Hartgen was surly and antagonistic. "How dare you bring me to Wiesbaden for this!" he screamed at Jaworski. "I have done nothing for which I should be tried! I will apologize for nothing! I deserve better treatment than to be brought here and placed in jail!"

Jaworski would not be intimidated by the Nazi's outbursts. He proceeded to ask if Hartgen knew why he had been brought to Wiesbaden, and Hartgen said yes. But Hartgen said it was pointless because there was no evidence against him.

Jaworski reached into his files and pulled out a statement written in the hand of a German witness, describing how he had seen Hartgen participate in the beatings and then shoot the airmen in the head. He silently pushed it across the table to Hartgen and let him read it.

"This is nonsense. This is just the work of political enemy," Hartgen said, chuckling with derision. "You are stupid to rely on such garbage as proof."

Without comment, Jaworski reached into his files and pulled out a second witness statement, sliding it to Hartgen. The German read the document, then scoffed and dismissed it just as he had the first.

Then Jaworski pulled out another witness statement. Hartgen scoffed again, but less this time. He still insisted the statements were not enough evidence.

So Jaworski pulled out a fourth statement. Then a fifth. And a sixth, seventh, and eighth. With each witness statement, Hartgen grew less cocksure, less belligerent, more reflective.

Hartgen's bravado disappeared as he realized how many of his fellow Rüsselsheim residents had given him up. Jaworski knew this was the time to move. He gave Hartgen several sheets of paper and a dull, stubby pencil.

"Write your version of what happened," he told Hartgen. "Just tell us your side of what happened that day and it may help you."

Jaworski had found that allowing Germans to write their own accounts yielded far more information than even a brutal interrogation, so he was hopeful that Hartgen would admit his involvement, even though he probably would try to justify the attacks.

"I'll be back at three o'clock," Jaworski told him, giving him about three hours. "I truly hope that by then you will have made a complete confession of your knowledge of this affair."

Jaworski got up and a guard let him out of the interrogation room. The normally mouthy German said nothing as he left. Jaworski instructed the guard to allow Hartgen to take the paper and pencil back to his cell but to search the room again for any items he could use to hurt himself.

The prosecutor went back to his office and began a round of conferences on other cases, but he found himself distracted. He kept thinking about Hartgen and feeling that he should go check on him. Jaworski tried to continue with his work, but by 2 P.M. he couldn't stand it any longer and left a meeting early, calling his driver and his interpreter.

They rushed back to the jail, where Jaworski instructed the interpreter to go to Hartgen's cell and bring him back to the interrogation room. Within seconds, Jaworski heard the interpreter screaming from the second floor that he needed help.

"I found him in a pool of blood!"

Jaworski and the driver raced upstairs, Jaworski trying to figure out how Hartgen could have gotten anything to cut himself with. He found Hartgen semiconscious, his wrists more torn open than cut, blood all over the floor.

The driver called for help, and soon Hartgen was carried downstairs to a Jeep and rushed to the local hospital. Jaworski stayed behind in the cell, trying to figure out what the Nazi had used to attempt suicide. Everything in the room had been removed except a bed, table, and chair. He kept looking and saw that there were blood splatters underneath the bed. Kneeling down and feeling around, Jaworski realized that Hartgen had put his arms underneath the bed and jammed the flesh of his wrists up onto the sharp ends of the bedsprings. *He must have had to do that over and over again, jerking his arms back and forth to rip the flesh,* Jaworski thought. *It must have been agonizing.*

Getting up from the bed, Jaworski saw the paper he had given Hartgen laying on the table. Smeared with blood, it said: "Heil Deutschland! Ich werde zeigen nichts."

Heil Germany! I will reveal nothing.

CHAPTER 11

THE TRIAL

July 18, 1945

AFTER A WEEK IN THE HOSPITAL, Hartgen was well enough to be released. On July 18, 1945, eleven defendants—nine men and two women, the sisters Witzler and Reinhardt—were charged with the murders of the six *Wham! Bam!* crewmembers found in the cemetery. No one had been able to locate the bodies of Adams and Brown. Jaworski assumed they had been buried elsewhere for some reason, and if they could be found, charges might be brought against the same defendants for their deaths.

As the trial date neared, local radio and newspapers picked up the story and gave it wide play. German citizens were being put on trial for killing American servicemen during war, and already Jaworski was seeing a sampling of the arguments that would come up during the trial. Was there really enough evidence to prove what any individual did? Were the witnesses lying, possibly exacting vengeance or carrying grudges against the defendants? How terrible was it, really, for beleaguered citizens to react with anger when an enemy bomber crew marched through their freshly bombed town?

A few days before the trial was set to start, American officials received reports that some people were planning to disrupt the trial with violence. The Americans knew that some diehard Nazis still had hand grenades and other explosives, not to mention the small arms that the Allies could not round up. The threat of violence was very real, and the

War Crimes Branch briefly considered delaying the trial. But Jaworski insisted that it go on as planned, because delaying it would not eliminate the threats and because it was vital to show the German people that the Allies valued justice and were determined to make the murderers pay for their crimes. Holding the trial without allowing the public to attend was completely unacceptable to Jaworski and his superiors. Instead, they would post heavily armed guards in and around the courtroom, and they required that all bags be examined before they could be brought into the courtroom.

The trial was moved to Darmstadt, because the Rüsselsheim jail and courthouse had been severely damaged in the bombing. Darmstadt also had been hit hard and was largely abandoned by its residents, but the four-story courthouse building was mostly intact. The courtroom was relatively large, and Jaworski wanted to hold the trial in a space that would allow as many Germans to witness the proceedings as possible, so that they could see its fairness for themselves. A six-member military commission—one brigadier general, one general, three colonels, and one lieutenant colonel—would serve as the jury. The judge was Brigadier General Garrison H. Davidson, a handsome, leading-man type with a head of thick, almost white hair. Davidson had been the West Point football coach from 1932 to 1938 and now served as chief of engineering in the Seventh Army. The Germans were represented not only by American officers equal in rank to their prosecutors but by German defense attorneys of their choosing. Several outstanding members of the German bar, including Heinrich von Betrano, who would later become foreign minister for West Germany, participated.

The American defense counsel was Lieutenant Colonel Roger E. Titus, who had graduated with Jaworski from the Army's Judge Advocate training program. Titus had seen combat with the 103rd Infantry, but Jaworski had not been in combat. During his time with the infantry, Titus participated in liberating several concentration camps, which caused him to detest Germans and what they had done to Europe. He was not happy about being assigned to the defense of eleven Germans accused of murdering American fliers. Titus was determined, nonetheless, to provide the best defense he could. He expressed his concerns to his wife in a letter dated July 20, 1945:

> *It is most discouraging to be counsel for eleven people who will probably be hung. Even though they are Germans, you get to know them personally in talking to them, preparing their defense. As well as all their families who weep all over you.*
>
> *As I said before, two of the defendants are women. All have families. Two with as many as four children. An eye for an eye and a tooth for a tooth is hard to take when you are on my end of the case. It doesn't help any, either, when everyone in the Army that you talk to wants to know why you are spending any time worrying about a bunch of damn Germans, who most likely are guilty and should be hung anyway.*

Titus went on to tell his wife that, although he knew some or even most of the defendants were guilty, he was worried that a few might be innocent. Witnesses' memories were imperfect, he said, and some anti-Nazis might be taking revenge on their pro-Nazi neighbors.

THREE INTERPRETERS—two serving the court and one specifically for the defense—were present at all times during the trial to interpret the English and German spoken by the participants and to check each other's translations. The interpreters were instructed to speak up if they thought one of their colleagues had mistranslated a word or phrase, and they were ordered to provide only verbatim translations of what was said, not their interpretations of it. The translators had to resolve any disagreements before the commission would accept the translation. Several of the German defense attorneys spoke English, and one brought along his daughter to help translate.

Case number 12–1497, *United States v. Josef Hartgen,* et al., opened at 9:35 A.M. on July 25, 1945. On that day, and on every following day of the trial, the court was packed to capacity with German citizens who wanted to see how the victorious Americans would deal with Germans accused of war crimes. Jaworski knew that this was a history-making trial, and he prayed for guidance every morning and evening, asking God to help him carry out justice.

After Davidson called the court to order, Jaworski read the specification and charge.

> Charge: Violation of the laws of war. Specification: In that Josef Hartgen, Friedrich Wüst, Margarete Witzler, Kathe Reinhardt, August Wolf, Johannes Seipel, Heinrich Barthel, Georg Daum, Johann Opper, Karl Fugmann and Phillip Gütlich, German civilians, acting jointly, did, together with other persons whose names are unknown, at Rüsselsheim, Germany, on or about 26 August 1944 willfully, deliberately and wrongfully encourage, aid, abet and participate in the killing of John N. Sekul, William A. Dumont, Thomas D. Williams, and Elmore L. Austin, members of the United States Army, and two other members of the United States Army whose names are unknown, each of whom was then unarmed and a prisoner of war in the custody of the then German Reich. Signed by Luke P. Rogers, Captain, CMP.

Jaworski then turned to the defendants, who were sitting on two benches on the right side of the courtroom, behind their defense attorneys. They were a pitiful-looking group, not at all resembling the violent mob that the crew of the *Wham! Bam!* faced on the streets of Rüsselsheim. Accused of murder were two women, seven men who looked more grandfatherly and frail than vicious, and two men in their forties. They were, in fact, a perfect snapshot of the civilian home front in Germany in the late stages of the war. Only women and old men were left at home, along with a relatively young party member here and there to enforce Nazi doctrine, while nearly all men below retirement age and even barely teenage boys were sent to fight. Reinhardt's husband, Witzler's brother-in-law, was fighting on the Russian front, and the family had not heard from him in a long time.

Jaworski asked each of the accused how they pled to the charges. He started with Hartgen, sitting in the front row on the far right, his arms folded and a defiant look on his face. Jaworski stated Hartgen's name and asked, "How do you plead to the specification of the charge?" The defense prosecutor translated and then the Nazi nearly shouted "Nicht schuldig!"—"Not guilty." Jaworski then asked, "How do you plead to the charge?" Again Hartgen answered with a sharp "Nicht schuldig!" Jaworski continued in the same manner with all eleven defendants, getting the same answer from each one. The only real difference came from the two sisters, who spoke softly through muffled sobs. The sisters were close to one another, spending their daily lives together and helping each other cope without the men of the family. The slim Reinhardt was dressed in an attractive patterned dress with a dark sweater and white heels, her brown hair pulled back. Her older sister, Witzler, sat next to her in the front row, dressed in the manner of a much older woman: a long, dark, simple dress that buttoned up the front, with a light jacket over it, and black low-heeled shoes. Her gray hair was pulled back in a bun, and her face was one of complete despair. Reinhardt cried more than her older sister, who seemed almost resigned to her fate, as did many of the men.

It was then time for Jaworski to present his opening statement to the court. He faced the commission, six Army officers sitting at a long desk on a dais perpendicular to where the defendants sat. A large American flag hung behind them. They listened as Jaworski began his historic prosecution.

On the morning of August 26, 1944, six, perhaps more, although this prosecution is based only on the death of six, American airmen who previously had been shot down and had been taken prisoners of war some two days prior to August 26, 1944, were in the process of being transferred to a place of detention. They were unarmed, were prisoners of war in every sense of the word. They were then in the custody of soldiers, guards, of the then German Reich. While en route to their place of detention they were taken through the city of Rüsselsheim. The prosecution expects to prove that as these fliers, under guard, these prisoners of war, came to a place within the vicinity of the Parc Hotel on Frankfurterstrasse in the city of Rüsselsheim on the morning of August 26, 1944, there were two women, who are the women accused in this case, who came running out from their places of abode, and in loud shouts implored others who were on the street to set upon the fliers and to beat them and to kill them; that through their cries and shouts, joined in by others, they soon gathered a group who began to beat and molest and mistreat these airmen; that the two women accused also joined in this beating; that rocks and missiles of various types and kinds were employed for the purpose of beating the fliers and were also thrown at them; that others of the accused joined in this mob action as the fliers proceeded along Frankfurterstrasse.

As they came to the intersection of Frankfurterstrasse and Wilhelminstrasse they turned south on Taunusstrasse where others of the accused also joined in death; that clubs and cudgels of various kinds were used; that one of the accused would use one type of club, another ac-cused, another type of club; some the handles of shovels, some broom-sticks, whatever happened to be available to them, for the beating of these victims.

As they proceeded along Taunusstrasse, most of the victims were al-ready badly hurt; they were bleeding. One was being carried on the back of his comrade; that they or some of them would fall to the ground to be lifted up by their comrades as they proceeded on their march along Taunusstrasse; that one of them, who fell by the wayside, was kicked by one of the accused in the head.

As they came to the corner of Grabenstrasse and Taunusstrasse they were each badly wounded and crippled. As they turned the corner of Grabenstrasse to proceed west along a wall adjoining a railroad track, still others joined in the beating, among them being some of the accused; that three of the accused came over the wall that adjoins Grabenstrasse; that from damage done by the previous air raid there were boulders, large rocks, there were beams, large pieces of wood, along this wall. Some of these were picked up by some of the accused and tossed at the victims; that after additional severe beatings and poundings received by these vic-tims on Grabenstrasse, they fell prostrate to the ground, whereupon, as they lay on the ground, some of the accused proceeded with clubs to beat them on the head; that after they appeared, to all intents and purposes, to be in a state of unconsciousness or perhaps dead, there was rolled up a cart and these bodies of the victims were thrown on to these carts or placed in this cart. Some of the bodies lifeless, others still having a spark of life, piled one on top of the other, they were rolled, pushed to the ceme-tery where they were left on this cart for the remainder of the day. Finally the cart, with the bodies, was pushed around to the rear of the cemetery where they remained until the following morning, at which time they were all placed in a common grave. That, in substance, is the case the prosecu-tion expects to present to the commission.

Jaworski would call the prosecution witnesses first. His goal was to establish that the defendants were seen abusing the airmen and/or urg-ing others to abuse them. He began by calling Margarete Zogner, a housewife with five children—including one who was sixteen days old on the day in question—who lived on Frankfurterstrasse at the time of the assault. Jaworski asked what first indicated to her that something was happening on the street that day: "Suddenly someone cried out, and I went outside in front of the door, and we thought they were peo-ple who were looting, and they came up to our house and then I saw that they were soldiers."

Jaworski asked what she heard the people shouting.

"I saw that they were hollering, 'Beat them to death, beat them into pieces.'"

"Did you notice anyone in particular calling out, 'Beat them to death, beat them to pieces'?" Jaworski asked.

"Mrs. Witzler and Mrs. Reinhardt."

He then had the witness point out the two sisters sitting with the defendants and confirm that they were who she saw shouting that day. Jaworski then asked about attacks on the soldiers.

"Did you or did you not see anything thrown at the American soldiers on the occasion in question?"

"Yes, Mrs. Reinhardt threw something," Zogner replied.

"Did you see whether or not the stone struck any of the soldiers?"

"Yes, it hit him over there on the head. He was bleeding."

"Can you give me some idea as to the size of that stone?"

"It was a stone which is used for building houses."

"Will you indicate its size?"

"Just like these stones are [indicating]. It was a brick."

Jaworski went on to ask Zogner about Hartgen, and she said she had seen him pull his pistol and fire but that she didn't know if the bullet had struck anyone. Zogner told the court that several of the soldiers were bleeding and one was being carried on another's back.

"Did you hear any of the American soldiers make any statement or any outcry to the group?" Jaworski asked.

"One of them told one woman to help him. Someone called he was a Jew and he called back, no, he wasn't a Jew, he was a German."

Jaworksi ended his direct examination by asking Zogner to confirm that the American soldiers were under guard by two German soldiers. (The defendants had been informed that the servicemen were American, not Canadians, as most had thought at the time.) She called them corporals and said they had yellow shields or badges. It was critical to establish that the men were prisoners of war at the time of their murders.

It was then time for the defense to cross-examine Zogner. Otto Albrecht Sturmfels, the German attorney representing Witzler and Reinhardt, took the lead. He tried a few questions to shake Zogner's conviction that it was the two sisters who were inciting the crowd, suggesting that it could have been some other women.

"I only saw these ones because they were the only women who were participating," Zogner said.

"You state that otherwise there were no women present?"

"There were other women present but they were the only ones who were yelling."

"The rest of the crowd of the men, they were quiet?" Sturmfels asked.

"It is possible that somebody else was yelling, but I didn't pay too much attention to it because I was just concentrating on the soldiers. I was concentrating on the soldiers because we couldn't help them."

When asked whether she saw Reinhardt with a brick in her hand, Zogner said she didn't know. But she did remember that Reinhardt never dropped the loaf of bread she was carrying.

Sturmfels went on to suggest that Zogner was exacting revenge on Reinhardt over a slight involving ration cards. He alleged that Zogner was angry because she had sent one of her boys to Reinhardt and Witzler's shop with a ration card to buy tobacco, but he was told there was nothing to smoke and sold a half pound of butter instead. He then traded the butter for a cigarette from Reinhardt. Zogner confirmed that she thought the transaction was shady but said she had no grudge against the sisters.

The defense attorney moved on to recounting the extensive damage in the city and the long air raid of the night before, to establish that the residents of Rüsselsheim were on edge that day. Then he went back to asking Zogner about what she saw of the Americans, trying to get an estimate of the crowd size.

"Would you say there were a hundred?"

"I don't know. We were crying, all of us who were standing there. I can't say accurately any more."

"Were you crying hard?"

"Yes."

"Because you were so upset and nervous?"

Zogner did not answer and the attorney asked the question again.

"No. No, we were very excited and we were crying because we had pity on the soldiers and because I have soldiers out in the field myself."

After a few moments, the president of the commission—Davidson, acting as judge—interrupted and asked Sturmfels what point he was trying to make.

"Right now, sir, I am just laying a little background to show hysteria, mob hysteria, the result of the night before," the defense attorney explained. "People up all night fighting fires. I don't like to bring it out at this time, but it is part of the picture, if these accused or any of them are found guilty, which might be considered by the court in mitigation—the state of mind of these people."

Davidson allowed him to proceed but Sturmfels was soon finished with Zogner. Jaworski called his next witness, Hanna Schur, a wife with no children. Schur testified that she was walking west along the wall adjoining Frankfurterstrasse when she saw a crowd of about twenty people walking in the middle of the street. She said she soon realized they were following a group of foreign soldiers and she heard people shouting, "These are the terrorizers of the night! Kill the dogs! We cannot have any pity on them!"

When Jaworski asked her to relate what she saw Reinhardt and Witzler do, Schur replied that they were "needling these other people to participate and then started attacking the Canadians" (still referring to the airmen by the nationality the crowd assumed at the time). The defense objected to the word "needling," so the court had her go into more detail. This would be a mistake for the defense. Jaworski asked her what shouts she heard.

"'These are the terrorizers of last night! Knock them down!' And they repeated these cries, these cryouts, all the time as long as I could watch them."

"Aside from these cryouts, did you see these two women or either of them do anything?"

"Yes."

"Tell the commission what it was."

"They attacked the soldiers and first went over them with their fists, first from the front, and then from the side, and also from the rear."

Jaworski elicited more detail and then asked Schur if anyone in the crowd had tried to discourage the attack on the airmen, to which she replied, "Yes, many." The prosecutor asked if any of the airmen had their boots taken off, and Schur explained that there were three "Canadians" in the first row and one of them had his boots torn off. They were left in the road, she said, and "that Canadian went limping along in socks." Jaworski asked who removed the man's boots, and she said, "One of these two women."

On cross-examination, the defense questioned how it was possible for a woman to remove the boots of a marching soldier.

Schur explained, "The soldiers were so badly maltreated already that they were just dragging along, and in the first row, two comrades were carrying one whose legs were wounded. And this one whose legs were injured was bleeding out of his mouth and nose when I saw him already. Because of that, I walked up to him, because he was bleeding. That soldier told me, 'I am not a Jew as they say. I am a German.'"

Sturmfels complained that her response didn't answer his question about how a woman could take the boots off a grown man as he marched along.

Schur put it plainly. "The Canadians moved very slowly because until then they were beaten very much. It is possible that she just had to bend down and the boot had a zipper, but I can't put an oath to that. It was a flying boot. It was fur-lined."

On redirect, Jaworski had Schur confirm that the men were being guarded by German soldiers. She said they were, that she had even talked to one guard and asked why he was permitting the assault. Jaworski did not ask her what he said in reply.

The next witness was Karolina Jung, a married mother of three who lived on Frankfurterstrasse. She also pointed out Reinhardt and Witzler as inciting the crowd, remembering that they yelled, "They are the ones who destroyed all our things last night!" She added that Gütlich was doing the same thing and also was carrying a stick. She noted that she recognized him because he owned a restaurant in Rüsselsheim. She said she saw Gütlich beat the fliers with the stick.

Neither the prosecution nor the defense extracted much more from her, and Jaworski moved on to Lorenz Wendel, a carriage maker from Weilbach, who told of how he and his nephew had arrived in Rüsselsheim about 9 A.M. on his bicycle to visit a relative. They were just crossing in front of the Peter's Eck Inn when the nephew said, "Look, Uncle, they are bringing Canadians past us, prisoners." As the mob approached, Wendel saw two women he took to be mother and daughter shouting "These are the gangsters! These are the criminals! These are the ones who killed our husbands and these are the ones who destroyed our houses!" And then, he said, the women "picked up stones and threw them dead." Jaworski and Sturmfels haggled with the witness over the exact location where Reinhardt and Witzler were seen shouting and throwing stones, the defense seizing on any inconsistency between the witnesses to cast doubt on their veracity, but to no avail. The witnesses were establishing quite clearly and consistently that the two sisters were there, that they incited the crowd, and that they actively participated in the beating.

Before being dismissed, Wendel told how he had tried to stop the mob from beating the airmen. "I said, 'You don't do that. You do not kill the prisoner by throwing things at him,'" he recalled. "After I said that the crowd started threatening me and then I just disappeared."

DURING A RECESS in the first day of the trial, there was a commotion at one of the side doors to the courtroom. Jaworski called for the sergeant of the guard, who reported that Herr Witzler, husband of the older sister on trial, was trying to get in. He was carrying a battered black briefcase and insisted on bringing it into the courtroom with him, even after the guard at the door ordered him to leave it outside. The guard, exercising caution because of the threats against the trial, suspected that the briefcase might contain a bomb or weapons and refused to let Witzler in. Jaworski wanted Witzler's husband in the courtroom if possible, because he felt strongly that the German people, and particularly the relatives of the defendants, should see that the United States carries out justice in a fair and orderly manner. So Jaworski had a guard bring Witzler to him.

Witzler was a large, bull-necked man with very short hair, a large head, a heavy jaw, and piercing black eyes. He reminded Jaworski of a professional wrestler. The prosecutor offered the man a seat in the courtroom if he would leave the briefcase outside. Witzler begrudgingly complied after Jaworski promised that it would be returned to him at the end of the day. No one with the court ever found out what was in the briefcase.

When the trial resumed, Elizabeth Schadel, a married mother of five, told the court of seeing Gütlich beating the prisoners and calling for others to beat them too. Katharina Diehl, a married mother of one, described the same scene with Gütlich, adding that she thought the stick was the type one used to herd cattle, about three feet long and two inches in diameter. Jaworski asked whether she had seen Gütlich beating Dumont as he was being carried. No, she said. "He jumped from his back and then the other one got it, the one who was carrying him."

"Got what?" Jaworski asked.

"The beating."

Soon after Ria Bastian, who worked in the butcher shop on Taunusstrasse at the time of the assault, told how defendant George Daum had been shoveling away ruins in the back of the shop. "Then he went outside and he was beating them" with the shovel he still carried, she said. She also told of seeing defendant Johannes Seipel on his way back from the assault, and how he told her of kicking one of the soldiers. Jaworski asked her how he had relayed this information.

"He was glad," she replied.

Two more witnesses testified that they saw Johann Opper strike an airman with a broom so hard that the bristles on the end went flying off, and Wilhelmina Biendl recalled how Gütlich stopped by her window afterward and said, "My hands hurt so from the beating." Anna Breideband, a mother of six, told the court of seeing Opper beat the fliers with a stick, and she said the airmen "were bleeding pretty strongly." She also saw Hartgen beating the Americans with what looked like the handle of a pitchfork.

"Just describe to the commission how he went about beating with this instrument."

"He was pretty wild," Breideband said.

"Did you notice whether he struck more than one or only one?"

"He beat several, not only one."

"Did you hear anyone or see anyone attempt to intercede on behalf of the fliers?"

"Yes."

"Did you hear whether or not the accused Hartgen said anything to that person?"

"Yes, he told them to keep quiet or to keep his mouth shut up, something like that, otherwise the same thing would happen to him."

"Did you hear any of the fliers say anything?"

"Yes."

"What was it?"

"He said, 'Don't kill me. I have a wife and two children.'"

THE NEXT WITNESS for the prosecution was Anne Willnow, who lived on Taunusstrasse and spoke English. She recalled seeing the fliers as they made their way up the street, looking like they were trying to go toward Grabenstrasse.

"I was unloading debris and when I heard, 'Let him come up and I am going to beat him to pieces.' I put down my pail," she said. "I walked up three houses and I stood like this [gesturing] and said 'Don't go up there. They will beat you to pieces.'"

She saw one airman who was bleeding badly, one shoulder and his chest badly injured, and with a piece of brick sticking out of his head. "I wanted to help him." She made eye contact with the airman and he lifted his arms up in the air, a look of desperation in his eyes, and said, "We did not bomb Rüsselsheim. We bombed Osnabrück."

The airman fell to the ground, and before Breideband could help him, Seipel came up and kicked him hard in the throat and chin, she testified. Jaworski asked how many times Seipel kicked.

"Twice, and then I felt faint and I went home."

Ludwig Willnow, a mechanic, testified next, telling the court that he lived on Taunusstrasse and was at home when heard women's voices calling, "There are fliers coming! Let's beat them to death!" He identified Witzler as one of the women shouting but did not recognize

Reinhardt. Willnow did not join the crowd, but he ran into defendant Opper later in the day and Opper told him, "We busted in their brains."

Willnow's testimony ended the first day of the trial, and Jaworski was quite satisfied with the day's proceedings. The German witnesses were establishing with certainty that the defendants had committed war crimes against American airmen. He was confident that as the trial progressed, the barbarity of the crimes against the *Wham! Bam!* crew would be pieced together with unmistakable clarity.

CHAPTER 12

A SLIP BY THE CENSOR

THE FIRST DAY OF THE TRIAL brought media attention back in the
United States. On July 26, 1945, the *New York Times* ran a front-page article headlined "11 Germans Tried for Killing Fliers." The article described how "in the biggest war crime proceeding held so far in the
American zone, two German women and nine men, including a former
resident of Yorkville, in New York, went on trial for their lives in the
bombed court house of bomb-wrecked Darmstadt."

The article went on to say that the Germans were accused of "the
brutal death march-lynching of six American fliers in the streets of nearby Rüsselsheim a year ago."

A couple of paragraphs later, the article said that only four of the
bodies had been identified. "The bodies were in a mass grave found in
the Rüsselsheim cemetery. They were named in the trial simply as John
N. Sekul, William A. Dumont, Thomas Williams and Elmore Austin." It
also described the defendants as "an inferior-looking group of middle-
aged and elderly persons." The *Times* article was picked up by the Associated Press and carried in hometown newspapers across the country.
It described how the fliers were beaten to death by enraged citizens as
they were marched through Rüsselsheim, relating much of the more

sensational testimony from the first day of the trial, including accounts of a flier with a piece of slate sticking out of his head being chased by an angry mob and one flier carrying an injured comrade on his back as they ran for their lives. It was a graphic, disturbing account of the deaths of young American servicemen.

And this article was how the family members of the *Wham! Bam!* crew found out that their loved ones were dead.

The military still had not officially notified any of the families, so they all had held out hope that the men might be found. That outcome looked less and less likely as time wore on, but the dreaded telegram with the secretary of war's sincere regret had not come yet. And then family members picked up their newspapers and saw the names in black and white.

For the families of Sekul, Dumont, Williams, and Austin, the news was both devastating and, in a way, a relief. Their sons were dead, as they had long feared, but at least now they knew. For the families of the rest of the crew, there would still be endless wondering, waiting for the story to end but fearing it would not be the conclusion for which they prayed so fervently. The families of the men not named in the article realized that this was the crew headed by Rogers. Helen Rogers almost had to assume that one of the unidentified bodies was that of her husband, but there could be no end to the wondering until the military made it official.

Many family members were shocked and disheartened to find out about the deaths through a newspaper article, especially since the circumstances of the airmen's deaths were so gruesome and sad. The families learned that their boys were gone and that they had died in terror, in pain, afraid, and with no one to comfort them in their last moments. The Williams family wrote to the Army to complain about the newspaper's publishing the names before they were notified that their Tom had died, and the Army replied with an apology. It wasn't supposed to happen, they were told. The Army said it was a mistake, a slip by the censor in France, which oversaw correspondence from Germany as well. There was no explanation for why the Army still had not officially notified the families.

The article also shocked Brown and Adams. They had no idea that the War Crimes Group was investigating the events in Rüsselsheim or that a trial was under way until they saw the *Times* report. They realized that their vow of silence was moot, that the crimes in Rüsselsheim would not be forgotten.

ON THE DAY THE families of the crew were learning of the horrors of Rüsselsheim, court reconvened at 9:30 A.M. and Jaworski continued calling his twenty-eight witnesses for the prosecution. As on the first day, the statements of the witnesses were devastating in their description of the brutality. Jaworski was steadily building a case against each defendant, establishing through eyewitness testimony that each had participated in the beatings and that several had been instrumental in inciting the crowd to further violence. Much of Jaworski's questioning was aimed at establishing certain important details, such as how Daum was seen beating the airmen with a shovel. Many of the witnesses testified against lifelong friends or acquaintances, such as when sixty-seven-year-old Gerog Burck told the court that he had known Johannes Seipel since they were small boys. Burck testified that he saw Seipel coming down Taunusstrasse and stopped to talk with him. "Well, what have you done?" Burck asked. "I also beat at them," Seipel replied.

Gottlieb Wolf, a forty-five-year-old saddler from Rüsselsheim, told the court of watching the scene from an upper floor of his home on Steinstrasse and seeing Friedrich Wüst with a hammer, or its handle.

"He was supporting himself on the wall and made a try as if he was going to beat someone, but he didn't hit anyone."

"Who was he trying to hit with that something that looked like the handle of a hammer?" Jaworski asked.

"The fliers were standing there."

Jaworski went on, "Did Wüst strike one or more than one time?"

"Struck several times."

"Did he strike lightly or with force?"

"He struck with force."

The defense tried to get Wolf to say that he was uncertain about what he had seen or that his memory must be faulty after a year, but the witness stuck to his story. Barthel's defense attorney got Wolf to concede that the flier hit on the rear end continued walking after the blow. "It had no significance at all?" the defense asked. "This wasn't the worst one," Wolf said. "From this they were not killed."

Much of Jaworski's effort was directed at showing that Hartgen was more than just another enraged citizen that day. It was important for the prosecution to show that Hartgen was in a position of authority and that he took direct action to incite the crowd and to assault the fliers himself. One of Jaworski's most convincing witnesses was a seventeen-year-old boy, Franz Rinkes, a member of the Hitler Youth, whom investigators had found only the day before. Visiting the scene of the crime, the investigators encountered Rinkes digging potatoes nearby and struck up a conversation. As they talked, the investigators realized that the boy had crucial information about the murders. The next day Rinkes appeared as a surprise witness for the prosecution.

According to his testimony, Rinkes did not see the early part of the attack but had a clear recollection of the ending. He told the court that he was at home when he heard yelling down the street and went to investigate. He arrived at the scene in time to see the airmen in their last moments on their feet. Rinkes identified Hartgen in the courtroom, sitting with his arms folded across his chest, his legs crossed, and an angry stare; then Jaworski asked what Hartgen was doing when the boy arrived.

"He asked all the people to beat and in the end when almost everyone was on the ground, he shot."

Staring directly at Hartgen as he spoke, Rinkes described how there were eight Americans, two on the ground and six standing "huddled together, protecting one another and bleeding hard. They began to sink under the many blows from sticks." Rinkes said he heard three or four shots, telling the court that Hartgen "took the pistol out of his pocket and he shot here in his head [indicating] so that black blood just came out."

After the shooting, Rinkes said, Hartgen encouraged the crowd to continue beating the airmen, at one point yelling "Give him a hit yet! He is still alive!"

Rinkes also established that Johann Opper incited the crowd, saying he "needled and encouraged them." That prompted another objection from the defense about the use of the word "needled," and the two sides debated the translation for several minutes, eventually accepting the translators' decision that it was the proper word, rather than "inciting."

Rinkes also testified that he had seen Barthel, whom he recognized because he had taken tools to the man's machine shop for grinding, and that "he talked to the people very excited" while pointing at the Americans. Jaworski asked if he were yelling at the crowd like Opper.

"Well, he did not. He was not the one who yelled so very loud. And he did not take part in the contest of who yells the loudest."

On cross-examination, the Hitler Youth also told of seeing Hartgen and another man load the fliers on a cart for the cemetery, saying, "When they were put on the cart I was right next to the cart." The defense tried futilely to establish that Hartgen had tried to disperse the crowd, at one point telling all the women and children to go away, but Rinkes said no, that did not happen. An elderly man tried to stop the mob.

"Well, the elderly man who had warned Hartgen to stop it, he said it wouldn't be right, and then Hartgen said, 'You bum,' or something, 'if you don't stop talking, you get it, too.'"

Rinkes testified that he knew Hartgen well from their association with the Nazi Party, having met him in 1939 when Rinkes was only eleven. He described Hartgen as a "big man in the party" and that he had the uniform insignia signifying his status, "a red colored patch and golden stars and a gold corner on his cap."

"Was he a higher leader?" Jaworski asked.

"Yes."

"Was he known as a higher leader in Rüsselsheim?"

"Yes."

Other witnesses would establish that Hartgen was, in fact, the propaganda chief for the Nazi Party in Rüsselsheim. After the attorneys finished, the president of the commission had a few question for Rinkes also. He asked if the fliers were still walking when Rinkes first saw them.

"No, some of them were already on the ground, and two just dragged along."

"You testified before that they were piled on top of each other. Did they fall that way or did somebody make them—place them that way?"

"They tried to protect each other, and almost crept together."

"During the time they were doing this were they being continually beaten?"

"Yes."

"Did the guards make any move, any effort to prevent the beating?"

"I heard when somebody said to the guard whether he couldn't do anything about it, but the answer was that he couldn't do anything, otherwise he would get it."

"Did you see any women beating the fliers?"

"No."

"Are you certain that there were eight fliers?"

"Yes. Six were together and two were beside them. Those two, they lived longer than the others and they were still alive when put on that cart. When they were put on the cart, the one still raised himself. He shook his head."

That meant that Rinkes was the boy Sekul looked up at, shaking his head no, as the fliers were about to be taken away. Most likely Rinkes was the last person on earth who looked Sekul in the eye.

Jaworski moved on to other witnesses, including Karl Barth, who told the court that Opper did not beat the airmen much. "He participated very little. He just had a little stick and beat only several times." Hartgen, however, was using a piece of wood to beat the fliers with "a lot of force" and using both hands. On cross-examination, the defense brought out the fact that Wolf, the hammer-wielding defendant, had lived in America for some time, enjoying a good life, and Barth said, "As far as I know, he is not an enemy of America. He might have been a friend."

However, nearly every attempt by the defense to undercut the testimony about Hartgen's ruthlessness either fell flat or backfired.

HAVING DRAWN A CONVINCING picture for the commission from eyewitness statements, Jaworski then moved to let the defendants' own words show their guilt. He offered into evidence four affidavits: the original German statements of Wüst and Wolf from their interrogations, along with English translations of each. As he offered the documents, Titus, the American lieutenant colonel leading the defense, objected and argued that the statements were inadmissible because the defendants had not been warned of their right against self-incrimination. "Now, it is against our principles of law to force an accused to make a statement against himself, and I object to the admission of these statements on that ground."

Davidson, the president of the commission, suggested that the members retire to another room and vote on the admissibility of the statements. But before they did so, Jaworski asked if he could speak on the issue. Davidson allowed it, and Jaworksi began an extemporaneous argument that can be applied to the current debate over trying international terrorists in civilian courts or in military commissions such as the one trying the Rüsselsheim defendants.

Jaworski argued:

> If the commission pleases, the objections that counsel has raised have absolutely no place in a proceeding that is before a military commission. The trial of these accused is under the laws of war; it is not under the Constitution of the United States of America. The matters that counsel refers to are rights that are accorded the American soldier in court-martial proceedings, and to a certain extent, the citizen in civil proceedings because they are expressly written into our Constitution, a constitution which has absolutely no reference or relevancy to this particular proceeding.
>
> The laws of war govern this matter, and the procedure normally followed by military commissions is here employed. This commission has the authority to call every single one of these accused to the witness stand, if it chooses to do so. Self-incrimination need not be recognized as an objection in trials held by military commissions.

Jaworski went on to point out that even under German law, the defendants would not have any protection against self-incrimination. Davidson acknowledged Jaworski's argument but said he still wanted to take a recess to discuss the issue with the commission. Before the court recessed, Titus brought up his second objection to the affidavits, arguing that the commission was supposed to use the court-martial manual as a guide, and the manual clearly stated that affidavits not made at the scene of the crime cannot be used against another joint conspirator or person being tried with the accused.

Jaworski disagreed. "Now the guide, the only guide, as to evidence that is laid before this Commission in the order appointing this court is precisely the same one that is set out in every order appointing a military commission. It was the same one that was set out by the President of the United States at the time that the military commission was appointed that tried the eight saboteurs," he said, referring to the 1942 military trial of eight Germans who came ashore in Amagansett, Long Island, and Jacksonville, Florida. "And it reads as follows: 'Such evidence shall be admitted as has, in the opinion of the president of the commission, probative value to a reasonable man.'"

The commission took a recess to consider the arguments and soon returned. The affidavits were accepted into evidence, and a court clerk read Wüst's statement to those gathered in the courtroom. It was brief, but it provided Jaworski with the evidence he needed in the defendant's own words.

> In the moment which the yelling and shouting started I was in my apartment repairing the air raid damage of the previous night. I looked out of the window and saw a police man and three guards, Hartgen, Rommich, in the street at the place where there was a turmoil. Wolf and Fugmann already had jumped on the railroad right of way and were running across. I was still behind the window when I saw Wolf and Fugmann holding rocks in their hands and throwing them into the heap. I followed them, running along the wall, where the crowd moved to the left. I still had my little hammer in the trouser pocket and hit across the wall, upon the second beat others joined and took the hammer away from me in order to hit hard, but the hammer flew away into the street. In that moment the crowd was on the ground. I cannot give the names of the people. We walked toward the crowd over the wall and it may be that I there delivered another stroke. When I had regained my hammer we returned to our apartment. Signed Frederic Wüst.

The court then heard Wolf's statement, which followed in a similar vein, acknowledging that he was there but minimizing his role in the beatings. However, his sworn statement described Wüst's involvement in a much different light than Wüst's statement had.

> My attention was attracted by a crowd consisting of about one hundred people, a part of whom shouted, "Beat them to death, beat them to pieces," when I just managed to see a few aviators dressed in a brown combination outfit, running in the direction toward the Geierssuhlstrasse.

I run in the direction toward the aviators together with the crowd. Here, I saw from a distance of twenty meters an altercation between Mr. Hartgen and teacher [Cristopple] Keil. Thereafter Mr. Fugmann and teacher Keil left the street in the opposite direction. An anti-aircraft soldier, unknown to me, beat the aviators, some of whom were already lying on the ground, with a club. At the same time I noticed that Friederich Wüst on his knees was crushing one of the aviator's heads with a hammer. In view of the brutality and cruelty toward the aviators I immediately returned to my home, to be sure, over the wall and across the railroad tracks.

This tone was to be echoed in many of the defendant's statements. They admitted their presence at the scene and perhaps some minimal involvement in the beatings but denied all of the most heinous accusations. By providing the statements to the commission, Jaworski showed how the truth could be woven together from the observations of those in the crowd who implicated each other even as they were trying to deny their own culpability. Wüst may have wanted the commission to think he struck only a few feeble and ineffective blows with his "little hammer," but Wolf's statement, which minimized his own guilt, noted that he saw Wüst "crushing one of the aviator's heads with a hammer." And so the pattern continued as Jaworski entered the other defendants' statements, all written in German in their own handwriting, into the record.

Witzler's affidavit was brief, explaining that she was standing on the street when she heard people shouting about aviators. "I wanted to see aviators for once because I had not seen any yet and I joined the crowd," she wrote. "There were many people around, but I did not observe who was present. Because the aviators walked so fast I went home via Taunusstrasse Waldstrasse." In the margin, she added, "I also saw Hartgen."

Witzler's sister, Reinhardt, tried to make her participation seem incidental to the violence. After seeing a commotion and hearing that aviators were on the street, "I followed fast for I, too, wanted to see the people. There was such confusion and shouting that it was impossible to pay attention to any individual person. I, too, shouted twice, 'Beat them.'" Reinhardt went on to mention that she saw Hartgen running past her at one point and she saw an anti-aircraft soldier beating the men. "When we left all the aviators were still alive and were running through the Taunusstrasse. The next day I heard that the people were dead."

In his handwritten statement, Fugmann denied any involvement whatsoever, stating that he had seen the mob but avoided it and went home. He denied throwing a stone or shouting anything. He did see Hartgen shouting at the seventy-six-year-old retired teacher, Cristopple Keil, and he saw Wüst returning with a hammer. After he returned home, he encountered a soldier who was very excited and told him, "I finished them off." When Fugmann asked why, the soldier replied, "I have lost my family and all my earthly possessions, and I now have avenged myself."

There was no statement from Hartgen, because his only contribution had been to scrawl "Heil Deutschland! I will reveal nothing," on a piece of paper as he tried to kill himself. There also was no deposition from him, as he had steadfastly refused to cooperate with the authorities. True to his word, Hartgen was revealing nothing.

But it didn't matter. Others were revealing plenty about Hartgen in their testimony. The picture emerged of a prominent local Nazi who was feared by the people of Rüsselsheim. The depositions—transcripts of statements provided by the defendants as they were being interviewed by the prosecution—were longer and more detailed than their handwritten statements, but they followed the same pattern of minimizing their own participation in the violence while implicating each other. Wolf, for instance, noted that he saw Hartgen threaten the teacher, Keil, for saying that the assault was wrong and Hartgen should stop it. Wolf also volunteered that Wüst was "a good Nazi." Wüst, in fact, had been a member of the SA since 1932.

Wüst did himself no good with his deposition. After repeating his story about how he "hit one of the fliers one or two cracks with the hammer," Wüst went on to say that the head flew off the hammer and he was left holding only the handle. "At this time all the fliers were already unconscious on the ground. It is possible that then I struck one of the fliers a couple of blows with the hammer's handle." Wüst also recounted how he had turned to Wolf at one point during the assault and said, "It serves the fliers right because they bombed a city so that women and children have to go away," and "I can understand why they bombed the Opel works but I cannot understand why they bombed a city where the farmers live."

In her deposition, Reinhardt tried to claim that she merely came upon the mob as it was already attacking the fliers, countering the notion that she was the one who had whipped the crowd into a frenzy. She said that she and her sister joined the crowd and moved along the streets with them but that she did nothing more than to twice shout "Beat them!"

That was not the conclusion others were coming to about Kathe Reinhardt. Depositions from witnesses also shed light on events of the day. Ludwig Willnow, the mechanic who testified on the first day of the trial, gave a deposition in which he recounted hearing the sisters call for the crowd to beat the fliers. "These women continued to yell and incited the crowd. These two women were the older Witzler, who has the tobacco store on the Frankfurterstrasse, and her sister Frau Reinhardt. These two women were definitely the leaders of the crowd and if it would not have been for these two, nobody would have done anything."

Jaworski's next witness was Raab, the cemetery caretaker, who testified that Stolz, the SA man who had brought the cart, beat the men after they reached the cemetery. He also said Hartgen had come to the cemetery late in the evening. Jaworski tried to determine if Hartgen had shot the men again that evening. There had been reports to investigators that Hartgen had gone to the cemetery that night and shot some of the men to make sure they were dead, but Raab could only say that, that evening, he saw Hartgen go to the area where the cart had been left and that he had a pistol in a holster. He also explained that the next day, he had ordered Russian POWs to bury the airmen in one mass grave in a corner of the cemetery. Rüsselsheim residents were being interred at the same time, he said, but in individual graves.

The cemetery was always busy, he said, because every bombing raid was followed by people bringing carts of the dead to be buried.

CHAPTER 13

"IT WAS NOT MY TASK"

FOLLOWING TESTIMONY BY CAPTAIN MAX BERG about his autopsies of the bodies, Jaworski rested his case on the third day of the trial. It was time for the defense to bring its witnesses in hopes of disproving or mitigating the mountain of evidence that Jaworski had brought forth. The defense began by calling Cristopple Keil, the retired schoolteacher, to testify about his encounter with defendants Fugmann and Opper. He said he ran into Fugmann, who told him, "You are not one of the people who lets a thing like this happen." But Keil added that "this was not in a serious tone."

The defense attorney asked if Keil understood the comment to mean that Fugmann also did not agree with the assault. Keil stated:

> The excitement was so big that you couldn't base any judgment upon things. I went to the scene and I saw a dying person lying there, who was beaten upon, and someone yelled "Scram!" or "Get away!", something like that—I can't remember the actual wording any more—"otherwise similar things will happen to you." Because I am an anti-fascist and known as that in Rüsselsheim and because I had involvements with the police several times and because I took this threat seriously, I left the scene, because I was afraid they would carry out their threat.

The attorney pressed Keil to say that Fugmann's comment could be construed to mean that he did not agree with the action either, but Keil would neither agree nor disagree. He did concede that Opper's yelling for him to get away could have been intended as a friendly warning and not a threat.

The most important witnesses for the defense were the two members of the clergy in Rüsselsheim, Georg Jung, the city's district priest for the past twenty-five years, and Jacob Hoffman, the local evangelical minister for the past sixteen years. The defense intended to ask them about the members of their congregations who were on trial, hoping to elicit kind observations from irrefutable sources about how the defendants were peaceful, loving people. The defense did achieve some of that goal, but the clergy also ended up adding to the unflattering portrait of Rüsselsheim. Defense attorney Heinrich von Brentano tried to establish that Fugmann was a man of good Christian spirit who provided religious instruction to his children even though doing so put him in danger with party officials, who discouraged it. "He was known as a peace-loving person," Jung said. Jung explained that he did not hear of the attack immediately and was never notified that the bodies were at the cemetery. No one prevented him from performing last rites there, he said, but he did not know the men were there until it was too late. He recalled having a conversation with someone on the evening of the attack, before he knew what had happened, and the priest made the comment, "It looks very sad in Rüsselsheim," referring to the bombing. The other person replied, "You do not know the worst yet."

The other clergyman, Hoffman, then took the stand and testified to the good character of Wolf, who he said was "not a person who likes to fight." He also spoke in support of Reinhardt, saying he knew nothing unfavorable about her. Otto Kattler, the German attorney for Opper and Gütlich, then asked Hoffman, "Is it true, Father, that you once said Gütlich entered into the whole action only because of his stupidity?" Jaworksi objected to the question as irrelevant, and the minister was not allowed to answer. Regarding Opper, the minister said, "I don't know that in any way he is a fighting person." Hoffman had little more to offer the defense, being unfamiliar with some of the defendants, so Jaworski then began his cross-examination. If the defense was going to paint the defendants as harmless and peace loving, Jaworski would have to put the minister on the spot.

"Reverend Hoffman, would you call persons who were shouting to arouse a mob to beat to death unarmed prisoners of war peaceful and law-abiding citizens?" he asked.

"No."

"Would you call people who threw rocks at unarmed prisoners of war who were being led through a town peaceable and law-abiding citizens?"

"No."

Jaworski then established that Hoffman was at home during the assault, still putting out fires from the previous night's bombing. The parsonage was near the Parc Hotel and the church, so Jaworski—a devout Christian whose faith guided every facet of his life—pointed out that the airmen and the mob had passed right by. The reverend admitted that he knew an assault was occurring just outside his home.

"Did you, as a minister of the Gospel, go out and make any attempt to stop the murder of these men?"

"I couldn't do that."

"Did you make any *attempt* to do it?

"No."

Jaworski was finished showing that the reverend himself exemplified the callousness to be found in Rüsselsheim, but the commission questioned the witness further, asking why he did not attempt to stop the attack. Hoffman's response was not a credit to himself or his position as a spiritual leader.

"It was not my task," he said. "It was the task of the persons who were leading these prisoners of war to step in for the safety of these prisoners of war. It was the task of the local police to look out for the order in the town. It was not my task."

A member of the commission then asked Hoffman exactly where he was when the assault took place in front of his church and home. He replied that he was in his study. He was then asked how he learned of the assault, and he replied that parishioners had come inside to tell him what was going on. Still he did nothing.

Then there was this telling question for the man of the cloth: "Did anybody prevent you from giving any assistance or rites to the people that had been killed?"

"No."

Yet he did not. Even as the violence ended, the reverend did not step outside to say a word of prayer over the dead and dying young men. After the clergy, Kattler called to the witness stand Dr. Frederich Spuck, assistant chief of the public health office at Darmstadt and also the prison doctor, and began questioning him about his interaction with the sixty-six-year-old defendant Seipel. When the court got impatient, Titus, the lead American defense attorney, explained, "I believe this doctor will indicate that in his opinion this accused is very senile and has reached a state of decay, whether he may or may not be responsible for his acts." The questioning continued, and Spuck testified, "I have an impression that this is a very senile person." He added, "I am of the impression that he is not fully responsible but only partly responsible for his actions."

Jaworski would not stand for such a dismissal of responsibility. He asked the doctor how many times he had examined Seipel. Twice, he replied. And for how long? About half an hour the first time, no more than fifteen minutes the second time.

"And on the basis of that you are giving your opinion to the commission of his mentality?"

"Yes."

"You don't mean to say that Johannes Seipel does not have the mental capacity to distinguish right from wrong, do you?"

"No."

"And you don't mean to say that he does not have the ability to adhere to the right and depart from the wrong, do you?"

"I am of the opinion that he can differentiate between right and wrong."

Daum's wife, forty-year-old Lonie Daum, a nurse in the German Red Cross, then testified that her husband, like many residents that morning, was trying to extinguish stubborn fires from the bombing the night before. As the air attack ended, she came to help, and the effort continued long into the morning, she said. She related how she had been near the front gate of their house when the airmen and the mob passed, but in what would become an important point later, she said that her husband was working in the back of the house, in the barn, trying to keep the stored hay from burning.

Lonie Daum also said she was wearing her uniform dress when the airmen came by and that one approached her at the gate seeking help. "One of the fliers was hurt in the head and had on a very thin bandage, and the blood came through it much and therefore I gave him another two packages of first aid bandages," she claimed. No one else reported seeing an airman receive a bandage prior to encountering Lonie Daum, and no one spoke of seeing her commit such an act of kindness. She emphasized in her testimony that she was the only one at the front gate when the airmen passed by and that her husband was in the rear of the house. She did not call him until the mob had already gone by, she said, and then they merely stood at the gate together while the crowd continued down the street.

Jaworski knew she was lying.

"Are you positive that your husband was working in the barn toward the rear of the house?" Jaworksi asked her.

"Yes, otherwise there was a danger that all the straw we had in the barn would burn down because the barn was full of straw."

"Are you *positive* that he was not working in the front of the house at that time?"

"Yes."

"If your husband in a sworn statement says that he was working in the front of the house, then your husband is mistaken?"

"Yes. I called him."

Jaworski then had George Daum's own statement read into evidence. In it, Daum stated: "On the day when the fliers in Rüsselsheim were murdered, I was working in the front of my house on the damage which had been done by the attack during the night." He then claimed that he watched the crowd go by, making no mention of his wife even being there with him.

On the third day of the trial, the commission members were able to hear the testimony they had really been waiting for. The defendants had been given the choice of testifying to the commission in either a sworn or unsworn statement. The commission would give more weight to sworn testimony, and the defendants could be questioned by the prosecution, the commission, and the defense. The defendants could not opt out of testifying; if they did not volunteer to speak, the commission would require them to take the stand, and a refusal to speak would weigh heavily against them.

Daum was the first to speak on his own behalf, choosing to be sworn, and he began by telling how he had left his cellar shelter to fight the fires at his house, and when the crowd came by he was standing at the front gate with his wife and only watched the people go by. He did absolutely nothing to participate, he said.

Daum also expressed concern for his wife.

"My wife was standing next to me," he said. "I am very sorry now that I had to call her here in front of the court, and that I had to call her because she is suffering from a heart disease since a longer period of time, and since she had fainting spells very often. I always have to think of my three children; the youngest one is going to be five years old, and I don't want the children shall lose their mother through this case, because we suffered very badly during the last three years. Nothing was saved from us because of strokes of fate."

The defense then recounted how eyewitnesses had testified to seeing Daum beat the men with a shovel.

"No, that is not true," he said, the anger in his voice rising with every word. "I want to say something. At first, I never intended to get a lawyer, Mr. van Basshuysen, as my lawyer. I also did not intend to bring my wife in front of this court. But during these hearings and during the questionings, I found myself forced to use Mr. van Basshuysen because the people in Rüsselsheim are so bad, because they are so brutal. They bring somebody innocent into this, who has nothing to do with it, and they don't know what they are doing by doing so!"

Davidson interrupted to warn Daum not to raise his voice to the court.

"No, I don't want to do it," Daum said, calming himself. "I am far away from that. I see that the commission functions here very orderly and very decently. I have to recognize this fact."

On cross-examination, Jaworski hammered Daum about inconsistencies in his testimony and his earlier statements, showing how Daum sometimes said he was standing at the gate when the fliers came by and sometimes said he was working in the barn behind the house. The man eventually denied having signed the pretrial statement, although he agreed that it was his signature on the document. The longer he talked, the more credibility Daum lost.

One of the members of the commission asked Daum if he knew why any of the four witnesses who testified regarding his participation would have reason to lie.

"It can only be bad feelings," he said. "And if you would put fifty witnesses in front of me, I would testify just like I did."

Barthel was next to give his sworn statement, telling the commission that he had been present at the assault but "saw a horrible thing" as the fliers were beaten while pinned against the brick wall and then left the scene.

"And are you telling the commission you did nothing?" Jaworski asked.

"No, I didn't do anything. I was a soldier myself, and I didn't want to look at this."

"But you did look at it."

"That is why I also left."

The questioning of Barthel continued for some time, addressing both his involvement and his earlier statements that he had seen the defendant Wolf at the scene carrying a stick.

When Barthel's testimony concluded, Davidson announced that the court would go to Rüsselsheim after lunch to see the scene of the crime. Davidson, all of the members of the commission, the attorneys, and a few court personnel drove to the city and walked the route of the death march to see for themselves how the fliers had tried to escape the crowd and the wall they were trapped against near the railway station, where they finally collapsed and where several were shot in the head.

The court reconvened at 3:10 P.M. Gütlich was the next defendant to speak, but he chose to make an unsworn statement. His comments were some of the most surprising and pathetic of the entire trial. After

stating that he had heard the commotion of the mob and went closer because he wanted to see foreign fliers, Gütlich admitted that he had hit
one of them. But he had a reason. "I must make the remark that I was
very excited from the attack from the night before, and there, one of the
fliers made some kind of face to me, and I felt that he tried to make fun
about all the damage which had been done the night before. Then I beat
him once with the hand."

Jaworski was dumbstruck by this claim. When it was his turn to
cross-examine, he asked Gütlich to explain further. "Do you want this
commission to believe that one of those boys walking along there under
guard with a crowd of people surrounding them picked you out to insult you?"

"I do not know whether he wanted to insult me. He looked at me
with a face and laughed."

"Are you sure that the grimace you are talking about wasn't an expression of pain that came from the flier after you struck him with that
club?"

"The face came before I had beaten him with my hand, and all those
who were together, they were not wounded at that time yet."

Gütlich was indignant and defiant throughout his time on the witness stand, adamantly denying that he had had a club or that he had
made any inflammatory statements that day. His story was that he merely
went to see the fliers out of curiosity and slapped one when the flier in-
sulted him. After a bit more questioning from Jaworski, Gütlich revealed
that he also had another reason for following the fliers.

"My entire interest was only that I wanted to find out where those
fliers are being led to, because I did not know that those fliers were supposed to leave Rüsselsheim again. And I believed they came in one of
our prison camps and would be used for work, because I needed one to
drive my car. And at that time I couldn't find one, and therefore, I
thought that if they stayed here I could get one to work for me."

After Jaworski and the commission asked a few more questions,
Gütlich offered more comments in his defense. "As I said before already, I was very much excited from the attack during the night. I had
not slept before, and there was a lot destroyed in my house. I have never

been a soldier, otherwise it might be that I would have known what it means to beat a prisoner. I was never a party member nor took part in any formations, and I never took part in any persecution of the Jews. In other words, I made myself difficulties with the party because I bought from Jewish stores long after it was not allowed any more. That I would like to say."

And one more thing.

"I would like to ask whether you are interested that I was very long in treatment from an American doctor because of a paralysis of the spinal cord, column, sir?"

Opper was next, also choosing to make an unsworn statement. In his version of events, he had put his broom down before encountering the crowd and never beat anyone. He also volunteered that he saw the defendant Wolf there, and he also was not involved in the beating. Opper told the court that he would never do such a thing because he has two sons in the army and he was a member of an antifascist party. The key witness against him, Wilhelmina Biendl, must be mistaken, he said.

"I am a very good friend of Mrs. Biendl's and still am today. I always came up to her. I killed her hares for her, and all of that, and I am very sure that Mrs. Biendl must have made a mistake. During the whole World War I, I was outside. I had twenty-five Belgian workers working for me. When the Taunusstrasse was demolished and the French prisoners were working for the masons, every morning these prisoners not only from me but from the whole population got their coffee and bread."

Johannes Seipel also chose to give an unsworn statement, revealing to the court that he had unexpectedly found himself in the middle of the mob and ended up getting hit in the face with a stone, then hit on the head with a wooden beam. He then left the scene and went home.

Jaworski asked about the eyewitnesses who said that Seipel had walked up to a flier who was sitting or lying down and kicked him. Seipel never denied that it happened, but he said maybe he did it because he was dazed from the blow to the head.

"When I was kind of dizzy from that beam on my head, I might have made like this [indicating], but no flier. Out in the woods I gave my bread and my coffee to two fliers a few days earlier."

"Did you see a flier either sitting or lying on the sidewalk who had a piece of slate sticking out of his skull?"

"I did not see what he had in his head."

"You saw him either sitting or lying there on the curb?"

"Yes, I wanted to bend down and look at him when I went over there."

"And that is the one you kicked in the throat and the chin?"

"I cannot say that I kicked him."

"Neither will you deny that you kicked him."

"That I cannot say. I cannot say. Why? Because I had that hit here [indicating] and I was dizzy."

Seipel went on to deny the accounts of his boasting that he had kicked the flier, but he never came right out and said that he didn't do it.

Up next was the first of the two female defendants, Reinhardt, who also chose to give an unsworn statement to the court. Reinhardt told of encountering the airmen, and she once again admitted to shouting "Beat them!" twice, but she claimed that afterward she left the scene and went home, never having any close contact with the airmen. Her testimony suggests that she did not fully understand the significance of admitting that she yelled "Beat them!"; she seemed to think that she could establish credibility with the admission and then deny the seemingly bigger accusation that she had beaten the men. Jaworski was thinking along a different track.

"You did see that the fliers were beaten considerably *after* you shouted, 'Beat them'?"

"I couldn't say that either because a lot of people were around there."

"Did you see that any of the fliers were beaten at all?"

"I don't know that for sure." Reinhardt was either being obtuse or had realized where Jaworski was headed with this line of questioning. She certainly had seen the airmen being beaten.

"You didn't see any beating taking place?"

"I saw the excitement and saw motions."

"But you didn't see a single blow that anyone gave these fliers?"

"Yes, I saw the anti-aircraft soldier, as I said before."

"Oh, I see. But that didn't happen until *after* you shouted, 'Beat them'?"

"It was a little bit further down when he did that."

"A little bit further down from the point where you hollered, 'Beat them.'"

"Yes, it was a piece further down."

"What did you mean when you were shouting, 'Beat them, beat them'?"

"I don't know myself. I was very excited from the night before, and I hadn't had any news from my husband for a long time, and I don't know myself."

When Jaworski asked Reinhardt about testimony that she had been seen beating soldiers with her fists, she said she would never do that because her husband had been a soldier for six years already. When she claimed to have walked away and not to have heard the fate of the soldiers for some time after, Jaworski asked her why she hadn't been more curious.

"After that I was sorry that I followed them because I was thinking of my husband," she said.

"Were you sorry that you had shouted, 'Beat them, beat them'?" Jaworski asked.

"Yes, I was sorry for that."

Her sister, Witzler, was the next to speak, choosing also to give an unsworn statement. She told a similar story of seeing the mob but not becoming actively involved. Then Jaworski asked her if she threw a tile at the airman, as a witness had testified. Witzler said she couldn't be certain whether she did or not. But she flatly denied yelling "Let's beat them to death," as a witness reported she had. When Jaworski asked how she could be so certain of one thing but not the other, she replied, "Because I have a brother-in-law in Russia who hasn't come home yet." The answer puzzled Jaworski, but Witzler couldn't explain what she meant. Her testimony continued in a confusing manner, with Witzler denying most of what the witness claimed she said or did, often suggesting that the accusers were vengeful because she would not sell them tobacco without a ration card. But with the testimony of Johannes Schildge, who stated that she had thrown a stone, Witzler would not deny the charge.

Witzler continued for some time, saying that she could not remember whether she threw a stone or not, but after much questioning, she eventually said that the man must have been mistaken. She also stated that her sister was "very excitable. She is very, very nervous." She added that "I am also nervous" and "My sister is more excitable."

Wüst followed with his unsworn statement, in which he denied using his hammer to assault the airmen and confirmed that he and Hartgen were both members of the Nazi Party. When confronted with his previous statement, in which he said "I bent over the wall and gave one of the fliers one or two hits with the hammer," Wüst said that was not true. "The right thing is that they were moving there and I couldn't reach it, so I pushed at him," he said.

HARTGEN WAS THE NEXT defendant to take the stand. So far the accused had tried to help themselves by leaving out details, obfuscating some of their actions, and downplaying their involvement in the worst of what transpired that day. Hartgen was about to try the much bolder action of making up an entire story that painted him not as the ringleader and primary murderer but as the civic leader who tried to stop the madness and restore order to the streets of Rüsselsheim.

In great contrast to his cocksure, antagonistic attitude up to that point, from the witness stand, Hartgen spoke calmly and tried to appear cool, an innocent man simply telling a story. He recounted how he came upon the fliers and stopped the Luftwaffe guards, who told him the men had been shot down and the guards had orders to march them through Rüsselsheim. Hearing this, Hartgen said, he walked across the street with his bicycle and with his left hand hit one of the fliers on the back with his fist. Afterward, he told the Luftwaffe sergeant to get the men out of town by way of Frankfurterstrasse because everyone in town was very worked up from the previous night's raid. Hartgen said he told the guard "that he should get out of town then and proceed because I saw the excitement of the crowd. I myself was very excited. In order to avoid another catastrophe, I said that."

Hartgen claimed that he then went back to the ready point at the police station to continue his air raid work. He admitted to striking one airman on the back with his fist, a seemingly minor blow, but no other witness reported seeing him doing so. It seemed that Hartgen was fabricating this innocuous physical contact so that he could admit to something minor, in order to make his denial of the much more serious charges seem more believable. He was only admitting that he let his anger get the best of him—for just a moment—and then he went on his way. The story, however, completely contradicted every other statement from numerous witnesses and the other defendants. Nearly every one of them swore that they had seen Hartgen in the crowd from the beginning to the end of the assault, and many testified that they had seen him beating the airmen and encouraging others to attack.

Hartgen went on with his story, saying that he went back to the police station and a short time later got word that there was a disturbance in town. When he went to investigate, he found the fliers trapped against the wall near the railway station, with a crowd furiously beating them. He told the court that he couldn't stop the assault because there were too many people and they were too frenzied. He did argue with some of the people present—some who were for the assault and some who were against it—and he told some that the mob was "not our fault," meaning not the Nazi Party's fault. He then became concerned that women and children should not see such a terrible sight and asked them all to leave, he said.

The defense asked him if he could see the fliers on the ground in front of the wall. Hartgen said no because "there were too many people around." Incredibly, Hartgen was portraying himself as a disapproving bystander so far back in the crowd that he couldn't even see the airmen. Page after page of eyewitness testimony made such a claim unbelievable. But according to Hartgen's story, he waited there until the crowd began to disperse on its own and then the Luftwaffe sergeant said, "Now we have got to see what happened." The two men approached the scene and when Hartgen propped his bicycle against the wall, he was shocked— *shocked!*—to see that the crowd had beaten the airmen to death. He heard no groaning and assumed all the airmen were dead. He turned to the remaining crowd and calmly announced, "Now they are beaten to death. They can't remain here. Now help bring them away."

Hartgen then testified that he laid the men out next to each other on the sidewalk and went off to borrow a farmer's cart. Once he returned twenty minutes later, he and a few other men, including Stolz, loaded the airmen onto the cart, and it was taken away. In response to repeated questions, Hartgen said he never heard groans or saw any movement from the airmen after they had been beaten. Hartgen and the Luftwaffe sergeant then returned to the police station, he said, and that was the end of his involvement in the whole sordid matter.

After more questioning in which Hartgen declared that all the accusations against him were just lies or mistakes, he stepped down. Wolf took the stand next and gave a sworn statement in which he denied any wrongdoing but indicated that he had seen Hartgen during the assault, including the time he was threatening the teacher, Keil. He also saw the German soldier beating the airmen with a piece of wood and saw Wüst "kneeling on the ground and beating the head of that flier with a hammer."

Jaworski challenged him on his story. "In other words, you were just what is known as an innocent bystander?" he asked.

"Yes. I am sorry I was that," Wolf answered.

Wolf went on to deny the statements of Wüst, Karl Barth, and Heinrich Barthel. Of Wüst's statement, he said, "That is completely invented. That is all invented, the story of Wüst."

Jaworksi had Wolf confirm that he spoke English well. Then he ordered the defendant, "You tell this commission what those poor boys were saying as they were being beaten and stoned." Wolf said he could not hear them because of all the commotion and that if he had heard anything, he would have reported it at his first questioning.

"Did you see any of those boys turn to the crowd and plead and beg with them not to strike them any more?" Again, Wolf declined to answer, saying he could not see them clearly at all times.

Fugmann was the last to be called and chose to make a sworn statement. He again denied throwing a stone or anything else at the fliers, but after much discussion with the attorneys he confirmed that he had seen Hartgen threatening Keil, Wolf with his hammer, and Wüst and Opper in the crowd.

After Fugmann, the commission recalled Barthel to the stand. Davidson, acting as the judge, wanted to clear up a point from his earlier testimony. After Barthel took the stand, Davidson asked, "Mr. Barthel, yesterday in your testimony concerning the accused August Wolf you started by saying you thought he was among the crowd."

"Yes."

"Later you said it could possibly have been August Wolf who was beating the fliers?"

"I heard. I heard."

"Lastly you definitely said that it was August Wolf you saw beating the fliers."

"That I messed up. I *heard.*"

"Did you or did you not see August Wolf beating the fliers?"

"No, I did not see that. I only heard it."

Barthel went on to confirm that he had seen Wolf carrying a stick.

In the defendants' box, Wolf muttered in English, "You rat."

With the defendants' testimony complete, the court ended the fifth day of the trial at 5:35 P.M. Closing arguments would begin the next day.

CHAPTER 14

"CONDUCT SO BRUTAL"

July 31, 1945

JAWORSKI WAS INFORMED EARLY THE NEXT DAY, July 31, that Wüst had tried to hang himself at the jail, but the guards stopped him in time. Apparently the evidence against Wüst was too great and he wanted to cheat the executioner, as many Nazis had done and continued to do.

After five days of testimony, the court convened at 9:35 A.M. on July 31, 1945, to hear closing arguments. The prosecution went first, and Jaworski began by underscoring how the American government had gone to great lengths to ensure that the German defendants received a fair trial.

> Counsel were permitted to ask leading questions almost to the point where counsel was testifying rather than the witness. No objection was raised, no obstacle was thrown in their pathway. That was their system. That is what they were accustomed to. It was probably helpful in bringing out all the facts. If so, all were willing for that practice to be engaged in. I am alluding to this only because I cannot help but say today, after reflecting over what has occurred in the last few days, that every single person who witnessed the spectacle of this trial must say that it was a splendid tribute to the system of military justice that is meted out by a great democracy, and there is no one seated among those who stand accused before this court who must not concede that they have been given a fair trial.

Jaworski went on to say that the trial benefited from a lack of burdensome rules regarding what evidence could be admitted, the only restriction being that the evidence must have probative value in the mind of a reasonable man.

> With that, this court was enabled to get at the very heart of this matter. I know, speaking for the prosecution, that we are not here to seek revenge. I know that that is true with every single member of this commission. I say in the same breath, however, that we are here to vindicate justice, and we are here to do that which is demanded by way of vindication to the memory of those boys, those lads, who suffered and endured so much. Now, it isn't a simple matter when one stops to think about the cross that those boys bore, about their burdens. I say it isn't a simple matter to lay aside all feeling and passion. But I say again that so far as is humanly possible we, of the prosecution, have been determined to let our goal be only that of bringing out the facts and letting justice take its course.

Jaworski also addressed head on an issue that the commission, and observers, must have been considering.

> There are among the accused in this case two women, two men of somewhat advanced age. I know that that offers a fertile field to some for asking that consideration be given to that fact, for seeking perhaps—oh, what might you term it—sympathy. A little mercy. It was not I, it was not the members of the commission who are responsible for who sits in that box which holds the accused, and I can only say that if it was the women and men of advanced age in Germany who undertook to assail, to assault, to beat, to mistreat, to murder our lads, then of necessity it must be the women and the elderly men who must pay the penalty. And I must say further that in the light of conduct so brutal and so dastardly as has been portrayed to this commission, age and sex become a matter of no consideration to me.

The prosecutor then reviewed the provisions of the Geneva Conventions, as summarized in Army Field Manual 27–10, and noted that Germany was a signatory. The Geneva Conventions stated that all prisoners of war "must at all times be treated with humanity and protected, particularly"—Jaworski repeated and emphasized *particularly*— "against acts of violence, insults and public curiosity." The Conventions also provided that all war crimes are subject to the death penalty, although a lesser penalty could be imposed.

Jaworski discussed how the defendants, though they were accused of the same crime, did not participate in the same or equal ways during the attack. Some may have participated more and contributed more directly to the violence, but from a legal perspective, the difference was not significant, he said. When a mob commits murder,

> no distinction is drawn between the one who incited the mob, if it please this commission, and the one who dealt the fatal blow. It must, of necessity, be so. Who is there who can tell which particular act was the most responsible for the fatality that ensued? . . . Every time that a member of a mob takes any action that is inclined to encourage, that is inclined to give heart to someone else who is present to also participate, that member has lent his aid to the accomplishment of the final result. . . . In the human experience that every member of this commission has had, this commission knows that there are many things that a group, a pack, a mob of men and women, if you please, will do that men and women acting singularly and alone wouldn't dare to do. The mere fact that someone else is standing there shouting words of encouragement or acting as though he or she is approving the act that is being done, that alone gives courage, gives courage to that coward who wouldn't do that abominable act standing alone. That is why the law must be so, and that is the way it operates in the light of human experience. Just as soon as they see one man run up with a shovel, for instance, and strike someone, that gives heart, it stimulates others to join in and also do something. That is the way mobs operate. Does this court or anyone who has heard the testimony in this matter think for a moment, would one think for a moment, to use an extreme example, that the accused Josef Hartgen would ever have stooped to the brutality that was displayed on this tragic occasion had he not had a group of men there and group of women, if you please, who he thought were giving approbation to what he was doing? Would he have dared to do it standing alone? Of course not.

Nevertheless, the prosecutor said, there was convincing evidence that the defendants were guilty of specific acts of violence toward the airmen, which made the cases against them that much more convincing. Jaworski went on to address some of the evidence against the accused, beginning with Margarete Witzler. He pointed out that Johannes Schildge's testimony was convincing in his account of how Witzler had thrown a piece of slate, and Witzler could not discredit him.

> I don't know and Johannes Schildge didn't know, and no member of this commission knows how many other pieces of slate she may have thrown at those fliers, and it isn't reasonable to me to assume that an accused such

as she, shouting for blood as she was on that day, should have thrown one piece of slate and then satisfied herself. The stubborn fact remains that she pursued them for some time, and I am sure that the circumstances in this case warrant the deduction that there was more than one piece of slate thrown. And we do have the sad, sad, tragic spectacle of there having been found one of those lads with a piece of slate sticking from his skull.

Witzler and Reinhardt were culpable for the murders regardless of what they threw or what blows they landed on the airmen, Jaworski said.

> I submit to this commission that there can be no doubt but that these two women, under the evidence in this case, touched off the spark that resulted in this shocking holocaust. They were continuously shouting for blood, and they got it. . . . And the circumstances very definitely show that the action of the mob did not begin until after Witzler and Reinhardt had whipped them into a frenzy.

Jaworski went on summarizing the evidence against each defendant, recounting the testimony provided against each one and addressing what he said were the unsuccessful efforts of the accused to discredit the witnesses. When discussing Seipel, Jaworski said, "There we have an elderly man sink to so low a depth as to step up and kick in the chin and throat a suffering lad who is lying prostrate with a piece of slate sticking from his skull. That is just the acme of brutality. Oh, and they talk about senility. Let's see how senile he was on that particular day."

As for Wolf, Jaworski was frank in admitting that it was difficult to determine the true extent of his participation.

> Oh yes, I'll grant you it is much more shocking to think of a man having participated to that extent than it is to see a man standing there with a club, lending encouragement to others because he's got a club in his hands and making a motion at striking and perhaps failing to connect. But so help me, I see no difference between the two! Is a man to be given any credit because his aim was poor? Is a man to be given any credit in a situation of this kind because he couldn't quite reach the fliers?

As for Hartgen, Jaworski called him

one of the ring masters in this exhibition of Nazi brutality. I don't know what caused him to show such viciousness, such ruthlessness, such heinousness on the occasion in question. He must have thought it was expected of him to do that in order to prove himself a good standard bearer. He must have thought it was incumbent upon him to just make a blood-curdling and gory affair of this whole thing. I almost feel that I am unnecessarily taking the time of this commission to review any of the evidence against that man.

Hartgen sat with his arms folded and his legs crossed, staring at the prosecutor as he spoke. When Jaworski turned toward him and gestured, Hartgen looked directly at him, never averting his gaze. He would not be cowed even as he was portrayed as a monster.

While summarizing the evidence against Hartgen, including the cemetery caretaker's testimony that Hartgen had come there later that evening, possibly to shoot the fliers again, Jaworski sidetracked to address an issue that had been nagging at him since the trial began. "One of the things that I have never understood, and one of the things that I know the commission can't understand, is that the evidence fairly points to the fact that there were more than six fliers involved in this great tragedy. We never did find more than six of the bodies. I don't know definitely that there were others."

After speaking for two and a half hours, Jaworski completed his closing argument by declaring that the evidence was convincing against each defendant. The court broke for lunch at noon, and the defense would make its final arguments that afternoon.

WHEN THE COURT RECONVENED at 3:15 P.M., Titus began the closing argument for the defense. He began by agreeing with Jaworski.

> Mr. President and members of this commission, it isn't very often that you get the defense to agree with the prosecution. However, I will have to agree that these accused have had a fair trial on the part of everyone concerned. I must concur in his opening remarks to that extent. Everybody has tried their very best to see that they knew what was going on, to see that all their rights were protected. To that extent, I am proud of our judicial system.

Titus proceeded to stress that the defendants must be found guilty beyond a reasonable doubt, and he insisted that there was an abundance of reasonable doubt because of the conflicting stories and lack of evidence other than eyewitness testimony. He told the court that he would speak primarily for Hartgen, because he was the only defendant not represented by civilian counsel. The story about Hartgen going to the cemetery on the evening of August 25, supposedly to shoot the fliers and make sure they were dead, was unconfirmed, he said, nothing more than a rumor braced by speculation. And the alleged shots to the head while the men lay on the street? Also not proven, he said.

Titus continued by addressing the elephant in the room: Hartgen was a Nazi, not merely a German.

> There has been a lot of stress laid on the fact that he was a member of the Nazi Party. Is he on trial for that here? Of course not. He is on trial for the charges as put before the commission. In fact, I have to kind of admire his stand. There are very few people in Germany today who will ever admit that they were members of the Nazi Party. But he has told you gentlemen frankly that he was, and he showed you that he had certain duties to perform in connection with that party, and those were the duties that he was performing that day.

The defense attorney pointed out that Hartgen admitted to being excited that day, as everyone was, and that he did hit one of the fliers. What he said next may not have sat well with the commission members.

"But also, he recovered himself, and if they [the Luftwaffe guards] would have followed his instructions they would have gone straight up Frankfurterstrasse, and they would have soon been on the edge of town and this tragedy wouldn't have occurred. Apparently they weren't following him."

Titus was implying that the airmen and their Luftwaffe guards brought the tragedy on themselves by not following the instructions of the well-meaning Nazi. Hartgen only wanted to get them through the town safely, and they just didn't listen.

Titus continued by reminding the commission that Hartgen claimed to be on the outside edge of the crowd and that some scant testimony supported that idea. Rather than being in the middle of the crowd beating the airmen, Hartgen actually was on the outside trying to restore order, doing his duties as a local authority, Titus said. The fact that he was unsuccessful should not be held against him.

"How would anyone, any one of you gentlemen, have tried to break up a mob of one hundred, one hundred and fifty people—screaming, yelling maniacs? What could you do? He did what he could. He was on the outskirts of the crowd trying to get the women and children away, lest some of them got hurt."

Titus then spoke about the dangers of faulty identification and how it was well known that eyewitnesses can identify a person as the suspect and be absolutely certain, yet the facts prove the witnesses are mistaken. Such a mistake must have happened with those witnesses who identified Hartgen as one of the people beating the fliers, he said. Having the witnesses stand up in court and point out Hartgen as the man they saw may have been dramatic, Titus said, but it was meaningless. "Now, of course, a witness can walk in this courtroom and look around. What are they looking for? They are looking for a blond man of medium build. How many in that accused box there are blonds with medium build, fairly young in age? Would it be difficult to pick out a man of that general description out of that box?"

In closing, Titus addressed the issue of sentencing. He asked the commission to consider the mental state of the defendants—their exhaustion and excited state from the previous night's air raids and firefighting, not to mention having lived for years with bombing in a war zone—as mitigating factors when deciding whether to sentence them to death if found guilty.

Defense attorney Otto Kattler, representing Gütlich, Opper, and Seipel, then spoke to the commission, pleading rather eloquently for its members to understand that the people of Rüsselsheim should be judged in light of what had been happening in Germany for years and to consider who was truly responsible for the tragedy.

The main fault lies with the German government of their time and with the propaganda minister Goebbels. It is probably known to the commission that during the last years, this German propaganda minister has excited the German people and has put hatred into them against all foreigners, and mainly against American and English fliers. In that connection, may I call your attention to a speech of the year 1943 in which Goebbels stated that the German people will know how to finish those gangster fliers. Could that statement mean anything else but a request to lynch all those fliers who are being shot down over Germany? There is no doubt that certainly that speech made a deep impression on all German people. Those words were brought to everybody's attention through every small worker of the party, and everybody was told that those attacks are against international law and that everybody could act as he pleased against those attackers. From your point of view, you can hardly imagine how big the hatred against the foreign fliers amongst the bigger parts of the German people was.

Kattler said another of the true guilty parties was the person who ordered the fliers marched through the city that day. He also pleaded with the commission to consider the defendants as what they were: war-weary citizens of a country very unlike the United States.

You cannot judge those people who are accused here according to measurements of the American people, the citizens of the most liberal republic in the world, which educated its people for tens of years according to liberty and humanity. You have in front of you German workers, peasants and small workers, who were excluded from every spiritual connection with the entire world, and who were under propaganda which inflamed the darkest instincts in the human being, and who did not awaken anything else in the human being but hatred. And we see, I am sorry to say, who lays the seeds will get some results.

The extreme stress from the previous evening's air raid also must be considered, Kattler said. The residents were in shelters for more than an hour and then came out to find the city on fire, their homes destroyed or burning, and they worked the rest of the night to save what they could. They got no sleep and were frightened of what might happen next. Then they saw fliers walking by and someone said they were the very people who had brought such terror to them last night.

"How do you think, gentlemen, after that night, that those primitive people felt?" Kattler asked. "How would they react when those fliers arrived at that time? One can almost say that the clash was inevitable, was bound to happen. And so those happenings occurred, those which I, as I told you before, am very sorry for even from the German point of view."

Kattler went on to reiterate some of the points Titus had made about false identification and faulty memory, also noting that some of the witnesses themselves were at first suspected of being involved in the crime. Their clear and firm testimony against others could have been an effort to deflect any effort to probe deeper into their own involvement, he said. After reviewing some of the evidence against his clients and refuting it for reasons that were brought out during the testimony, Kattler pointed out that, although he considered the trial to be as fair as possible, the German defense was at a disadvantage. The defense counsel did not learn about most of the witness statements until they heard them at trial, and the American system of cross-examination was new to them, he said.

Attorney Otto Albrecht Sturmfels spoke next. He also cast doubt on the value of eyewitness testimony given a year later, especially when the events had taken place in a chaotic, moving crowd of violent people. And he informed the commission of a typically German sentiment: the idea that the local businessman or shopkeeper is cheating you on a regular basis or showing favor to some, a particularly serious issue during the war when rationing and shortages were so severe.

Sturmfels defended Witzler and Reinhardt at length, saying it was clear that the prosecution was trying to portray the women as having set off the whole incident with Reinhardt's shouting at the crowd to beat the fliers. But that theory did not make sense, he said, because there were so many people shouting at the same time that it was impossible to know whether the woman's shouting touched the spark to the gunpowder. And then Sturmfels made a surprising and intriguing statement to the commission. He suggested that the whole incident had been put in motion intentionally by others who knew that if the fliers were paraded through Rüsselsheim, they would not make it out alive. If that was so, the sisters could not fairly be said to have caused the attack, he argued.

Sturmfels said there was no point in denying that Wüst attacked the airmen or at least tried to, but he said that Wüst was "a primitive person" with no initiative of his own and that because he had been a Nazi brown shirt since 1932, he was "a subject of temptation, to all the temptations which are being offered in such a crowd."

Van Basshuysen spoke next, defending Barthel and Daum. He recounted the evidence against them and dismissed it as unreliable, explaining how he had gone to the home of one witness and stood at the window from which she supposedly saw Daum among the crowd. Van Basshuysen reported that he could not see the point in question from that window at all, much less identify an individual in a crowd. He also argued that Barthel had gone to the scene merely to see what the commotion was and had not participated in any violence or jeering. Last he implored the commission to use their discretion to impose lighter sentences on his clients if they were found guilty.

He was followed by Heinrich von Brentano, representing Wolf and Fugmann. Brentano reviewed the evidence and arguments in Wolf's favor, then turned his attention to Fugmann, saying that in the statements and testimony of forty-six witnesses and the defendants, Fugmann's name was mentioned only twice. He also noted that Fugmann gave sworn testimony in court, unlike some of the other defendants. In addition, he cast doubt on the handwritten statement in which Fugmann seemed to invite suspicion; Fugmann had written that he didn't throw anything but that even if he did, it was "as a result of the excitement I do not know anything about it." The attorney said Fugmann added that last line only after repeated prompting by the interrogator, who suggested that maybe Fugmann just couldn't remember throwing something at the fliers, an interrogation technique commonly used by police even today to extract quasi-confessions or to make the denial look weak in court.

Then the prosecutor was allowed to address the court for a final time.

Jaworski told the commission that it should give no weight to the argument that the defendants were merely puppets of Nazi leaders. "It is an easy thing now to say, 'Oh, we were confused, and we were influenced by the policies of Goebbels' or what have you. They are grown people, and if Goebbels or anyone caused them to commit murder, then they are just the same responsible."

Jaworski also scoffed at the argument that the witnesses could not be trusted to remember details of an event from a year earlier. He said he was sure the witnesses were left with lasting and terrible memories after seeing "those who could so ruthlessly assault those bleeding fliers. And I dare say that not only for one year, but for many years to come will they be able to speak of that day and what they saw on that occasion."

Giving no quarter, Jaworski also derided the defense attorneys' pleas for leniency from the commission.

"To me, it is a very strange plea," he said, adding that the accused were "in effect, asking for sympathy. Before they asked for sympathy, for mercy. There was at least one flier who was begging for mercy on behalf of his wife and two small children. That much was definitely established by the evidence. How many others begged for mercy, we do not know. There was no sympathy, no mercy shown them by these accused, and I can see no reason for their expecting sympathy to be extended to them."

Jaworski also told the commission that it was his policy not to suggest the penalty to be assessed once a defendant was found guilty, but that he couldn't resist noting that "a graver case could not have been presented against the accused present here, and that penalties commensurate with the gravity of the offense committed can appropriately be imposed."

With all the closing arguments completed late in the afternoon, Davidson ordered the defendants returned to confinement until he sent for them and ordered the counsel to be available in the court until 8:30 P.M. in case they were needed. The general closed the court, and the six members of the commission began discussing the case

Their task was immense. Six men had to determine the fate of eleven German citizens, most of them seemingly everyday people, in the first war crimes trial to be brought after the end of the war in Europe.

THE MEMBERS OF THE commission serving as the jury had to consider the state of mind of the people of Rüsselsheim and ponder how seemingly normal citizens could become involved in such violence. To be sure, the commission started out with limited sympathy for the German defendants. The commission members were all Army officers who had seen the worst of the war, and they knew what brutality and atrocities came not just from the German military but sometimes the citizenry as well. But the commission members also had seen firsthand the toll exacted on the German people from Allied bombing and occupation. They may have had little sympathy for the killers of Rüsselsheim, but at least they understood some of what drove them to violence.

Also important for the commission members to consider was the frightening nature of mob violence and vigilantism. Everyone agreed that the men of the *Wham! Bam!* were killed not as a singular act by any one person or even several, and not solely by the eleven defendants. The men had been beaten mercilessly by many hands, debris had been thrown by scores of people, possibly a hundred or more. Each blow may have contributed to the deaths of the six airmen, and, except regarding the shots fired by Hartgen, it was difficult to ascribe any definitive culpability for the deaths. There was little doubt, even from most of the defendants' own testimony, that they had all contributed to the terror and participated in a mob action.

But was that enough to convict these eleven people of murder?

CHAPTER 15
VERDICTS

July 31, 1945

THE U.S. NEWSPAPER COVERAGE OF THE TRIAL continued, and the *New York Times* ran a lengthy front-page article on July 31, 1945, summarizing the final day's arguments. Under the headline "Fliers' Death Laid to German Hatred," the article described how "hate, revenge, sadism and nearly every ignoble trait of mankind had its turn in the musty courtroom." The article recounted the defendants' testimony and portrayed the Germans as brutish, simple people turning on each other and showing little remorse.

The six Army officers on the commission deliberated for eight hours and then late in the day on July 31 they notified Davidson that they were ready with verdicts for all of the defendants. On each count, four of the six commission members had to agree on the verdict.

Davidson recalled the attorneys to hear the verdicts, but the defendants remained in the jail. As the attorneys and other court personnel took their positions, Jaworski was fairly confident that they would all be found guilty. Davidson explained that the defendants would be brought into the court one at a time to hear their verdicts and sentences, then removed. He ordered Fugmann brought into the courtroom first. Entering with an MP guard, Fugmann was dressed in a simple civilian suit, not handcuffed or otherwise restrained, and stood before the commission. Davidson instructed a court clerk to read the verdicts.

"Upon secret written ballot, two-thirds of the members present at the time the vote was taken concurring in each finding of guilty, finds the accused Fugmann, of the specification, not guilty. Of the charge, not guilty."

As he heard the sentence translated into German, Fugmann's shoulders slumped in relief, his head falling forward as he raised his hands to his face and muttered something the court could not hear. The defense attorneys breathed a sigh of relief, but Jaworski remained stone-faced, showing none of the disappointment he felt. He knew that, although he thought there was enough evidence to show that this man had participated in the violence, Fugmann was the one defendant against whom the evidence was the weakest. There had been enough testimony to cast doubt on his involvement, so Jaworski, while not pleased, was not entirely surprised at the verdict.

Fugmann was escorted out of the courtroom, now a free man again, and Davidson ordered the most prominent defendant, Hartgen, brought into the room. Dressed in a loose-fitting jacket that buttoned up to his neck, Hartgen stood in front of the court with an MP at his side. Appearing neither frightened nor defiant now, merely stoic about his fate, Hartgen looked at the commission members. Jaworski braced himself for this verdict. He knew with absolute certainty that Hartgen was guilty of all charges, but for a fleeting moment he worried that Fugmann's acquittal might signal the commission's attitude toward the rest of the group.

Hartgen turned his head to look at the clerk as he began to read the verdict. "Of the specification, guilty. Of the charge, guilty."

Even after the German translation, there was no visible reaction from Hartgen. Jaworski held his breath waiting for the next words. What would the sentence be?

"And upon secret written ballot, two-thirds of the members present at the time the vote was taken sentences the accused Hartgen to be hanged by the neck until dead."

The prosecutor could finally breathe. Hartgen remained emotionless and calmly walked out of the courtroom with the MP.

Wüst was next. Guilty. Sentenced to death by hanging.

Then came Witzler, the first of the two women on trial. Jaworski was confident that he had proven their guilt in inciting the crowd and in participating in the beatings. Witzler walked in to the courtroom wearing a long, shapeless, dark dress with a lighter sweater unbuttoned over it, holding a piece of rolled-up paper in her left hand. Her gray hair tied back in a bun, she could have been anyone's grandmother. She stood and waited a moment for the clerk to speak. Then she looked to the translator: "Schuldig in beiderlei Hinsicht." Guilty in both respects.

Witzler raised her right hand to her face, closed her eyes, and slowly shook her head.

But would the court sentence a woman to be executed?

" . . . sentences the accused Witzler to be hanged by the neck until dead."

"Nein! Nein!" she cried out after the translation, shaking her head. "Nein, nein, nein. . . ."

As she began to sob, the MP took her by the right elbow and led her from the courtroom.

Reinhardt followed her older sister. She came into the courtroom unsteadily, obviously shaking with nerves. Dressed in a gingham dress, a dark sweater, white heels, and light-colored hose, she clasped her hands together at her waist and heard her fate. Reinhardt shook harder and let out a small cry as she heard that she was guilty in both respects. When the translator said "to be hanged by the neck until dead," Reinhardt gasped and her knees buckled, prompting the MP to reach out and steady her. When the MP was confident that she would not collapse, he guided Reinhardt out of the courtroom as her sobs grew louder.

Jaworski could hardly believe the verdicts. The court was taking the most aggressive position possible with these war crimes. His emotions were conflicted, part of him again feeling the human spirit redeemed, the same assurance that civilized, God-loving people would triumph over evil as he had felt on Easter Sunday at the Eiffel Tower. But he also took no joy in hearing men and women sentenced to death. He only prayed that justice had been done.

At this point, Jaworski was confident that if the court treated the two women with such a firm hand, the rest of the defendants would also be found guilty. Seipel, the elderly and possibly senile man accused of kicking an airman in the chin and throat while he lay on the ground with a piece of slate in his head, was found guilty in both respects and sentenced to be hanged. Opper, who had wielded a broom against the airmen so fiercely that the bristle end flew off the handle, received the same verdict and sentence.

As for Gütlich, the man who testified that he went to see the airmen because he wanted to force one to work for him, perhaps as his driver, and then slapped one because he supposedly made a disrespectful face at him: guilty in both respects, sentenced to hang.

As the court clerk read on through the list, a few defendants received some mercy from the commission in the form of lighter sentences. Wolf, accused of hitting the airmen with his hammer, was found guilty in both respects but sentenced to confinement at hard labor for fifteen years. Barthel, who hit an airman on the rear end with a stick or board and was seen shouting at the Americans, was found guilty on both charges and also sentenced to fifteen years at hard labor. Daum, the husband who left his air raid shelter to save his house in the middle of the bomb attack and then beat the airmen with a shovel, was found guilty on both charges and sentenced to twenty-five years of hard labor.

Seven sentenced to hang, three sentenced to years at hard labor, one acquitted. The death sentences were a sad but appropriate result, Jaworski thought, and the entire experience left him not jubilant over his victory but deeply disturbed by what he had seen of his fellow man. He was confident that he had done his job well and fought for the crew of the *Wham! Bam!*, though, and he fervently hoped that this showing of the American way of justice, conducted openly and fairly with a defeated enemy, might help Germany move from the cruel insanity in which it had wallowed for years back to a place among the righteous.

THE AMERICAN MILITARY COMMISSION system required that death sentences automatically be reviewed by a higher authority before they were carried out. The review would take months, but the defendants did not realize this and expected to die very soon, so all seven of the condemned requested permission to receive Communion from a priest. The requests were granted, and the likely delay was explained to them as well. When Jaworski heard of the requests for Communion, he was pleased.

They had been believers in Christ, and now they are returning to Him.

Jaworski also ordered that the around-the-clock guards assigned to Hartgen during the trial to prevent his suicide be removed. He felt that Hartgen had been brought before the bar of justice and justice had been done, so the man was now free to choose his course.

The verdicts and sentences were reported in the press back home, with the New York *Daily News* running a large picture on the front page—just below the banner headline about Yankees pitcher Bill Bevens's throwing a one-hitter for a 7–1 win over the Boston Red Sox—of Witzler holding her head as she received her death sentence, next to the headline "Death for Nazi Killers." The paper also ran a large, gruesome photo on the front page of the six crewmen's bodies after they had been dug up in the cemetery.

WITH HIS WORK IN DARMSTADT complete, Jaworski returned to the War Crimes Group headquarters in Weisbaden, housed in what was formerly a bank because it offered extra security. The Army knew that the group was at risk from those who wanted to thwart its postwar work, so a tall, barbed wire fence had been erected around the entire premises, and anyone entering had to pass through a single gate where both a guard and an officer would check identification. Jaworski had been assigned to an office in the back of the building, furnished almost as it had been when some bank manager called it home. Two days after the trial, Jaworski was in his office, still feeling deeply depressed over the images he had conjured of the Rogers crew being chased and beaten. He continued to pray that he had served justice and his Lord well, even as he went over every step of the trial and judged himself with a critical eye.

Jaworski was deep in this train of thought when he looked up from his desk and saw someone in civilian clothing approaching from down the hall. As the figure got closer, he was astonished to see it was Herr Witzler, Margarete Witzler's husband, who had made a disturbance at the entrance to the courtroom one day during the trial. Now he was standing at the door to Jaworski's office carrying the same battered black briefcase that had concerned the prosecutor in court that day. Jaworski's mind flashed with many possible scenarios for how the next moments would play out, and he was puzzled by how Witzler could have gotten past security and walked right to his office.

Like all officers, Jaworski was required to carry a .45-caliber sidearm. But like many officers sitting at a desk, he took the pistol off for the sake of comfort. Jaworski glanced from Witzler to the pistol in its holster hanging on the wall fifteen feet away and quickly decided he shouldn't make a grab for it. Whatever was in that briefcase could get him before he got to the pistol. For what seemed like a long few seconds, the two men just looked at each other. Then Witzler started shouting in German, the guttural sounds spilling forth with great energy.

"Die Zeugen gegen meine Frau gelogen! Sie wollten uns weh! Meine Frau sollte nicht bestraft werden. Ich habe hier um dich zu mir zu helfen. Sie müssen. . . ."

Jaworski did not need a translation to understand the man's cries. "The witnesses against my wife lied! They wanted to hurt us! My wife should not be punished. I have come here to get you to help me. You must . . ."

Jaworski interrupted and said, loudly enough to counter Witzler's shouts, that he must calm down if he wanted to be heard. Witzler lowered his voice and said he would remain calm, so Jaworski invited him to sit in a chair next to the desk. Witzler spoke urgently, but with control, for the next ten minutes about why his wife had been wrongly convicted. He held the black briefcase firmly under his arm the whole time, conspicuously keeping it secure and away from the American officer. Jaworski listened patiently, but he reminded Witzler that the record of the trial would be reviewed by the Army commander and also by the theater commander and that they had the authority to vacate the verdicts or change the sentences. That might take weeks to complete, he told Witzler, but he could be assured that his wife would get a fair review. Jaworski could not resist briefly recounting the evidence against his wife and saying that he had no doubt about the accuracy of the testimony. He did express concern for the distraught husband and assured him again that his wife still had an opportunity for clemency. Jaworski then shook Witzler's hand and told him it was time to leave, calling for a sergeant to escort the man out.

As soon as Witzler was gone, Jaworski called the security officer and demanded an explanation. They soon determined that the guards and officers charged with checking visitors had made a series of mistakes and assumed that Witzler was an approved messenger delivering documents to Jaworski. Witzler had claimed to know where Jaworski's office was and so didn't need an escort.

After the encounter was over, Jaworski berated himself for not having taken the opportunity to question Witzler more, to learn more about this kindly looking woman who was to be hanged for war crimes. And he wondered—would wonder for many years—just what was in that briefcase that Witzler held so firmly under his arm.

THREE WEEKS AFTER THE TRIAL, Brigadier General Davidson received an astonishing two-page handwritten letter. He immediately sent it to Jaworski.

> *Dear Sirs:*
> *After reading of the trial of the eleven Germans for the murder of six American fliers in Darmstadt, the last week of July 26th, we would like to inform you that it was Lt. N. J. Rogers' crew of the 491st Bomb Grp. The paper gave the names of only four members. Here is the full crew and those that were killed:*
>
> > *2nd Lt. Norman J. Rogers*
> > *2nd Lt. John N. Sekul*
> > *F/O Haigus Tufenkjian*
> > *Sgt. Thomas D. Williams*
> > *Sgt. William A. Dumont*
> > *Sgt. Elmore L. Austin*
>
> *According to the report in the paper the Germans gave the right reports. Here is our story: We are two members of the crew that escaped after we were carried to the cemetery.*
> *We all got out of the ship O.K. Were picked up right away and on the night of August 24th we stayed at a German air corps base. Two members of the crew were wounded by flak, one in the stomach and they kept him at the base there. The next morning the rest of the crew, 8, started by train to the interrogation center down near Frankfort-on-the-Main. We rode until about 12 o'clock on the night of August 25th and about 6 o'clock came to*

town of Rüsselsheim and we think the tracks were bombed out ahead and we had to get out and walk. William A. Dumont broke his ankle when he jumped out and we were taking turns carrying him when we went into this town, and the people attacked us. There must have been better than 150 people. After they beat us down we were carried to this grave yard, and everybody walked off and left the cart. William M. Adams and myself managed to get off the wagon and leave. We were picked up four days later.

We had a box with us with all our watches, rings, wallets and other personal belongings in it and also our escape kits. This was taken away from us during the attack. There should be about ten times the number on trial.

The two members of the crew that wasn't identified were the Pilot, 2nd Lt. Norman J. Rogers, and the navigator, F/O Haigus Tufenkjian.

The names of the rest of the crew were released in the New York Times *before the War Department notified their next of kin.*

If it is possible, we, Sgt. William M. Adams and Sgt. Sidney E. Brown, would like to come back and do anything we can to help in the trial.

We would appreciate if you have reports sent to us on the outcome of the trial.

Thanking you,
Sincerely yours,
Sgt. William M. Adams
Sgt. Sidney E. Brown

Jaworski was astounded. Out of all the horror, against all odds, two of the men had survived to return home to their families. There was mercy in this terrible story, after all.

Jaworski read and reread the letter, grateful that two of the victims had survived, that they were home with their families. Reading the letter in Brown's own hand lifted Jaworski's heart, alleviating some of the depression he felt after the conclusion of the trial in Darmstadt. There was a candle in the darkness of the Rüsselsheim story. Jaworski called in Rogers, the lead investigator of the case, and showed him the letter. Rogers reacted in the same way, utterly surprised and thrilled to hear why the other two bodies could not be found at the cemetery. The two men discussed what a shame it was that they had not found Adams and Brown earlier, Rogers musing that they could have helped considerably with the investigation. More than anything else, Rogers and Jaworski were immensely satisfied to hear that two of the men they had come to know through the terrible images painted by the defendants had, in fact, survived the ordeal. For the first time during a discussion of the Rüs-selsheim case, the men had big grins on their faces.

Although the trial was over, Jaworski and Rogers still wanted to hear what the survivors had to say. Clearly there had been more attackers than the eleven who had just been tried, so there was still the possibility of identifying and trying more defendants in the case if Adams and Brown could provide sufficient information. Jaworski cabled the Office of the Judge Advocate General in Washington and requested that Adams and Brown be questioned. The Foreign Positive Intelligence Section, Secu-rity and Intelligence Division, at Dover Air Field in Delaware sent agents to Klingerstown, Pennsylvania, and Gainesville, Florida, to interview the men. Their interviews confirmed the facts already known about the Rüs-selsheim lynching, but the survivors could offer little more detail. By the time of the interviews in October 1945, both of the men had settled back into civilian life, with Adams marrying his sweetheart soon after return-ing from the war. Although they were eager to cooperate and provide an account of their experiences, both Adams and Brown told the investiga-tors that they could not identify any of their assailants.

Brown and Adams gave rather short, straightforward statements about their experience to investigators, who asked only about the assault itself and what additional evidence they might provide. In his statement, Adams stressed that he and Brown only left their fellow crewmembers in the cemetery because they were sure they were dead; leaving your crew-mates behind to save your own hide would be unforgivable. "After every-one had left, Sgt. Brown and myself escaped," he said. "I am sure that those men we left behind were dead because their brains were laying around and their heads were all cut open."

Military officials never heard the story of their days and months after escaping because it was inconsequential to the investigation in Rüs-selsheim, but Brown would tell the story to his family, many years later, when he was more comfortable talking about some of the worst moments in his life.

CHAPTER 16

"NORM KNEW"

AS REQUIRED BY THE MILITARY COMMISSION SYSTEM, the sentences of the court were reviewed at the top levels of the Army: the commanding general of the Seventh Army and the commanding general of the European theater. All of the verdicts and sentences were upheld, with the exception of the two sisters'. Perhaps because death by hanging seemed too harsh for women whose primary offense was shouting rather than physical assault, or perhaps because of fears that hanging two women would look vengeful and as sadistic as what the Nazis did regularly, General Geoffrey Keyes, commanding general of the Seventh Army, commuted the death sentences of Reinhardt and Witzler to thirty years in prison.

Luke Rogers, the war crimes investigator, and Jaworski were disappointed to hear that the sisters would not hang. Although neither would have rejoiced at seeing women step to the gallows, they felt strongly that Witzler and Reinhardt were instrumental in the murders of the American fliers. If not for their encouragement, Rogers and Jaworski still contended, the lynching might never have happened. Nevertheless, five men would hang for what they did to those boys. The execution date was set for November 10.

In August 1945, as the Rüsselsheim killers awaited their fate, the Rogers family was still waiting for official notification of Norm's death. They strongly suspected that he was one of the unidentified fliers mentioned in the *New York Times,* but they wanted to know for sure. The grim confirmation came in the form of a letter not from the government but from Sidney Eugene Brown. The next day, Norm's mother, Jennie Rogers, wrote to her other children to break the news.

> *Well Darlins', our hunch about that newspaper article was O.K. Helen had a letter yesterday giving us definite word that Norm is gone. He was one of the six killed by German civilians on Aug. 26th. Please don't tell how we heard it because we haven't been officially notified yet, but it was Norm's tail gunner who wrote.*
>
> *He asked us not to let the Gov't know who told us because it was against regulations for them to tell us anything, so be careful of what you tell and you'd better destroy this letter right away after you and Norma read it.*

Forrest Brininstool was discharged soon after returning to the States, and he set off on trips around the country, traveling with his wife, to meet with the family members of the men in his unit who had died. He had no specific goal, no new information to pass on, but he felt that he owed it to his friends to knock on the door, shake their parents' hands, and answer any questions they had. He visited several families, and most were welcoming, sensing that Brininstool had a deep-seated survivor's guilt, understandable in his situation. Williams's mother broke his heart by screaming in anger, "Why did you come back and my son didn't?"

Brininstool's resolve faltered after the encounter with Williams's mother, but not before he visited with the Rogers family on Thursday, August 9, 1945. Helen Rogers was still hurt by Norm's last letter having been stolen and destroyed before it reached her. Although she had heard from Norm's letter to his father that he knew about the baby, she still wanted to hear it from someone who had been there with him when he got the news. Helen was holding nearly six-month-old Madeline in her arms when Brininstool finally put her mind at ease.

"Norm knew. He got your letter and he was very happy," Brininstool told her. "Norm was excited about being a father."

On Saturday, Jennie Rogers wrote to her children.

Dear Boy and Girl,
I suppose you are anxiously waiting for more news. Well, now we have all
the facts first hand. We still haven't been officially notified but that will
come too. . . .

Norm's engineer came to see us Thursday afternoon. He and his wife
are driving around to tell all the families about their boys. It's a mighty swell
thing for them to do and if you saw him, you'd realize how terribly hard it
was for him to do it. He never knows how he'll be received but was pleased
with the reception in Rochester. One couple in Pa. who lost their only child
told him they didn't see how he could get back and their son couldn't. He told
them one of the boys was the second son lost in one family and they said,
"Well that's not hard for them. They have others. Ours was our only one."
They were the first ones he met and after that he hated to go any farther. He
came here and knowing Dad to be a fireman, he inquired at a firehouse and
a fireman guided them here. At first he didn't want to see Helen but I told
him he must. He and his wife had both known Helen down South and I told
him Helen wouldn't be hysterical or cry all over him but would be bitterly
disappointed if he didn't come.

I called Helen up and after giving them some supper, I rode down with
them. Later he brought me home and his wife, Helen, and Bernice came
along and we sat up in Dad's bedroom until 11 o'clock and had a couple
glasses of beer and of course Bernice was the life of the party and there wasn't
a gloomy minute. We had all heard the whole story and then dropped it. They
stayed all night at Monna's and left about seven last night. They made us feel
better and certainly made a big change in Helen. That terrible wondering
has ended and we are all relaxed again. Now I'll try to tell his story.

The letter went on for another two and a half pages as Jennie Rogers recounted the story Brininstool told them about the mission, being shot
down, and how he was separated from the others, and then gave a fairly
detailed account of the killings as relayed by Brown and Adams. She
ended the letter with this:

Well Darlins', that's the story and it doesn't make nice reading but Norm is
not suffering now and wouldn't come back if he could. God has always been
so good to us and His goodness is not just in giving us the things we like but
the things we need. I feel positively no bitterness and my heart is more quiet
and content than it has been in nearly a year. We have two boys gone on
ahead to get a new home ready for us and just pray that we'll all be found
worthy to join them when God calls us. It certainly gives us something to
look ahead to.

As the Rogers family tried to make peace with their loss, the war in the Pacific was coming to a close. Japan refused the demand for unconditional surrender, and so the United States delivered prompt and utter destruction in the form of two atomic bombs dropped on the cities of Hiroshima and Nagasaki in early August. Japan surrendered on August 15, 1945, and would sign the documents on the deck of the American battleship USS *Missouri* on September 2. The war was over.

Spontaneous celebrations broke out all over the country as Americans heard the news that the long ordeal was finally over, that their boys were coming home. As the residents of Rochester, New York, danced in the streets, honked car horns, and waved newspapers shouting news of V-J Day, Rogers's parents and his wife, Helen, carrying the infant Madeline, slowly made their way through the party to go to Mass. They still had to pray for Norm.

On August 18, three days later, Norm Rogers's mother wrote to her other children.

Well Chilluns, peace day was pretty wild and noisy here. It was announced at 7 pm and shortly after, Dad and I went to confession. We went to St. Monica's to avoid questions over here, and on the way down kids were yelling at Dad, "Blow your horn!" Everyone was hilarious but us. I guess maybe we looked like Nazis or Japs. We were happy without a doubt but just didn't feel like raising the roof.

The families of the *Wham! Bam!* crew continued to stay in touch with the occasional letter, and in October, Anoosh Tufenkjian wrote to Brininstool to confirm that she had been notified of her son's death. He wrote her back with a letter dated October 22 that was very generous, considering that, like the other crew members on the *Wham! Bam!* that day, Brininstool did not know Tufenkjian. Because Tufenkjian wasn't mentioned in the July *New York Times* story, and because he wasn't a regular crewmate of the men who were mentioned, there had still been some question about whether his was one of the unidentified bodies. Earlier in October, the Army had written Mrs. Tufenkjian to say that her son was now presumed dead because he had been missing for more than a year. Brininstool wrote to her,

My Dear Mrs. Tufenkjian,
I've received your letter that you have received word of your son's death in
Germany. I can confirm this. I am very sorry that my letters from Germany
gave everyone false hope. Of the nine men in our crew there are now only
three of us left. Six of these boys died in Germany and I regret this very
much. The men you fly with and live with mean very much to you. One can
not explain these feelings.

I returned to the States in July. I'm now at Dayton, OH. Would like
very much to visit you and I promise you that at my first opportunity I shall
call on you. I expect to receive my discharge soon and then I will call on you
if you would like to talk with me. The other boys to survive the ordeal are
S/Sgt. G. Brown and S/Sgt. Wm Adams and myself.

Respectfully yours,
S/Sgt. Forrest Brininstool

BY THIS POINT—October 1945—the family of Thomas Williams was growing dissatisfied with how long it was taking to carry out the executions. On October 2, Thomas Williams Sr. wrote to Major General Edward F. Witsell, acting adjutant general of the Army.

Dear Sir:
Mrs. Williams and I have been greatly concerned as to the ultimate fate of
the seven prisoners that were to hang for the murder of my boy.

We have been watching the newspaper every day but have failed to find
any account of the deaths by hanging. In your letter of August 8th, 45, you
stated swift justice was being meted out. If these people are still alive, and
we have every reason to believe they are, I don't think I would call that swift
justice.

After all, these people got a fair trial and were found guilty. My boy got
no trial. Is that justice?

It would give Mrs. Williams and myself a great deal of comfort to know
if my boy received a proper burial and where his body is resting. We intend
bringing his body home when we are allowed to do so.

We would greatly appreciate it if you can answer these questions for
us. We are not blood thirsty people but we do want to see justice done.

Sincerely,
Thomas D. Williams, Sr.

Major Clarence L. Yancey of the War Crimes Group replied to Williams on November 9, 1945, the eve of the execution date, writing that "the reason for the delay in carrying out the decree of the court is that the perpetrators of this crime are being continually questioned as to their knowledge and identity of other individuals who may have committed certain other crimes and mistreatment of American military personnel." He assured the Williams family that "I, too, am interested in meting out swift justice to guilty parties who have brutally beaten and in many instances killed American military personnel."

HARTGEN AND THE OTHER men sentenced to death would meet their fate at the hands of Master Sergeant John C. Woods, a lively Texan who took exceptional pride in his work. Originally serving as an engineer in the Army, Woods had eagerly stepped forward when the military needed a hangman—his occupation before the war. By the time he was called to carry out the Rüsselsheim death sentences, Woods had already executed 212 criminals in the United States and 87 in Europe, before and during World War II. Having long since accumulated enough service points to be discharged and go home, Woods told the Army he wanted to stay on and maybe have a go at hanging Hermann Göring. He was more than happy to string up the Rüsselsheim murderers in the meantime.

Woods was an interesting character. He was a short, stocky man of Irish descent, jovial except when talking about Germans and others who needed to die, his doughy face breaking into a big grin often. An American officer who worked with Woods in executing German war criminals after the Nuremberg trials later described how he had been warned that Woods was an unpredictable troublemaker with a violent temper, but he found that the executioner actually was respectful and friendly, quite controlled when on duty, professional, and knowledgeable about his difficult task.

"He did have a predilection for beer, and was given to verbal and physical outbursts when he was drunk," Lieutenant Stanley Tilles wrote. "He freely expressed his hatred of Germans, a hatred rooted in the fact that he had lost several friends at the Malmedy Massacre, which occurred in Belgium when 190 American POWs were herded into a field, stripped, and machine gunned to death."

A career soldier, Woods was secretive about his personal life because he knew some people didn't like what he did for a living and he didn't want anyone harassing his family. He never spoke to anyone about his family or much else of his life before the war, but he did once tell Tilles, after many beers one night, how he had gotten into the execution business. According to the story, Woods had grown up next door to the hangman for a Texas prison, who once invited the teenage Woods to witness an execution. Woods took him up on the offer, then saw several more, and eventually became the hangman's assistant. He saw combat in North Africa and Normandy during the war but had been the Army's part-time hangman for twenty years.

As the most experienced and somewhat famous executioner in American military history, and probably in American history altogether, Woods was a quintessential American archetype—brash, loud, full of piss and vinegar, with not an ounce of regret or misgiving about his job. He stood in contrast to his British counterpart of the era and professional rival, the famed Albert Pierrepoint, who executed more than 400 men and women between 1931 and 1956, including many German war criminals after the war. Where Pierrepoint was the proper British gentleman, as fastidious about his appearance as he was about the details of his work, Woods was more down to earth and no-nonsense. Both took their profession seriously and considered their work an unpleasant but important contribution to society, but Pierrepoint fretted more about the delicacies of ensuring that the condemned prisoner not suffer emotionally or physically any more than necessary. The British executioner considered hanging to be both a science and an art, priding himself on an extensive knowledge of the materials used, the different methodologies, the precise calculations used to determine the correct rope length, and highly choreographed movements that allowed him to have a dead body hanging from a rope as little as twenty seconds after first laying eyes on the prisoner. Woods knew most of the information just as well, but he did not make a fetish of the procedural aspects or worry too much about making the condemned's last moments comfortable. He knew how hanging worked, and he could be counted on to kill the condemned efficiently and definitively. Beyond that, he didn't make much of a fuss over the details. Pierrepoint and Woods knew of each other, and their paths crossed during the postwar executions, when there were more Nazis to be killed than Woods could handle alone. They did not admire each other. Pierrepoint held great disdain for Woods's cowboy personality and what he saw as the American's primitive and unprofessional style of hanging, particularly a more lax method of calculating the rope length—based on the body weight of the condemned and other factors—needed to provide instantaneous death from snapping the spinal column rather than from slow strangulation. The British executioner thought too many of Woods's victims died a slow and painful death, and that Woods didn't mind. Even the gear was different: The British used a specially designed metal eye through which the rope slid, and the Americans stuck with the classic hangman's noose of rope coiled around itself. Pierrepoint also thought the whole way of hanging in the U.S. military was odd, so contrary to everything he thought important about how the British did it. Pierrepoint's hangings were all about speed and efficiency, taking the condemned straight from the holding room to the scaffold, putting on a white hood, and releasing the trapdoor as quickly as possible. In the U.S. military, everything was drawn out in a big affair. Rather than a speedy and simple procedure, a U.S. military hanging often included troops assembled as witnesses, and a military band playing the "Dead March" escorted the prisoner to the scaffold, according to the Army's manual on executions. Then the prisoner had to stand on the scaffold as an officer read the charge, finding, sentence, and orders aloud to him, which could take a while. After the prisoner was proclaimed dead, the troops and the band retired "with the band playing a lively air."

From the other side, Woods saw Pierrepoint as a British dandy who tried to make the job more complicated than it had to be and who was too concerned about the feelings of vicious Nazi beasts, who would usually get a quick, clean death from Woods—but who gained no pity from him if they happened not to die easily. All the American ceremony served a purpose, Woods thought, and if the condemned had to stand on the scaffold a few minutes longer than Pierrepoint liked, well, he shouldn't have committed the crime. As for his victims' slowly suffocating instead of enjoying a quick and painless death, Woods was good enough at his job that such deaths didn't happen unless he wanted them to. When he was killing ten of the men convicted in the Nuremberg trials, nine got a clean death. The tenth, Julius Streicher, was the publisher of an anti-Semitic newspaper and had spent time in prison for beating and killing Jews before the Nazis came to power. He had been belligerent throughout his incarceration, and as he was led to the gallows in Nuremberg, Streicher pulled away from his escorts and snapped a one-armed salute at the tribunal that had convicted him, screaming "Heil Hitler!" The other nine condemned had used their last words to proclaim their innocence, express love for their families, or wish the best for Germany. Streicher's display didn't sit well with Woods, and Tilles watched as Woods put the hangman's noose over the German's head and positioned the coils toward the back of the head rather than directly in line with the left ear, as was standard. Tilles realized Woods was doing this so that the rope would not snap Streicher's neck but would leave him to dangle until he suffocated. He saw Woods grin slightly as he pulled the lever for the trapdoor. Streicher dropped at 2:14 A.M. The witnesses heard him gasp and gurgle for the next nine minutes. No one moved to help him, no one complained, and for years afterward, everyone would deny that they heard Streicher make a sound.

The Woods brand of hanging would come to the Rüsselsheim killers in the courtyard of Bruchsal Prison in Baden, Germany, where they had been held since the trial. The gallows were constructed within the outer stone wall, beneath a corner turret. Late in the afternoon on November 10, 1945, in a cold, pouring rain, thirty soldiers and other witnesses stood in overcoats. The Army opted not to have a military band. Woods spent more than an hour executing the men sentenced to death for their roles in the lynching of the crew of the *Wham! Bam!* Accompanied by a clergyman, two MPs, an interpreter, and officers assigned to the proceedings, each man was led to the scaffold, which was a simple wooden structure measuring eight feet by ten feet, the platform ten feet off the ground and the lower portion shrouded by dark drapes.

First to mount the scaffold was Johannes Seipel, convicted of kicking an airmen in the chin and throat while he lay on the ground with a piece of slate in his head. The MPs wore long overcoats in the chilly rain; Seipel, like all the prisoners, wore a simple dark jacket and a white skullcap with no brim. An officer read the charges, findings, and sentence to him. He was asked if he had last words, and he shouted, "I saw a fellow Engel throw rocks at them," his voice shaking with fear and frustration. "I did nothing! Nothing!" Woods pulled the black hood down over his head as Seipel continued shouting "Nothing!" Woods pulled the lever on the trapdoor and Seipel dropped to a quick death. After he was taken down and put in a waiting coffin, Woods readied the gallows for the next man, Opper, who had beaten the airmen with a broom. His last words were a request: "If the military won't give me another trial, could I be tried by the church?" Woods answered by pulling the lever.

Wüst was next—the man who had knelt down to beat a flier on the head with a hammer. His diminutive stature was made even more noticeable by a six-foot-five-inch, burly MP escorting him. Asked for his last words, he said, "With this I die with a clear conscience," the last words muffled as an impatient Woods pulled the black hood down over his head.

Gütlich, who admitted hitting an airman, looked at the soldiers present and said, "I only did one thing and only because an American stuck out his tongue at me." Woods put the hood on, adjusted the noose, and gave the lever a firm yank.

The last to be executed was Hartgen, the Nazi Party member who encountered the crewmen as they were being escorted through town and had the authority to stop the violence but instead encouraged it and ended up shooting several airmen in the head. Accompanied by a Catholic priest in a white lace surplice and stole carrying an open Bible and reciting the Lord's Prayer, Hartgen walked steadily, with his head held high. Night was falling early on the rainy day, and the courtyard was dark as the last condemned murderer from Rüsselsheim approached the steps to the scaffold. He paused and kissed the silver crucifix held by the priest, then he firmly mounted each step to the scaffold. He stood on the trapdoor, looking small and powerless, the opposite of what he had sought to make of himself in Rüsselsheim. An officer asked for his last words.

"God forgive you because you don't know what you're doing."

Photographers took pictures of Hartgen's last moment, the flashes lighting up the German killer standing there in a black suit, his hands tied behind his back. The image of Hartgen lit so harshly against the scaffold and the dark sky lent his death an almost glorious, Valkyrian air.

The hood went down over Hartgen's head. The noose was placed carefully. Woods released the trapdoor. Hartgen fell to his death, a death far more merciful than any of the American airmen had received.

After checking to confirm that his last prisoner of the day was dead, Woods smiled and proclaimed the day "a perfect hanging."

EVEN AFTER THE DEATHS of some of the Rüsselsheim killers, there was still unfinished business. Rogers and Jaworski had not known during the investigation of the killings that one of the people most responsible for the airmen's deaths was Otto Hermann Stolz, the man at the cemetery who beat some of the fliers in the head with a club or board in an effort to finish them off. His name and role in the killings came out during the trial of the Rüsselsheim defendants, mostly through the testimony of Jakob Raab, the cemetery caretaker, and of Hartgen. In addition, the statements of Brown and Adams clearly described a man beating the fliers at the cemetery. The War Crimes Group found Stolz and put him on trial for the killings on May 15, 1947, at the Dachau War Crimes Court in Germany, as part of what would be almost three years of court proceedings against 1,672 Germans in 489 separate trials. In the end, 1,416 men and women were convicted, 297 received death sentences, and 279 were sentenced to life in prison. The trials were held inside the walls of the former Dachau concentration camp to highlight the depravity of the Nazi regime.

Before the war, Stolz had been a carpenter in Rüsselsheim. During the Nazis' rise to power, Stolz joined the SA, and he knew Hartgen well. When he went to trial, Stolz was charged with the same violations as the original eleven defendants, and the evidence from the first trial was introduced. Importantly, the statements of Adams and Brown also were used in Stolz's trial. Witnesses from the first trial—Gottlieb Wolf, Karl Barth, and others—testified that they saw Stolz in the crowd assaulting the fliers. Several testified that they saw him beating the men with a wooden club about the same size as a table leg. A cemetery worker, Adam Schmitt, testified that he was present when Stolz arrived with the airmen in the cart and that Stolz had a club with him. Raab also testified, and the two cemetery workers described how Stolz beat the men in the cart with his club. Then Raab asked Schmitt who the man was. Schmitt told Raab that it was Stolz and that he knew him.

Raab also offered new information not heard in the first trial. He explained that when the cart arrived, he remarked that some of the airmen were still alive and told Stolz, "We only bury dead people and not half-dead ones." It was after that comment that Stolz began beating the men, he said. Stolz first beat the men while standing beside the wagon, then climbed up on the wagon to hit them some more, he said. He also said that Stolz remained in the cemetery after the air raid alarm and that he saw Stolz beat the men more.

The prosecution rested its case on the first day. Civilian defense counsel Donald Ross began his case that day, and on the following morning, Stolz took the stand in his own defense. He testified calmly, speaking very politely to the court, explaining that his wife had died just four months earlier, leaving him with one child. As the defense began questioning him about his involvement with the Rüsselsheim murders, Stolz painted a different picture from what anyone had heard of him so far. He said he was on his way to the Opel factory when he came upon the mob and was stopped by one of the Luftwaffe guards, who asked him to help stop the American fliers, because they were running away. Stolz claimed that he ran to catch up with the fliers, got in front of them, and then stood there with his arms spread wide to stop the prisoners from escaping. The Americans went around him, he said, and then the crowd began beating them. Having no weapon himself, he was unable to protect the fliers, and so he simply left and went on his way to the factory. He came back to the area twenty minutes later looking for his Opel factory pass, and that is when Hartgen asked him to help take the bodies to the cemetery, he said.

Stolz told the court that when he arrived with the bodies and moaning was heard, Raab left on his bicycle to get someone who could administer first aid to the airmen—a claim Raab never made in either trial. Stolz flatly denied ever hitting the airmen.

The trial was brief, with closing arguments on the second day. "He took these people out to the cemetery and he got up on the cart and beat the people some more just because he heard a little noise there," chief prosecutor Lieutenant John Pohlman said. "I submit to the court that this is one of the most brutal and vicious killings I have ever seen, and this man should be given the extreme penalty under the law."

The defense countered that the evidence against Stolz was vague, saying that far from being a killer, the defendant actually was performing an act of mercy by taking the men to the cemetery for a proper burial.

"In many respects, Stolz is the sucker in this case," Ross said. "Through decency and blindly following an order, he took these corpses to the cemetery."

The court adjourned at noon, and the commission came back with a verdict at 1:30 P.M.: guilty. When the court asked if Stolz had any evidence of extenuating circumstances before being sentenced, he told the court that he was "the only one who brought the fliers the way it should have been done to the cemetery and that I have an eleven-year-old child at home, and that my wife has been paralyzed since 1938 until now when she died."

After adjourning for only a few minutes, the court reconvened and pronounced sentence on Stolz: death by hanging.

The War Crimes Group also found one of the three or four German soldiers who had been seen in the crowd assaulting the fliers. Rinkes, the Hitler Youth who testified in the first trial, reported to Rogers that he had identified one of the soldiers as Franz Umstatter. Rogers found him in the town of Denheim, about thirty miles from Rüsselsheim. The investigator arrested Umstatter and found that he was "the worst looking criminal of them all and was built like a gorilla." He was tried in the Dachau War Crimes Court in 1946. Two witnesses testified that he had kicked the Americans so hard that he broke the heel of his boot, an image that Brown remembered even years later. Other witnesses testified that Umstatter returned home carrying his old boots with the broken heel and wearing brown shoes he had taken from the pilot, who had worn shoes instead of boots because they were easier to fly the plane in.

Umstatter was found guilty and sentenced to death by hanging.

EPILOGUE

THE THREADS OF THE RÜSSELSHEIM MURDERS continued spreading for years. Everyone involved with the murders and the trials would find that that terrible day would stay with them forever, an event that changed their lives and how they saw their fellow human beings.

There would be one more hanging to end the Rüsselsheim executions. Stolz was hanged in March 1948 for administering the final death blows to the fliers in the cemetery. Umstatter, however, was released from prison that same month, when the War Crimes Group of the European Command overturned the commission's verdict, without citing a reason in the official records. The only serious claim made during Umstatter's appeal concerned a technicality: the charge against him did not specify where the crime took place. The omission was a clearly an error, and the military court system did not require a verdict to be overturned on such a technicality if it had no meaningful impact on the case. Yet it appears that the War Crimes Group let one of the most vicious of the Rüsselsheim killers go free for lack of a few words in a charging document.

Others of those convicted in the Rüsselsheim trials lived long enough to look back and marvel at how close they had come to being hanged for their crimes. The sisters Reinhardt and Witzler were paroled on December 19, 1953, taking jobs in the tobacco shop they formerly owned. Reinhardt died on November 11, 1958, and Witzler died on January 7, 1976.

The men who served prison time for their roles were eventually released from prison and led quiet lives thereafter, although they were known in Rüsselsheim and people still whispered behind their backs, debating exactly what they had done during the assault. Barthel and Wolf were both paroled on December 21, 1953. Barthel died on February 2, 1965, and Wolf on May 11, 1981. Daum was paroled on February 5, 1954, and died a year and a half later, on July 27, 1955.

Jaworski would remember the Rüsselsheim case as a distinct challenge for him both professionally and personally, drawing him deeper into his faith in his effort to understand and accept that people could be so brutal with one another. He was satisfied that he had carried out the prosecution with integrity, bringing justice to the murderers and honoring the memories of the men who had died. As the Allies continued prosecuting war crimes, Jaworski took the lead in many more cases, including some of the most notorious, such as the Hadamar euthanasia center, where 10,072 people were gassed or killed by other means because the German government deemed them defective in some way. In the October 1945 trial, just two short months after the Rüsselsheim case, Jaworski told the commission of how Hadamar workers would lie to children and adults alike, many of whom were mentally deficient or ill, telling them they were about to receive helpful medical treatment. Outraged by the cruelty, Jaworski was in fine form before the commission:

> Oh, what a vicious falsehood, what a terrible thing, what an evil and wicked thing to do to a person who is already suffering and already carrying burdens, to build up the false hope that sunshine was to enter their hearts. They told them they would be given medication that would help them. Oh, yes, they were given medications, medications of poison that gripped their heart and closed their eyelids still; that is the sort of medication they were given.

However, when Jaworski was assigned as a prosecutor in what would become the most well-known and historically significant war crimes trial, he refused to participate. The Nuremberg trials, in which prominent members of the political, military, and economic leadership of Nazi Germany were charged with war crimes, would become known as the best example of how the Allies held the Nazis responsible for their reign of terror. Held in the city of Nuremberg, at the Palace of Justice, the first and best-known of these trials was the Trial of the Major War Criminals, which tried twenty-two of the most important captured leaders of Nazi Germany. Jaworski could have added to his already substantial record by prosecuting criminals like Hermann Göring and Martin Borman, but he insisted that the charges against the men were invalid. The crimes they were accused of—a conspiracy for a crime against peace and waging wars against peace, among others—did not exist at the time the defendants allegedly committed them, Jaworski said. While he had no doubt that the Nuremberg defendants were guilty of terrible crimes, Jaworski said the charges were improper and therefore he could not prosecute. Titus, the lead defense counsel in the Rüsselsheim case, also was tapped to prosecute the Nuremberg defendants but refused for the same reason.

After the war, Jaworski went on to a prominent law career, building his Austin, Texas, firm, Fulbright & Jaworski, into the largest in the country. His greatest fame came when he was appointed special prosecutor during the Watergate investigation of President Richard Nixon. True to the character he displayed during the Rüsselsheim case, Jaworski pursued his duty with the utmost integrity, convinced that he was serving God. Jaworski died on December 9, 1982, at his ranch near Wimberley, Texas, while chopping wood.

Hangman John Woods would never get to tell his story in retirement the way his British counterpart Albert Pierrepoint did. After finally accepting discharge from the Army, he continued to work as a civilian contractor for the military—in construction, not hangings. In the 1950s, he was accidentally electrocuted by a high-voltage power line while working in Eniwetok, Marshall Islands. His grave site is unknown and his part in history remains enigmatic.

THE SURVIVORS OF THE *Wham! Bam! Thank You Ma'am* lived with their memories of Rüsselsheim every day of their lives. Adams, Brown, and Brininstool remained the closest of friends, reuniting often, their wives and children becoming like family. The memories of Rüsselsheim and the prison camps were always with them, just beneath the surface. The three men could understand each other like no one else could, not even their wives. They knew why Adams couldn't stand being alone even for a minute, and they understood why none of them could look at a German shepherd without feeling fear and a little bit of anger. All three survivors avoided feelings of hatred or anger toward the people of Rüsselsheim who attacked them, however. They said they understood, that it was a time of war and the people of Rüsselsheim had been through hell. What they did was wrong, all three men said, but they could understand the anger and the urge for retribution from people who had suffered so much.

Brown and Brininstool were at Adams's side in Pennsylvania when he died of cancer on March 8, 1980. They saw that their friend passed without resentment in his heart.

Brown lived a full life in Gainesville, Florida, raising a family and working as a machinist. He returned with the same attitude as most veterans from World War II: "You come home, you get a job, you have babies, you get on with your life," he often told his daughter Rachel whenever she would ask about the war. That was all she would learn for many years, although she knew there was more to her father's story. Even at a young age, she suspected that there was some connection between the war he wouldn't talk about and the way her father could become so troubled around the August 24–26 anniversary of the crash and lynching. For the whole month of August, every year, Rachel and her brothers and sisters knew that their father needed time to himself. "Your father's feeling bad," their mother would say. "Just leave him alone." They knew there was something under the surface, something he wouldn't talk about. Later, Brown revealed to close friends that he was always troubled by the memory of leaving his crewmates behind in the cart, knowing some of them were still alive—if only barely. There was nothing he could have done for them; he couldn't even have carried them to safety. But still it troubled him deeply.

Rachel's first real clue came when she was six years old and enjoying time with her father, in a good mood that day. Rachel loved to brush her daddy's thick, wavy hair, and on this day he was glad to sit on the floor and let his girl run a brush across his head. Rachel pulled the brush through his locks over and over, but after a few minutes she had a question.

"Daddy, what are all these marks on your head?" she asked. "There are so many."

Brown tensed up and tried to dismiss the girl's question.

"It's nothing, baby doll," he said. "I just got hit on the head a long time ago."

Brininstool returned home to Munith, Michigan, just outside of Jackson, working as a tool and die maker while also a partner with his brother-in-law in the family's dairy operation. His wife often reminded the children that their father had done a very brave thing by fighting in the war and that, if not for a quirk of fate, he might have been among the crewmembers of the *Wham! Bam!* who died. She told them many times about visiting the families of the dead crewmembers with her husband after the war and what a profound effect it had on him. Brininstool spoke often of his devotion to the families of his lost crewmates.

"These people are our family, and they always will be," Brininstool once told his son David. "Sometimes you get dealt the lucky hand and sometimes you don't. It's our job to support the guys and the families who didn't get the lucky hand."

FORTY YEARS AFTER THE survivors came home from the war, the massacre in Rüsselsheim had faded into obscurity. It was little more than a footnote, if even that, in any account of the bombings in Europe during World War II, a terrible event forgotten only because there were so many other terrible memories competing for prominence after the war. Not until 1985 was it resurrected, as part of the German people's struggle to come to terms with the sins of the past. Just as the generation of Americans who fought in World War II often chose to keep their dreadful memories to themselves, so did the Germans of that era choose to keep their own nightmares and transgressions locked away. But as the younger generation explored its history, the story of the Rüsselsheim murders came out in the open, much to the chagrin of many residents of the town, which had become a vibrant industrial city of 60,000. A prominent German magazine article made the killings a topic of debate and deep reflection in Germany, raising difficult questions about the extent of Allied bombing and whether the rage of the mob in 1944 could be justified in any way, or at least understood, by the destruction that had rained down on their city. Elderly Germans who remembered the war debated the same questions that evoked such strong reactions among their children and grandchildren. Was the vicious response by citizens on the ground any worse than the Allies' dropping bombs on civilians? The story of the lynching and the trial of the Rüsselsheim murderers resonates so strongly because it illustrates the great quandaries of war, questions that are as relevant in today's world as they were in 1944: Where are the boundaries? What is acceptable in times of war? How can rules be applied to what is essentially an exercise in savagery against one another? Can we blame civilians for fighting back against what they see as aggression and terrorism?

One particular question had loomed in the background of the Rüsselsheim trial but was never spoken aloud in the courtroom: How would American or English citizens have reacted in the same situation? What would they have done if they had been bombed mercilessly and then encountered an enemy bomber crew, one of the very bomber crews that had inflicted such horror on them only hours earlier (or so they thought), walking through the middle of their bombed-out town? Would American or British townspeople—or citizens from any other country, for that matter—have reacted differently from the people of Rüsselsheim, with more restraint and mercy?

Jaworski later wrote addressing this very question:

> I like to think that they would. Yet we must remember that the murderers of Rüsselsheim had been raised in Christian homes, had worshipped God earlier in their lives, and had been good, law-abiding people. How much exposure to Nazism, the Ku Klux Klan, or to any other group that feeds on hatred and prejudice does it take to transform fine and honorable people into beasts? I do not know.
>
> Of one thing I am sure. Somewhere along the way the murderers of Rüsselsheim had stopped going to church, had, I believe, lost their relationship with God.
>
> Might the same thing happen to any of us? Without a continuing and vital relationship with our Lord, we become a spiritual vacuum. And evil loves a spiritual vacuum.

The chief investigator in the case, Luke Rogers, saw less a spiritual explanation than one that was part and parcel of the German philosophy: They were better than everyone else. What the Germans did to others was justified, but what the Allies did to the Germans was cause for outrage: "I found in Germany an intense dislike toward flyers. This is because the Air Force taught the Germans their sternest lesson and the one they will remember longest. They speak often of the terrible raids on Germany, but few admit knowledge of Warsaw, the towns of Northern France or Coventry, and none I spoke to admitted knowledge of Rotterdam."

Rogers was referring to the destruction of Rotterdam on May 14, 1940, during the German invasion of the Netherlands. The Luftwaffe devastated the city, killing nearly 1,000 people and making 85,000 homeless. Rogers knew that there were endless examples of Allied communities being bombed just as thoroughly as Rüsselsheim had been, yet all of the stories of fliers being terrorized, beaten, and killed came from Germany. The deaths of the *Wham! Bam!* crew were not unique. Other crews had been abused, some killed, by townspeople, but in most cases there was not enough evidence to prosecute. American investigators suspected that many of the airmen listed as missing in Germany had met fates similar to those of the *Wham! Bam!* crew.

The abuse and lynching of air crews was actively encouraged by leaders in Germany, and War Crimes Group records have numerous examples of violence toward Allied fliers. But even extensive research on the other side of the war reveals no counterpart. The people of England might have been vengeful when Luftwaffe pilots drifted down to earth, considering the extreme destruction of their towns and their capital, especially since the attacks signaled Germany's effort to take over their country. Violence against the Luftwaffe crews might have been understandable to some degree, just as the rage of Rüsselsheim residents can be understood—but not condoned—in light of their bombing experience. But there are no stories like Rüsselsheim from England. No tales of Englishmen chasing Luftwaffe airmen through the streets and beating them to death, then bragging about it to their friends. Indeed, the only reported incident of a German flier being assaulted by English civilians turns out to be either highly exaggerated or entirely apocryphal. As the story goes, twenty-seven-year-old Oberleutnant Robert Zehbe of Kiel,

Germany, was the pilot of a Dornier Do 17, a light bomber designed with a twin tail fin configuration. Highly maneuverable and fast, the plane was capable of surprise bombing attacks. Zehbe was shot down over Kennington, England, on September 15, 1940, his parachute snagging on a telegraph pole and leaving him dangling several feet off the ground. Local townspeople, mostly women, rushed to the scene. There were some reports in local newspapers that they beat Zehbe, while others claimed that the women were merely trying to pull him down so they could get the highly coveted parachute silk. A police official soon arrived and took Zehbe into custody, or rescued him from a lynch mob, if more extreme versions of the story are to be believed. He was then taken to Millbank Military Hospital, where he died the next day. It is generally accepted that Zehbe died from wounds and burns suffered when his plane was shot out of the sky rather than injuries inflicted on the ground. Townspeople who were there reported later that Zehbe was seriously injured before he landed and that though there was a lynch-mob mentality among some of the crowd, no one abused Zehbe. No one disputes that a police superintendent arrived quickly and took the flier into custody, driving him away in a van. Historians consider the story of Zehbe being assaulted to be greatly exaggerated over time, prompted by the local newspaper accounts that played up the angry mob. Even the newspaper coverage itself sets the incident apart from the many cases of Allied airmen beaten in Germany. The English newspaper reported the supposed mob action in a critical tone, as opposed to the celebration of such incidents by the German government and press.

Thus, even the single example of Allied brutality against a downed flier is not remotely like what happened in Rüsselsheim. Such a story from Germany would have scarcely been noticed; there were too many concrete tales of abuse to waste time with one case in which women *might* have been violent toward an enemy flier before he was promptly rescued by authorities who then treated him properly. An important point for the Rüsselsheim commission was that the *Wham! Bam!* crewmen were in custody at the time they were assaulted. They had surrendered. They were POWs. If they had been shot or beaten before surrendering, even while running away after they landed, one could have argued that they were enemy fighters still engaged in combat who could legitimately be killed. It is acceptable by the rules of war to continue firing at your enemy even when he is in retreat, for instance, and both sides were known sometimes to shoot at airmen hanging from their parachutes in the air. But once the airmen were under the control of the Luftwaffe, they were POWs, so assaulting them was a war crime.

Although the debate continues, with some descendants of the executed murderers arguing that the prosecution was simply an act of vengeance by the victors, most residents of Rüsselsheim were shamed by the brutality of the murders and the complete disregard for the conventions of war. In 1987, after the military history magazine *After the Battle* detailed the murders, the brick wall where the fliers were trapped and beaten was torn down. The headstones marking the graves of Hartgen and the others executed for killing the airmen—in the same cemetery where the airmen were first buried—also were removed. Many residents of the town disavowed any guilt for the murders, saying that they did not participate and that the trials after the war forced those who did to pay the price. Nevertheless, a strong faction of Rüsselsheimers were determined to make amends.

In August 2001, the town of Rüsselsheim invited the only living survivor of the attack to return to the city and receive a formal apology. Seventy-six-year-old Sidney Eugene Brown had to think long and hard about returning to the city that murdered his friends and nearly killed him fifty-seven years earlier, but in the end he accepted and made the trip. He was accompanied by his wife, Dorothy, Tufenkjian's brother, Jack Tian, and his wife, Stella. (Tufenkjian's family had shortened the name to Tian.) Brown was received warmly by the people of Rüsselsheim, though he privately admitted to family and friends that the sound of the German language grated on him, reminding him of the angry, guttural shouts from that day long ago. Though there were many in Rüsselsheim who opposed the remembrance, Brown was the guest of honor at a memorial ceremony attended by more than one hundred people, where Mayor Stefan Gieltowski spoke on behalf of the city, saying, "We all have the responsibility to remember what happened in

Rüsselsheim. And we remember because remembering lays the ground for forgiveness—forgiveness we see from people like Sidney Brown."

Brown spoke to the crowd, his heavy Southern accent giving him the sound of a Southern Baptist preacher, pausing every so often to have his words translated into German. With a flair for diplomacy, Brown began by noting that Germany had been devastated during the war but that the United States had been instrumental in rebuilding the country, and that thereafter the two nations had been close allies, working together to defeat what Brown called a worse threat than Hitler: communism.

Brown assured the people of Rüsselsheim that he did not hold a grudge. "I have told everybody I have no animosity in my heart against the people of Germany or the people of Rüsselsheim. You have heard that I am a person who claims the name of Jesus, and if you claim the name of Jesus you must try to live up to his teachings. And the Scripture plainly says that you must forgive."

Sounding confident and assured, Brown explained that coming to Rüsselsheim was not easy for him but that it also was something he needed to do, a step toward accepting what happened to him in the city and forgiving those responsible.

"I didn't know what my emotions would be, coming here, but it was something I had to put behind me," he said. "I knew that if I came, I wanted to go to the cemetery and that would be the supreme test. If I could go into that cemetery and control my emotions, I knew for a fact I would have licked it."

Brown told those gathered that he had visited the cemetery the day before. He also stopped a rumor that had been going around the city, one that did not sit well with him. People had been telling a story about how, when he and Adams escaped, they were accompanied by a young woman from Rüsselsheim. Perhaps it was an effort to lend a dramatic, romantic air to an otherwise sordid story, but Brown didn't like it. He told the attendees that when he and Adams fled the cemetery, the last person they wanted to see was anyone—male or female—from Rüsselsheim. Brown went on to discuss how singular incidents can affect the rest of your life in profound ways, and he attributed his survival to God.

"I firmly believe God was calling the shots that day," he said.

Brown told how he and the rest of the crew found themselves trapped against the wall, and he saw that Austin was being beaten severely with a hammer and others were trying to drop a railroad tie on him from above. "Well, my momma didn't raise no crazy young'un, so I backed away from that mess," he said. But then he ran into a man he thought was reaching for a gun and moved away from him, only to be hit over the head with a bottle that contained some type of alcohol. The alcohol had the effect of cooling Brown off in the terrible heat and, he believed, disinfecting the terrible head wounds he had suffered. Brown knew that infections killed as many soldiers as bullets, and he was convinced that the alcohol saved his life.

"That was number one, the Lord taking care of me," he said.

He saw the vicious kicking of Adams as they lay next to each other on the street, he told them. Only when he brought up "my good buddy, Bill Adams" did Brown's voice waver. Brown had six brothers back home in Florida, and he told the audience that none of them was closer to him than Adams had been. It was terrible watching his friend being kicked over and over, he said. And then when the shooting began, Brown was sure he was about to be killed, but Hartgen ran out of bullets.

"That was number two."

Then Brown described how he had been spared the fatal blows from Stolz in the cemetery only because of the way he lay in the cart.

"That was number three, in the cemetery."

Brown continued relating his story, emphasizing that he had survived only because God was looking out for him, providing a series of what might have seemed mere happenstance to someone else. Brown knew it was not luck. It was the hand of God. In all, he recounted fourteen examples of how God had saved his life in Germany.

THE PATH TOWARD REMEMBRANCE and reconciliation continued, and on the sixtieth anniversary of the atrocity, August 26, 2004, the citizens of Rüsselsheim invited Brown and family members of the other survivors to return once again. Brininstool was unable to attend because of his health. At a formal ceremony near one of the locations where the Americans were beaten so savagely, the townspeople unveiled a memorial to the crew of the *Wham! Bam!* An inscription in German and English bluntly admits that the Americans were "driven and lynched by an enraged mob" and concludes: "May this memorial recall us to our common humanity."

The memorial stands near the site where the airmen were herded against a brick wall, the place where they suffered the most. On one side, the memorial looks like a simple stone wall similar to the one that stood there in 1944. On the other side, facing the train tracks, the memorial includes large photos of the men who died at the hands of Rüsselsheim residents. Everyone at the train station in Rüsselsheim sees those photos of the American servicemen, which serve as a reminder to the townspeople and a promise to everyone else that such a violation of human dignity will never happen again on those streets.

Brown died on April 4, 2009. Brininstool died in Michigan on October 14, 2009, at the age of ninety-three. The last survivor of the *Wham! Bam!* was in good spirits to the end, and he always became energized when speaking of his friends from the ill-fated plane.

WITH THE MEN OF THE *Wham! Bam!* gone, and even after such a positive experience in Rüsselsheim, the quest for understanding continues. Even sixty-six years later, the deaths of the *Wham! Bam!* crew continue rippling through the generations of men and women who came after, the sons, daughters, and grandchildren who were only a distant hope in the minds of men who just wanted to serve their country, get the job done, and then get back home to their families.

Like many other orphans of World War II, Madeline Rogers Ruf Teremy still struggles to understand the father she never knew and how his absence affected her, how it shaped who she is today. She still is piecing together parts of her father's life, trying to understand the man who was supposed to be with her, the young man who probably thought of his pregnant wife in his last, terrified moments. The loss of the *Wham! Bam!* crew affected dozens of lives and will continue to influence hundreds more.

Teremy, the daughter of pilot Norman J. Rogers Jr. and his wife, Helen, is just one of the many men and women who grew up without a father who never came home from the war. Living still in Rochester, New

York, she has met many more children of those lost in World War II, and in her quest to understand this missing chapter in her life she has found similarities in their longing for answers. Teremy struggled for years to learn the true story of her father's death, and she finds some peace from knowing it, terrible as it was.

Other family members of the *Wham! Bam!* crew were making similar discoveries, in their own time, all of them finding that the generation who fought and suffered through World War II spoke little of such horrors, keeping the disturbing secrets to themselves and not dwelling in the past. The knowledge of what had happened to their loved ones wore heavily on the relatives and friends of the *Wham! Bam!* crew, but they chose to keep their anguish private, maintaining an impassivity and distance that was meant to spare the children. Even the few who survived the bomber's crash and the subsequent mob attack were reluctant to talk about it with anyone who wasn't there, anyone who didn't have their own burden of memories.

The families still struggle to understand what happened to the men of the *Wham! Bam!* and to make sense of the way they died. The effect on the lives left behind was evident when the author visited Teremy's home. With the Teremy clan gathered at the house one evening, it was clear that the loss of this man on the streets of a German city sixty-six years earlier had left an indelible mark on the family. Madeline's mother and Norman's widow, ninety-year-old Helen Ruf, helped illustrate how the greatest generation handled such tragedies. Sitting in a small office, with the sounds of the raucous family gathering spilling through the closed door, I asked Helen about Norman. She told me of how her first husband's death at the hands of an enraged mob in Germany is always with her, even decades later and even though her life since has been full and satisfying with her second husband, Roy Ruf.

But still she thought of Norm. "I say the Stations of the Cross every day for Norm and the other boys," she once told her daughter in a moment of reflection. "I always thought what they went through was their own personal Stations of the Cross."

Such sentiments were rarely voiced, however. Stoic and humble in the face of a loss that would devastate many people, just as she was in

1944, she brushed off any suggestion that her husband's death was unique or especially meaningful. So many men died in the war, so many wives lost their husbands, she said. It wouldn't be right for her to act like her loss was special. That was part of the reason she never told Madeline much about what happened to her father. Plenty of other little girls lost their fathers, too, and there was nothing to be gained from dwelling on such a terrible story.

I understood that Helen came from a generation that didn't go on and on about their personal lives and problems, and I didn't press her to talk more about her emotions. But as we continued talking of the young man she had only just married, only just begun to envision spending the rest of her life with, her strong façade slipped, just for a moment.

It happened when I asked her if, after all these years, she still missed Norman.

"Your heart can only break once," she said in a voice edged with frustration, even anger, her eyes brimming with tears. "Why does this keep coming back to me?"

Because she remembers Norman.

Because she remembers.

ACKNOWLEDGMENTS

I MUST EXPRESS MY GRATITUDE to those who invited me into their lives and memories, those who provided their assistance with a cautious sense of trust that the story would be told with dignity. I can only hope that I have done right by the men of the *Wham! Bam! Thank You Ma'am* and the loved ones they left behind.

Madeline Teremy was gracious in her support of this project, and her assistance was beyond measure. Madeline has safeguarded so many stories and memories about her father and the other crew members of the *Wham! Bam!,* saving the bits of information, the documents and photos, the little anecdotes that reveal who these men really were. Thank you, Madeline, for welcoming me into your life and sharing your story with me. The other children of the crew members also contributed mightily to this book by providing memories of their fathers. My sincere appreciation goes to Barry Adams, Forrest Adams, Bill Brininstool, David Brininstool, Rachel Brown, and Becky Dietrich. Jennifer Teremy also was helpful in telling me of her perspective on the Rogers family, two generations removed from Norman Rogers Jr., and in conveying her memories of Gene Brown and William Adams. I also am indebted to the family of Gene Brown for the videotaped interview in which he told the story of his experience in Germany slowly but vividly while watching a football game in his favorite recliner.

I thank Helen Ruf, in particular, for allowing me to question her about memories from years ago, taking her back to a time and place that has long since passed but that I believe will always be with her.

I also thank the researchers who have helped me along the way at the National Archives and the Library of Congress, and also Winston Ramsey, editor in chief of *After the Battle*. My editors at Palgrave, Alessandra Bastagli and Colleen Lawrie, shepherded the book with a deft touch, and I thank them for their valuable input. My William Morris Endeavour agent, Mel Berger, deserves kudos for his work on this project and all that preceded it.

My wife, Caroline, and my son, Nicholas, inspire me every day, and I thank them for their support in this project. I will long treasure the memories of Nicholas coming downstairs to my office in his pajamas, very early in the morning, to find me working on this manuscript. (Yes, you can sit on my lap and watch me work.)

GAF

NOTES

INTRODUCTION

p. 1: first war crimes trial after World War II: There were six military commissions before the Rüsselsheim case, including two that involved fliers lynched by German citizens (Case No. 12–2422–1 [*US v. Peter Back*], concluded on June 16, 1945; and Case No. 12–1397 [*US v. Albert Bury et al.*], concluded on July 17, 1945). The Rüsselsheim trial was considered the first war crimes trial after World War II because it was brought after the end of combat in the European theater. The other cases had been investigated and the defendants charged before the conflict was completely over. Also, the Rüsselsheim case was significantly bigger; there were eleven defendants, as opposed to the previous trials that concerned one or two defendants, or in one case, six defendants. In his 1981 book *Crossroads* (Elgin, IL: David C. Cook), Jaworski wrote that the Rüsselsheim case was "the first war crimes trial of World War II" and "the first under the Geneva Convention of 1929" (pp. 101–102), making no distinction or mention of the previous six cases. Investigator Luke Rogers also wrote in *True Detective* in July 1947 that with the Rüsselsheim case, "for the first time, justice was visited upon the Germans for the murder of American prisoners of war" (p. 72). One could argue that the Rüsselsheim case was not technically the first war crimes trial after World War II, but those involved clearly drew a distinction between cases brought during the conflict, even in the final days, and those brought afterward, when it could be said that the cases were purely an effort by the legal system to seek justice rather than action by one side against the enemy during time of war.

p. 1: the residents of Rüsselsheim: The German pronunciation of the city's name sounds approximately like "roosels-shime."

CHAPTER 1

The account in chapter 1 is drawn from the information Sergeant Sidney Eugene Brown provided to the War Crimes Office in a statement after the trials.

p. 7: saying the rosary, quietly, in a voice muddled with blood: Family of Sidney Eugene Brown, videotaped interview with Sidney Eugene Brown. Gainesville, FL, 2004.

p. 8: "Hail Mary, full of grace": Ibid. Unfortunately, Brown suspected that Sekul's saying the rosary may have brought the German's attention and resulted in the beating. However, Brown also said that the men were making involuntary sounds that would have drawn attention anyway.

CHAPTER 2

p. 19: Could a German bomber possibly have made it there?: Allan G. Blue, "Ringmasters: A History of the 491st Bombardment Group (H)" (Summer 1964). Accessed online at: www.491st.org/491hist.html.

p. 20: ball turret, mounted on the belly of the plane: Ibid.

p. 21: B-24 proved its mettle: Jay A. Stout, *Fortress Ploiesti: The Campaign to Destroy Hitler's Oil Supply* (Havertown, PA: Casemate, 2003), p. 318.

p. 21: In the first two weeks of August 1944: Blue, "Ringmasters."

p. 22: moving to a nearby base in North Pickenham, in Norfolk: Ibid.

p. 23: *It seems sort of strange to me that I'll have kids of my own:* Norman J. Rogers Jr., Personal letter to Norman J. Rogers. North Pickenham, England, August 20, 1944.

CHAPTER 3

p. 27: another Soviet offensive forced German troops from western Ukraine and Eastern Poland: Steven J. Zaloga, *Bagration 1944: The Destruction of Army Group Centre* (New York: Osprey Publishing, 1996), p. 7.

p. 27: German troops crushed the largest one, in Warsaw: Ivan T. Berend, *Central and Eastern Europe, 1944–1993: Detour from the Periphery to the Periphery* (Cambridge: Cambridge University Press, 1999), p. 8.

p. 27: both countries shifted their allegiance to the Allies: U.S. Library of Congress, "Armistice Negotiations and Soviet Occupation." Accessed online at: http://countrystudies.us/romania/23.htm.

p. 27: pushing the Japanese back to the Chindwin River.: Daniel Marston, *The Pacific War Companion: From Pearl Harbor to Hiroshima* (Oxford: Osprey, 2005), p. 120.

p. 28: capturing the cities of Changsha in June and Hengyang in August: Philip S. Jowett and Stephen Andrew, *The Japanese Army, 1931–45* (Oxford: Osprey, 2002), p. 168.

p. 28: When they arrived in England: Blue, *Ringmasters.*

p. 31: "That's the last time this little old Southern boy": Family of Sidney Eugene Brown, videotaped interview with Sidney Eugene Brown, Gainesville, FL, 2004.

p. 32: each man taking the time to shave: Ibid.

p. 32: He had considered going on sick call: Ibid.

p. 32: he realized he had left his dog tags in the shower stall: Ibid.

p. 32: The men enjoyed the scrambled eggs with toast: Ibid.

p. 33: the Rogers crew would be among 72 bombers: Eighth Air Force Historical Society, *WWII 8th AAF Combat Chronology, July 1944 through December 1944,* p. 16. Accessed at: www.8thafhs.org/combat1944b.htm.

p. 33: ferocious gusts that could blow through a bomber: August Nigro, *Wolfsangel: A German City on Trial* (Dulles, VA: Brassey's, 2000), p. 14.

p. 35: the right strategy was to bomb civilian targets and destroy the German morale: A. C. Grayling, *Among the Dead Cities: The History and Moral Legacy of the WWII Bombing of Civilians in Germany and Japan* (New York: Walker, 2006), p. 74.

p. 35: considered a military target because it was assumed to have military or industrial assets: Ibid., p. 141.

p. 36: "dehousing" the citizens and making them refugees: Ibid.

p. 36: "The entire population got into the act": Ibid., p. 142.

p. 37: The August figure included 136 children and 392 women: Randall Hansen, *Fire and Fury: The Allied Bombing of Germany, 1942–1945* (New York: New American Library), 2009, p. 18.

p. 37: a general bombing campaign against urban targets, specifically with the intent of destroying British morale : Ibid.

p. 37: The bombs had destroyed more than 1.25 million homes: Ibid., p. 19.

p. 37: "No, we will mete out to the Germans the measure": W. Churchill, *Unrelenting Struggle: War Speeches* (London: Ayer, 1942), p. 187.

p. 38: The people who had seen the horrors of what area bombing: Grayling, *Among the Dead Cities,* p. 186.

p. 38: "These great war industries can only be paralyzed": Ibid., p. 199.

p. 39: "I can't feel that war is 'humanised'": Ibid., p. 204.

p. 40: Three times as many civilians were killed: Ibid., p. 257.

p. 41: resting their heads on the bundles they always carried to the shelters: Ibid., p. 82.

p. 41: "Hamburg's night sky became in minutes, even seconds": Martin Middlebrook, *The Battle of Hamburg: The Firestorm Raid* (New York: Scribners, 1980), p. 257.

p. 43: and the burned corpse of a child: W. G. Sebald, *Natural History of Destruction* (London: Modern Library, 2004), p. 29.

p. 43: Thinking at first that they had been blown out of a bomb shelter by a direct hit: Middlebrook, *Battle of Hamburg,* p. 275.

p. 43: Germans . . . could distinguish the different types of incendiaries: Grayling, *Among the Dead Cities,* p. 88.

p. 44: only to find that the phosphorous reignited instantly: Ibid., p. 89.

CHAPTER 4

p. 45: "Just keep working on it": Family of Sidney Eugene Brown, videotaped interview with Sidney Eugene Brown, Gainesville, FL, 2004.

p. 46: a point on the English coast where it met up with the rest of the 1,247 aircraft: Roger Freeman, Alan Crouchman, and Vic Maslen, *Mighty Eighth Diary* (New York: Jane's, 1981), p. 33.

p. 47: Brown had seen it happen to another gunner in training: Videotaped interview with Sidney Eugene Brown.

p. 47: discontinued when too many gunners accidentally shot other planes in their formation: Ibid.

p. 47: startled to see none of the 1,000-plus planes he had marveled at just moments earlier: August Nigro, *Wolfsangel: A German City on Trial* (Dulles, VA: Brassey's, 2000), p. 17.

p. 48: *Old Gene's the last one in the bunch,* he thought: Ibid.

p. 48: big, hinged metal ear flaps that came down over the ear cutaways: James C. Beyer, William F. Enos, and Robert H. Holmes, *Wound Ballistics.* U.S. Army Medical Department, Office of Medical History, Personnel Protective Armor. Accessed online at: http://history.amedd.army.mil/booksdocs/ wwii/woundblstcs/chapter11.html.

p. 49: almost standing the plane straight up on its other wing: Videotaped interview with Sidney Eugene Brown.

p. 49: he went back and manned one of the .50-caliber guns there: It is not entirely clear why Adams was manning a waist gun instead of being at his usual position in the nose when the flak burst hit the plane. This explanation is based on the supposition of his sons and veterans familiar with how flight crews performed during a mission.

p. 50: Rogers immediately radioed for fighter escorts: Eighth Air Force, 491st Bomb Group, Squadron 854, Individual Casualty Questionnaires: William A. Adams, Elmore L. Austin, Forrest W. Brininstool, Sidney Eugene Brown, William A. Dumont, Norman J. Rogers, John N. Sekul, Haigus Tufenkjian, Thomas D. Williams Jr., North Pickenham, England, August 24, 1944.

p. 50: with one engine smoking but Rogers and Sekul keeping the plane under control: Allan G. Blue, *Ringmasters: A History of the 491st Bombardment Group (H),* Summer 1964. Accessed online at: www.491st.org/491hist.html.

p. 50: he threw the flak suit back over Adams's shoulders: Videotaped interview with Sidney Eugene Brown.

p. 51: firing three ten-round volleys as the plane circled past: Winston G. Ramsey, ed., "The Rüsselsheim Death March," *After the Battle* (London) 57 (1987): 1–2.

p. 52: So this would be everyone's first jump: Videotaped interview with Sidney Eugene Brown.

p. 52: where they feared their chutes would become entangled in the B-24's twin tails: Ibid.

p. 52: Adams watched his friend disappear through the bomb bay: Supposedly, Dumont was too scared to jump and had to be shoved out by another crew member. Brown told others of Dumont's hesitation years later.

CHAPTER 5

p. 55: the engines traveling the farthest and settling in the farmyard: Winston G. Ramsey, ed., "The Rüsselsheim Death March," *After the Battle* (London) 57 (1987): 2.

p. 56: *That happens so fast that it's no wonder folks break their legs:* Family of Sidney Eugene Brown, videotaped interview with Sidney Eugene Brown. Gainesville, FL, 2004. The rest of Brown's account is derived from this interview.

p. 58: The stocky man, about forty years old: War Crimes Office, Judge Advocate General's Department—War Department, Perpetuation of Testimony of William M. Adams, formerly S/Sgt. Valley View, PA, July 4, 1947. The author assumes that Brown was beaten by the same man who later beat the men during their interrogations.

p. 59: where he was met by a farmer who was about 50 years old: Ibid.

p. 59: Soon the farmer placed some cornbread and buttermilk: Videotaped interview with Sidney Eugene Brown.

p. 60: it did not matter much because Adams was not going to tell him anything: War Crimes Office, Perpetuation of Testimony of William M. Adams.

p. 61: "This what you get for bombing our women and children!": Ibid.

p. 62: "I hope that won't mean anything to the Germans": Videotaped interview with Sidney Eugene Brown.

p. 62: "I'm not Jewish. I'm not Jewish": Brown described this scene to some family and friends but did not speak of it often. While it could be apocryphal, it also is understandable that Brown would not relate such an ugly scene often.

p. 63: "We'll get out of this": Videotaped interview with Sidney Eugene Brown.

p. 64: "Hard to believe they won't spring for first-class tickets, huh?" Ibid.

p. 64: the Dulag Luft aircrew interrogation center at Oberursel, north of Frankfurt: Ramsey, "The Rüsselsheim Death March," p. 3.

p. 68: 400,000 incendiaries on Rüsselsheim: Bomber Command Report, United States Strategic Bombing Survey, Table I, p. 1a, Adam Opel, Rüsselsheim, Physical Damage Division, January 1947.

p. 68: "All men, out of the shelter now!": The bunker scene is drawn from the testimony of several Germans during the ensuing trial.

p. 68: Pathfinders, elite squadrons of fliers: Ramsey, "The Rüsselsheim Death March," p. 3.

CHAPTER 6

p. 72: The group would never see the senior guard again: Family of Sidney Eugene Brown, videotaped interview with Sidney Eugene Brown. Gainesville, FL, 2004.

p. 72: four or five thousand people moving: War Crimes Office, Judge Advocate General's Department—War Department. Perpetuation of Testimony of William M. Adams, formerly S/Sgt. Valley View, PA, July 4, 1947.

p. 74: "Beat them! There are the terror fliers!": The narrative of the attack, including the quoted comments, is drawn from the testimony of multiple witnesses and the accused during the trial as well as the affidavits from Brown and Adams and the videotaped interview with Brown.

p. 74: "Just stay with us and take it like a man!": Videotaped interview with Sidney Eugene Brown. Many years later, Brown heard from Williams's girlfriend about Adams's dream of being beaten to death in Germany and felt guilty for having berated his friend for being emotional.

p. 75: "a flood of fury erupted": There is some speculation among the crew members' families that the attack was not spontaneous but rather was planned. According to this theory, the Luftwaffe alerted Hartgen or others in Rüsselsheim that the men would be marched through the town that day, and the townspeople were ready for the assault. Support for the theory includes the way the men were herded into what amounted to a "kill zone" from which there was no escape, with groups attacking from more than one direction, the armed guards' failure to fend off the mob, and the way the group apparently focused much of the violence on Tufenkjian, whom the interrogators had labeled a Jew.

p. 78: shouting that the Jew terror flier must die: Brown confirmed in his videotaped interview that the Germans thought Tufenkjian was Jewish. One of Madeline Teremy's daughters, Jennifer, is a physical anthropologist and bioarchaeologist and discussed the autopsy reports with the author. She says the reports indicate that Tufenkjian was beaten far more severely than the other fliers. Although they all had serious and potentially fatal head wounds, Tufenkjian's skull was completely crushed, leading Jennifer Teremy to conclude that the attackers targeted him and were especially violent with him.

CHAPTER 7

p. 81: whooping and hollering with joy about their triumph: August Nigro, *Wolfsangel: A German City on Trial* (Dulles, VA: Brassey's, 2000), p. 53.

p. 81: the SA were considered Hitler's own private army: John Simkin, SA. Spartacus Educational. Accessed online at: www.spartacus.schoolnet.co.uk/GERsa.htm.

p. 82: knee breeches, thick woolen socks, and combat boots: Ibid.

p. 82: "No one else would do it": War Crimes Office, Judge Advocate General's Department—War Department. Trial record, *United States v. Otto Hermann Stolz*, Case 12–3245. Dachau, Germany, May 15–16, 1947, p. 32.

p. 84: "Bill, we're gonna have to climb that wall": Family of Sidney Eugene Brown, videotaped interview with Sidney Eugene Brown. Gainesville, FL, 2004.

p. 85: dropping more than 2 million pounds of explosives: A. C. Grayling, *Among the Dead Cities: The History and Moral Legacy of the WWII Bombing of Civilians in Germany and Japan* (New York: Walker, 2006), p. 316.

p. 85: Their hearts were pumping madly: Sidney Eugene Brown, speech at reconciliation ceremony, Rüsselsheim, Germany, August 26, 2001. Brown acknowledged that he was uncertain about the correct sequence of some events during his escape, but he was clear on the details of the things that happened over several days. It is possible that some events did not happen in the order depicted here.

p. 88: "Hey, Brownie, what do you think's gonna happen to us": Videotaped interview with Sidney Eugene Brown.

p. 89: *We're going to be killed before we get to Switzerland:* Ibid.

p. 89: he suspected the boy had brought the girl up the hill for something else: Ibid.

224 I THE LAST MISSION OF THE WHAM BAM BOYS

p. 92: "It says the doctor gave you a tetanus shot": Videotaped interview with Sidney Eugene Brown.

CHAPTER 8

p. 98: an airborne assault in the Netherlands, but that effort was unsuccessful: I. C. B. Dear and M. R. D. Foot, eds., "Market-Garden," *Oxford Companion to World War II* (Oxford: Oxford University Press), p. 877.

p. 98: German troops in Greece and Albania to shift closer to prevent them from being cut off: Max Hastings and Paul Henry, *The Second World War: A World in Flames* (New York: Osprey, 2004), pp. 223–224.

p. 99: "He was here, but he left last week!": The War Crimes Office, Judge Advocate General's Department—War Department, Perpetuation of Testimony of William M. Adams, S/Sgt. Dover, DE, October 4, 1945, p. d–2.

p. 99: Allied naval victory during the Battle of Leyte Gulf: Daniel Marston, *The Pacific War Companion: From Pearl Harbor to Hiroshima* (New York: Osprey, 2005), p. 120.

p. 99: If successful, Hitler expected the Allies would be willing to end the war: Danny S. Parker, *Battle of the Bulge: Hitler's Ardennes Offensive, 1944–1945* (New York: Da Capo Press, 2004), pp. xiii–xiv.

p. 99: "the investigation of alleged war crimes, and the collection of evidence relating thereto": Leon Jaworski, *After Fifteen Years* (Houston, TX: Gulf, 1961, p. 65).

p. 100: pushing from the Vistula to the Oder River in Germany: Donald Sommerville, *The Complete Illustrated History of World War Two: An Authoritative Account of the Deadliest Conflict in Human History with Analysis of Decisive Encounters and Landmark Engagements* (London: Lorenz Books, 2008), p. 5.

p. 100: "Your letter certainly contained wonderful news": Sam Sekul, Personal letter to Anoosh Tufenkjian. Bronx, NY, February 6, 1945.

p. 101: *Your letter is the first I have received:* Helen Rogers, Personal letter to Anoosh Tufenkjian. Rochester, NY, March 4, 1945.

p. 101: *Please, God, I've been through so much:* Videotaped interview with Sidney Eugene Brown.

p. 102: encircling a large number of German troops, and the Soviets advanced to Vienna: Tom Buchanan, *Europe's Troubled Peace, 1945–2000* (Hoboken, NJ: Wiley-Blackwell, 2006), p. 21.

p. 102: The Reichstag was captured on April 30: Donald E. Shepardson, "The Fall of Berlin and the Rise of a Myth," *Journal of Military History* 62, no. 1 (1998): 135–154.

CHAPTER 9

p. 106: "So where are the others, the ones that you didn't mark as having fled?": Luke P. Rogers, "The Rüsselsheim Case," *True Detective* 47, no. 4 (July 1947): 72.

p. 107: "You're not going anywhere": Ibid.

p. 108: "Do not tell anyone why we were here or what we were talking about": Ibid.

p. 110: "Beat this one. He's still alive": Ibid.

p. 110: *All typical small-town louts:* Ibid.

p. 111: "They're going to do the digging": Ibid.

p. 111: "What did you do with them?": Ibid.

p. 112: The report identifies the bodies: Max Berg and Henry H. Mize, Pathologist's reports on the bodies of John N. Sekul, William A. Dumont, Body Unknown, Thomas D. Williams, Elmore L. Austin, N. J. Rogers. Bensheim, Germany, July 9, 1945.

p. 114: "the alternative for Japan is prompt and utter destruction": Herbert Bix, *Hirohito and the Making of Modern Japan* (New York: HarperCollins, 2001), p. 360.

CHAPTER 10

p. 116: he was stepping into a delicate situation: Leon Jaworski, *Crossroads* (Elgin, IL: David C. Cook, 1981), p. 93.

p. 116: mistreatment of aircrews that were taken prisoner after landing in or bailing out over Germany: Leon Jaworski, *After Fifteen Years* (Houston, TX: Gulf, 1961), p. 66.

p. 117: German police had been instructed not to interfere with civilians who attacked Allied airmen: Ibid., p. 66.

p. 117: Germany in the Hague Convention of 1907 as well as in the Geneva Conventions of 1929: Jaworski, *Crossroads,* p. 96.

p. 117: "If violators went unpunished, such treaties would become meaningless": Jaworski, *After Fifteen Years,* p. 66.

p. 118: "We understand there are over ten thousand of us here": Ibid., p. 101.

p. 119: "the power of the one whose life we were celebrating this Easter Sunday": Ibid.

p. 119: *What could change seemingly God-fearing, well-meaning humans into vicious beasts?:* Ibid.

p. 119: *neither can we imagine the depths to which we can sink without him:* Ibid., p. 100.

p. 120: "Unless we can get several witnesses to substantiate a charge, we will not prosecute": Ibid., p. 69.

p. 120: "Then I saw Johannes Seipel go up and kick him in the face": Luke P. Rogers, "The Rüsselsheim Case," *True Detective* 47, no. 4 (July 1947): 72.

p. 122: *If not, what caused him to become more beast than man?:* Jaworski, *After Fifteen Years,* p. 71.

p. 122: excelled in his schoolwork, coming home every afternoon to study: Jaworski, *Crossroads,* p. 97.

p. 122: "he was transformed into a vicious beast," Jaworski would write later: Ibid., p. 89.

p. 122: "How dare you bring me to Wiesbaden for this!": Ibid., p. 72.

p. 123: "This is nonsense." Ibid.

p. 124: "I found him in a pool of blood!": Ibid., p. 73.

p. 124: I will reveal nothing!: Ibid., p. 74.

CHAPTER 11

p. 127: expressed his concerns to his wife in a letter dated July 20, 1945: August Nigro, *Wolfsangel: A German City on Trial* (Dulles, VA: Brassey's, 2000), pp. 71–72.

p. 127: and one brought along his daughter to help translate: Leon Jaworski, *After Fifteen Years* (Houston, TX: Gulf, 1961), p. 76; and the War Crimes Office, Judge Advocate General's Department—War Department. Trial record, *United States v. Josef Hartgen,* et al., Case 12–1497. Darmstadt, Germany, July 25–31, 1945, p. 8.

p. 128: Jaworski read the specification and charge: The War Crimes Office, Judge Advocate General's Department—War Department. Trial record, *United States v. Josef Hartgen,* et al., Case 12–1497. Darmstadt, Germany, July 25–31, 1945, p. 9.

p. 128: "Charge: Violation of the laws of war": Ibid., p. 3.

p. 130: He began by calling Margarete Zogner: Ibid., pp. 10–14.

p. 131: Otto Albrecht Sturmfels, the German attorney representing Witzler and Reinhardt: Ibid., pp. 14–15.

p. 133: saw a crowd of about twenty people walking in the middle of the street: Ibid., pp. 21–29.

p. 134: Karolina Jung, a married mother of three: Ibid., pp. 30–32.

p. 135: Lorenz Wendel, a carriage maker from Weilbach: Ibid., pp. 34–39.

p. 136: No one with the court ever found out what was in the briefcase: Jaworski, *After Fifteen Years,* p. 82.

p. 136: Gütlich beating the prisoners and calling for others to beat them too: *United States v. Josef Hartgen, et al.,* pp. 39–42.

p. 136: the stick was the type one used to herd cattle: Ibid., pp. 42–46.

p. 136: Daum had been shoveling away ruins in the back of the shop: Ibid., pp. 46–53.

p. 136: "My hands hurt so from the beating": Ibid., pp. 63–67.

p. 136: she said the airmen "were bleeding pretty strongly": Ibid., pp. 69–74.

p. 137: Anne Willnow, who lived on Taunusstrasse: Ibid., pp. 74–77.

p. 137: "There are fliers coming! Let's beat them to death!": Ibid., pp. 77–83.

CHAPTER 12

p. 139: front-page article headlined "11 Germans Tried for Killing Fliers": Gladwin Hill, "11 Germans Tried for Killing Fliers," *New York Times,* July 26, 1945, p. 1.

p. 141: "I also beat at them," Seipel replied: War Crimes Office, Judge Advocate General's Department—War Department. Trial record, *United States v. Josef Hartgen, et al.,* Case 12–1497. Darmstadt, Germany, July 25–31, 1945, p. 93.

p. 142: "From this they were not killed": Ibid., pp. 97–101.

p. 144: "When they were put on the cart, the one still raised himself. He shook his head": Ibid., pp. 101–111.

p. 148: Wüst, in fact, had been a member of the SA since 1932: Ibid., Exhibit BB.

p. 148: "but I cannot understand why they bombed a city where the farmers live": Ibid., Exhibit AA.

p. 149: "and if it would not have been for these two, nobody would have done anything": Ibid., Exhibit J.

CHAPTER 13

p. 152: Opper's yelling for him to get away could have been intended as a friendly warning and not a threat.: War Crimes Office, Judge Advocate General's Department—War Department. Trial record, *United States v. Josef Hartgen,* et al., Case 12–1497. Darmstadt, Germany, July 25–31, 1945, pp. 148–155.

p. 152: The other person replied, "You do not know the worst yet": Ibid., pp. 155–159.

p. 154: "Did anybody prevent you from giving any assistance or rites to the people that had been killed?": Ibid., pp. 159–167.

p. 154: "this accused is very senile and has reached a state of decay": Ibid., pp. 173–176.

p. 157: "And if you would put fifty witnesses in front of me, I would testify just like I did": Ibid., pp. 224–230.

p. 157: he had seen the defendant Wolf at the scene carrying a stick: Ibid., pp. 231–246.

p. 159: "in treatment from an American doctor because of a paralysis of the spinal cord, column, sir?": Ibid., pp. 247–252.

p. 159: "every morning these prisoners not only from me but from the whole population got their coffee and bread": Ibid., pp. 252–259.

p. 160: but he never came right out and said that he didn't do it: Ibid., pp. 261–264.

p. 161: "Yes, I was sorry for that": Ibid., pp. 264–270.

p. 162: "My sister is more excitable": Ibid., pp. 271–280.

p. 162: "and I couldn't reach it, so I pushed at him," he said: Ibid., pp. 280–287.

p. 164: Hartgen declared that all the accusations against him were just lies or mistakes: Ibid., pp. 287–306.

p. 164: Again, Wolf declined to answer: Ibid., pp. 306–323.

p. 165: Barthel went on to confirm that he had seen Wolf carrying a stick: Ibid., p. 336.

p. 165: In the defendants' box, Wolf muttered in English, "You rat": "7 Germans Doomed for Killing Fliers," *New York Times,* July 31, 1945, p. 1.

CHAPTER 14

p. 171: Jaworski completed his closing argument by declaring that the evidence was convincing against each defendant: War Crimes Office, Judge Advocate General's Department—War Department. Trial Record, *United States v. Josef Hartgen, et al.,* Case 12–1497. Darmstadt, Germany, July 25–31, 1945, pp. 340–352.

p. 173: mitigating factors when deciding whether to sentence them to death if found guilty: Ibid., pp. 352–355.

p. 175: the American system of cross-examination was new to them, he said: Ibid., pp. 355–359.

p. 175: "a subject of temptation": Ibid., pp. 359–365.

p. 176: an interrogation technique commonly used by police even today to extract quasi-confessions: Ibid., pp. 365–371.

p. 177: in the first war crimes trial to be brought after the end of the war in Europe: Leon Jaworski, *Crossroads* (Elgin, IL: David C. Cook, 1981), p. 101. As discussed in the notes to the introduction, Jaworski and his colleagues consistently called this case the "first" war crimes trial after World War II, distinguishing it from the handful of earlier, smaller trials that were begun in the final months and weeks of the war.

CHAPTER 15

p. 179: "hate, revenge, sadism and nearly every ignoble trait of mankind had its turn in the musty courtroom": "7 Germans Doomed for Killing Fliers," *New York Times,* July 31, 1945, p. 1.

p. 183: *They had been believers in Christ, and now they are returning to Him:* Leon Jaworski, *After Fifteen Years* (Houston, TX: Gulf, 1961), p. 101.

p. 183: justice had been done, so the man was now free to choose his course: Ibid.

p. 183: New York *Daily News* running a large picture on the front page: "Death for Nazi Killers," *Daily News,* August 31, 1945, p. 1; and *Baseball Almanac,* 1945 New York Yankees Schedule. Accessed online at: www.baseball-almanac.com/teamstats/schedule.php?y=1945&t=NYA.

p. 183: he went over every step of the trial and judged himself with a critical eye: Jaworski, *After Fifteen Years,* pp. 96–97.

p. 184: puzzled by how Witzler could have gotten past security: Ibid., pp. 97–98.

p. 184: "The witnesses against my wife lied! They wanted to hurt us!": Ibid.

p. 185: just what was in that briefcase that Witzler held so firmly under his arm: Ibid., pp. 98–100.

p. 185: *After reading of the trial of the eleven Germans for the murder of six American fliers:* William M. Adams and Sidney E. Brown, Letter to Brigadier General C. Davidson, War Crimes Section, Seventh Army. Klingerstown, PA, and Gainesville, FL, August 1945.

p. 187: "I am sure that those men we left behind were dead": War Crimes Office, Judge Advocate General's Department—War Department. Perpetuation of Testimony of William M. Adams, S/Sgt. Dover, DE, October 4, 1945, p. d–2.

CHAPTER 16

p. 190: *Well Darlins', our hunch about that newspaper article was O.K.:* Jennie Rogers, Personal letter to her children. Rochester, NY, August 8, 1945.

p. 191: *I suppose you are anxiously waiting for more news:* Jennie Rogers, Personal letter to her children. Rochester, NY, August 11, 1945.

p. 192: *Well Chilluns, peace day was pretty wild and noisy here.:* Jennie Rogers, Personal letter to her children. Rochester, NY, August 18, 1945.

p. 193: *I've received your letter that you have received word of your son's death in Germany:* Forrest Brininstool, Personal letter to Anoosh Tufenkjian. Munith, MI, October 22, 1945.

p. 193: *Mrs. Williams and I have been greatly concerned:* August Nigro, *Wolfsangel: A German City on Trial* (Dulles, VA: Brassey's, 2000), pp. 119–120.

p. 194: "may have committed certain other crimes and mistreatment of American military personnel": Ibid.

p. 194: quite controlled when on duty, professional, and knowledgeable about his difficult task: Stanley Tilles and Jeffrey Denhart, *By the Neck until Dead: The Gallows of Nuremberg* (Bedford, IN: JoNa Books, 1999), p. 42.

p. 195: as little as twenty seconds after first laying eyes on the prisoner: Albert Pierrepoint, *Executioner: Pierrepoint: The Amazing Autobiography of the World's Most Famous Executioner* (London: George G. Harrap, 1974), p. 92.

p. 196: military band playing the "Dead March": War Department, *Procedure for Military Executions* (Washington, DC: 1944), p. 5.

p. 197: everyone would deny that they heard Streicher make a sound: Tilles and Denhart, *By the Neck until Dead,* p. 137.

p. 197: the platform ten feet off the ground and the lower portion shrouded by dark drapes: War Department, *Procedure for Military Executions,* p. 14. The description is based on the Figure 2–type scaffold depicted in the military manual, the closest, but not exact, match to the actual scaffold depicted in the photographs of the hangings.

p. 198: as Seipel continued shouting "Nothing!": Winston G. Ramsey, ed., "The Rüsselsheim Death March," *After the Battle* (London) 57 (1987): 16.

p. 199: saw him beating the men with a wooden club about the same size as a table leg: Deputy Judge Advocate's Office, 7708 War Crimes Group, European Command. Record of Testimony, *United States v. Otto Herman Stolz,* Case No. 12–3245. Dachau, Germany, September 18, 1947, pp. 8–28.

p. 200: Schmitt told Raab that it was Stolz: Ibid., pp. 28–33.

p. 200: "We only bury dead people and not half-dead ones": Ibid., p. 41.

p. 200: he saw Stolz beat the men more: Ibid., p. 36.

p. 200: Stolz flatly denied ever hitting the airmen: Ibid., pp. 50–62.

p. 201: he was "the worst looking criminal of them all and was built like a gorilla": Luke P. Rogers, "The Rüsselsheim Case," *True Detective* 47, no. 4 (July 1947), p. 72.

p. 201: Umstatter was found guilty and sentenced to death by hanging: War Crimes Office, Judge Advocate General's Department—War Department. Trial record, *United States v. Franz Umstatter,* Case 12–2381. Dachau, Germany, August 26–27, 1946, p. 12.

EPILOGUE

p. 203: Stolz was hanged in March 1948: Deputy Judge Advocate's Office, 7708 War Crimes Group, European Command. Record of Testimony, *United States v. Otto Herman Stolz,* Case No. 12–3245. Dachau, Germany, September 18, 1947, p. 5.

p. 203: without citing a reason in the official records: War Crimes Office, Judge Advocate General's Department—War Department. Trial record, *United States v. Franz Umstatter,* Case 12–2381. Dachau, Germany, August 26–27, 1946, p. 5.

p. 204: telling them they were about to receive helpful medical treatment: Leon Jaworski, *After Fifteen Years* (Houston, TX: Gulf, 1961), pp. 103–123.

p. 208: "And evil loves a spiritual vacuum": Ibid., p. 105.

p. 209: "none I spoke to admitted knowledge of Rotterdam": Luke P. Rogers, "The Rüsselsheim Case," *True Detective* 47, no. 4 (July 1947), p. 72.

p. 210: his parachute snagging on a telegraph pole and leaving him dangling several feet off the ground: John Sample, "The Story of Robert Zehbe." Accessed online at: http://johnsample.50megs .com/johnsample%20text/thestoryofrobertzehbe.html.

p. 210: though there was a lynch-mob mentality among some of the crowd, no one abused Zehbe: Luftwaffe Archives & Records Reference Group, Oberleutnant Robert Zehbe. Accessed online at: www.lwag.org/forums/showthread.php?t=469.

p. 211: The headstones marking the graves: Winston G. Ramsey, ed., "Update: The Rüsselsheim Death March," *After the Battle* (London), no. 66 (1989): 40.

p. 212: "forgiveness we see from people like Sidney Brown": Associated Press, "WWII Tailgunner Returns to Germany," August 26, 2001.

p. 212: "And the Scripture plainly says that you must forgive": Sidney Eugene Brown, speech at reconciliation ceremony, Rüsselsheim, Germany, August 26, 2001.

p. 212: "I knew for a fact I would have licked it": Ibid.

p. 213: "I firmly believe God was calling the shots that day": Ibid.

BIBLIOGRAPHY

INTERVIEWS AND CORRESPONDENCE WITH AUTHOR

Adams, Barry
Adams, Forrest
Brininstool, Bill
Brininstool, David
Brown, Rachel
Dietrich, Becky
Ruf, Helen
Teremy, Jennifer
Teremy, Madeline

BOOKS

Beck, Earl R. *Under the Bombs: The German Home Front 1943–45*. Lexington, KY: University Press of Kentucky, 1986.

Berend, Ivan T. *Central and Eastern Europe, 1944–1993: Detour from the Periphery to the Periphery*. Cambridge: Cambridge University Press, 1999.

Bix, Herbert. *Hirohito and the Making of Modern Japan*. New York: HarperCollins, 2001.

Buchanan, Tom. *Europe's Troubled Peace, 1945–2000*. Hoboken, NJ: Wiley-Blackwell, 2006.

Churchill, Sir Winston. *Unrelenting Struggle: War Speeches*. London: Ayer Company Publishing, 1942.

Dear, I. C. B., and M. R. D. Foot, eds. "Market-Garden." *Oxford Companion to World War II*. Oxford: Oxford University Press, 2002.

Dobbs, Michael. *Saboteurs: The Nazi Raid on America*. New York: Alfred A. Knopf, 2004.

Freeman, Roger, Alan Crouchman, and Vic Maslen. *Mighty Eighth Diary*. New York: Jane's, 1981.

Grayling, A. C. *Among the Dead Cities: The History and Moral Legacy of the WWII Bombing of Civilians in Germany and Japan*. New York: Walker and Company, 2006.

Hansen, Randall. *Fire and Fury: The Allied Bombing of Germany, 1942–1945*. New York: New American Library, 2009.

Hastings, Max, and Paul Henry. *The Second World War: A World in Flames*. New York: Osprey, 2004.

Jaworski, Leon. *After Fifteen Years*. Houston, TX: Gulf Publishing, 1961.

Jaworski, Leon. *Crossroads*. Elgin, IL: David C. Cook, 1981.

Jaworski, Leon. *The Right and the Power*. New York: Reader's Digest Press, 1976.

Jowett, Philip S., and Stephen Andrew. *The Japanese Army, 1931–45*. Oxford: Osprey, 2002.

Marston, Daniel. *The Pacific War Companion: From Pearl Harbor to Hiroshima*. Oxford: Osprey, 2005.

Middlebrook, Martin. *The Battle of Hamburg: The Firestorm Raid.* New York: Scribners, 1980.

Nigro, August. *Wolfsangel: A German City on Trial.* Dulles, VA: Brassey's, 2000.

Parker, Danny S. *Battle of the Bulge: Hitler's Ardennes Offensive, 1944–1945.* New York: Da Capo Press, 2004.

Pierrepoint, Albert. *Executioner: Pierrepoint: The Amazing Autobiography of the World's Most Famous Executioner.* London: George G. Harrap, 1974.

Sebald, W. G. *Natural History of Destruction.* London: Modern Library, 2004.

Sommerville, Donald . *The Complete Illustrated History of World War Two: An Authoritative Account of the Deadliest Conflict in Human History with Analysis of Decisive Encounters and Landmark Engagements.* London: Lorenz Books, 2008.

Stout, Jay A. *Fortress Ploiesti: The Campaign to Destroy Hitler's Oil Supply.* Haverstown, PA: Casemate, 2003.

Tilles, Stanley, and Jeffrey Denhart. *By the Neck until Dead: The Gallows of Nuremberg.* Bedford, IN: JoNa Books, 1999.

Zaloga, Steven J. *Bagration 1944: The Destruction of Army Group Centre.* New York: Osprey, 1996.

OFFICIAL DOCUMENTS

Berg, Max, and Henry H. Mize. Pathologist's reports on the bodies of John N. Sekul, William A. Dumont, Body Unknown, Thomas D. Williams, Elmore L. Austin, N. J. Rogers. Bensheim, Germany, July 9, 1945.

Bomber Command Report. United States Strategic Bombing Survey. Table I, p. 1a, Adam Opel, Rüsselsheim, Physical Damage Division, January 1947.

Deputy Judge Advocate's Office, 7708 War Crimes Group, European Command. Record of Testimony, *United States v. Otto Herman Stolz,* Case No. 12–3245. Dachau, Germany, September 18, 1947.

Deputy Judge Advocate's Office, 7708 War Crimes Group, European Command. Review and Recommendations, *United States v. Otto Herman Stolz,* Case No. 12–3245. Dachau, Germany, September 18, 1947.

Eighth Air Force, 491st Bomb Group, Squadron 854. Extract: Missing Air Crew Report. A.A.F. serial number 42–110107. Aircraft nickname "Whem Bam—Reclining Rabbit—Thank you Ma'am" [sic]. North Pickenham, England, August 24, 1944.

Eighth Air Force, 491st Bomb Group, Squadron 854. Individual Casualty Questionnaires: William A. Adams, Elmore L. Austin, Forrest W. Brininstool, Sidney Eugene Brown, William A. Dumont, Norman J. Rogers, John N. Sekul, Haigus Tufenkjian, Thomas D. Williams Jr. North Pickenham, England, August 24, 1944.

War Crimes Office, Judge Advocate General's Department—War Department. Perpetuation of Testimony of William M. Adams, S/Sgt. Dover, Delaware, October 4, 1945.

War Crimes Office, Judge Advocate General's Department—War Department. Perpetuation of Testimony of William M. Adams, formerly S/Sgt. Valley View, PA, July 4, 1947.

War Crimes Office, Judge Advocate General's Department—War Department. Perpetuation of Testimony of Sidney E. Brown, formerly Sgt. Gainesville, Florida, July 26, 1947.

War Crimes Office, Judge Advocate General's Department—War Department. Trial record: *United States v. Franz Umstatter,* Case 12–2381. Dachau, Germany, August 26–27, 1946.

War Crimes Office, Judge Advocate General's Department—War Department. Trial record: *United States v. Josef Hartgen, et al.*; Case 12–1497. Darmstadt, Germany, July 25–31, 1945.

War Crimes Office, Judge Advocate General's Department—War Department. Trial record, *United States v. Otto Hermann Stolz,* Case 12–3245. Dachau, Germany, May 15–16, 1947.

War Department. *Procedure for Military Executions.* Washington, DC: Author, 1944.

PERSONAL CORRESPONDENCE AND WRITTEN MATERIAL

Adams, Althesta. Personal letter to Anoosh Tufenkjian. Klingerstown, PA: February 10, 1945.

Adams, William M., and Sidney E. Brown. Letter to Brigadier. General C. Davidson, War Crimes Section, Seventh Army. Klingerstown, PA, and Gainesville, FL, August 1945.

Austin, Hildrid. Personal letter to Anoosh Tufenkjian. Enosburg Falls, VT, February 5, 1945.

Author unknown. Handwritten poem: "The deeper the darkness . . ." Among the possessions of Helen Ruf and Madeline Teremy.

Brininstool, Forrest. Personal letter to Anoosh Tufenkjian. Munith, MI, October 22, 1945.

Rogers, Helen. Personal letter to Elizabeth Jane Rogers and Norman Rogers Sr. Savannah, GA, April 18, 1944.

Rogers, Helen. Personal letter to Anoosh Tufenkjian. Rochester, NY, February 4, 1945.

Rogers, Jennie. Personal letters to her children. Rochester, NY, August 8, August 11, and August 18, 1945.

Rogers, Norman J., Jr., Personal letter to Elizabeth Jane Rogers and Norman J. Rogers. Savannah, GA, April 21, 1944.

Rogers, Norman J., Jr. Personal letter to Norman J. Rogers. Metfield, England, July 8, 1944.

Rogers, Norman J. Jr. Personal letter to Elizabeth Jane Rogers. Metfield, England, July 23, 1944.

Rogers, Norman J., Jr. Personal letter to Norman J. Rogers. North Pickenham, England, August 20, 1944.

Secretary of War. Western Union telegram to Anoosh Tufenkjian. Washington, DC, September 5, 1944.

Sekul, Rita, and Sam Sekul. Personal letter to Anoosh Tufenkjian. Bronx, NY, September 4, 1945.

Sekul, Sam. Personal letter to Anoosh Tufenkjian. Bronx, NY, February 6, 1945.

Tufenkjian, Haigus. Western Union telegram to Anoosh Tufenkjian. Dallas, TX, March 19, 1944.

PERIODICALS

Associated Press. "WWII Tailgunner Returns to Germany," August 26, 2001.

"Death for Nazi Killers," *Daily News* (New York), August 31, 1945, p. 1.

Hill, Gladwin. "11 Germans Tried for Killing Fliers," *The New York Times,* July 26, 1945, p. 1.

Middleton, Drew. "Fliers' Death Laid to German Hatred," *The New York Times,* July 31, 1945, p. 1.

Quinlan, Linda. "A Father—and the Horror of War—Remembered," *Irondequoit (NY) Post,* June 12, 2003, p. 1.

Ramsey, Winston G., ed. "The Rüsselsheim Death March," *After the Battle* (London) 57 (1987).

Ramsey, Winston G., ed. "Update: The Rüsselsheim Death March," *After the Battle* (London), no. 66 (1989): 40.

Rogers, Luke P. "The Rüsselsheim Case," *True Detective* 47, no. 4 (July 1947): 44–47, 72.

"Says Germans Shot 4 American Fliers" *The New York Times,* July 27, 1945, p. 1.

"7 Germans Doomed for Killing Fliers," *The New York Times,* July 31, 1945, p. 1.

Shepardson, Donald E. "The Fall of Berlin and the Rise of a Myth," *Journal of Military History* 62, no. 1 (1998): 135–154.

Teremy, Madeline Rogers. "Teremy Doesn't Give Up on Plaque for Father, Crew Killed in German Massacre," *The Star* (Indianapolis, IN), June 2008.

Volkan, Vamik D. "Linking Objects: Summary of Dr. Vamik D. Volkan's Speech at AWON Conference 2000," American WWII Orphans Network. San Diego, CA, November 12, 2000.

VIDEO

Bethge, Kurt. *Hessens Weg Nach 1945: Folge 1.* Hessischer Randfunk, 1986.

Brown, Sidney Eugene. Speech at reconciliation ceremony. Rüsselsheim, Germany, August 26, 2001.

Families of Helen M. Ruf and Madeline E. Teremy. *World War II Remembrance.* Rochester, NY, 2004.

Family of Sidney Eugene Brown. Videotaped interview with Sidney Eugene Brown. Gainesville, FL, 2004.

Klapproth, Mike. 491st Bomb Group and B-24 Video. Galena, MD, 1993.

ONLINE RESOURCES

Baseball Almanac. 1945 New York Yankees Schedule. Accessed online at: www.baseball-almanac .com/teamstats/schedule.php?y=1945&t=NYA.

Beyer, James C., William F. Enos, and Robert H. Holmes. *Wound Ballistics.* U.S. Army Medical Department, Office of Medical History, Personnel Protective Armor. Accessed online at: http:// history.amedd.army.mil/booksdocs/wwii/woundblstcs/chapter11.htm.

Blue, Allan G. "Ringmasters: A History of the 491st Bombardment Group (H)." Summer 1964. Accessed online at: www.491st.org/491hist.html.

Capital Punishment U.K. "Hanged by the Neck until You Are Dead in the USA." Accessed online at: www.capitalpunishmentuk.org/hanging.html.

Dougherty, Kevin. "Memorial Honors Victims of WWII Mob," *Stars and Stripes,* European edition, August 25, 2004. Accessed online at: www.military.com/NewContent/0,13190,SS_08 2504_Memorial,00.html.

Eighth Air Force Historical Society. *WWII 8th AAF Combat Chronology, July 1944 through December 1944.* Accessed online at: www.8thafhs.org/combat1944b.htm.

Luftwaffe Archives & Records Reference Group. Oberleutnant Robert Zehbe. Accessed online at: www.lwag.org/forums/showthread.php?t=469.

Mckinstry, Leo. "Did Lancaster Bombers that Killed 600,000 in German Cities Deliberately Target Civilians? A New Book Says YES," *Mail Online,* September 29, 2009. Accessed online at: www.dailymail.co.uk/news/article-1216788/Did-Lancaster-bombers-killed-600-000-German-cities-deliberately-target-civilians-A-new-book-says-YES-.html.

"Rüsselsheim Massacre." Accessed online at: www.b-29s-over-korea.com/Russelsheim/ Russelsheim01.html.

Sample, John. "The Story of Robert Zehbe." Accessed online at: http://johnsample.50megs.com/ johnsample%20text/thestoryofrobertzehbe.html.

Simkin, John. SA. Spartacus Educational. Accessed online at: www.spartacus.schoolnet.co.uk/ GERsa.htm.

Smith, Kingsbury. "The Nuremberg Trials: The Execution of Nazi War Criminals," International News Service, October 16, 1946. Accessed online at: www.mindfully.org/Reform/Nazi-Execution-Smith16oct46.htm.

U.S. Library of Congress. "Armistice Negotiations and Soviet Occupation." Accessed online at: http://countrystudies.us/romania/23.htm.

Wolfe, Robert. "A Brief Chronology of the National Archives Captured Records Staff." Accessed online at: www.archives.gov/research/holocaust/articles-and-papers/symposium-papers/ chronology-of-captured-records-staff.html.

INDEX